The

Spoor

of

Spooks

and

other

nonsense

ALSO BY BERGEN EVANS

The Natural History of Nonsense

The SPOOR

of SPOOKS

and other nonsense

BY BERGEN EVANS

London
MICHAEL JOSEPH

First published by
MICHAEL JOSEPH LTD
26 Bloomsbury Street
*London, W.C.*1
1955

Made and printed in Great Britain by Purnell &
Sons, Ltd. Paulton (Somerset) and London, and
set in Caslon type, eleven point, one point leaded

To
JEROME HEAD

The mixture of a lie doth ever add pleasure
BACON, *Of Truth*

Let the Reader be Wary

This book seeks to give aid and comfort to the
enemies of nonsense. The bitter taste which may
be detected here and there in its pages is gall.
The salty, smoky taste is caviar. It is a statutory
offence to show it to anyone below the age of
intellectual consent.

CHAPTER ONE

The Spoor of Spooks

SUPERSTITIONS, as Bacon said, like bats, fly best in twilight, and the twilight of a confused liberalism seems particularly favourable to them. Certainly we are suffering, or enjoying, a period of unusual supernatural activity. Mysterious writings and rappings, rocking chairs that keep on rocking, wild rushings of the sun about the sky, roses that never fade, barrels that never run dry, coffee-pots ditto, leaves that grow pictures, statues that sweat and weep, abominable snowmen, corpses that stay fresh and fragrant for fifty years, horses that answer three questions for a dollar, flat tyres that repair themselves, monsters and sea serpents, half-ton stones that drag themselves across deserts, ghostly hitch-hikers who suddenly disappear and are later discovered to have been persons long dead—in news stories, in table talk, in radio and television interviews, from pulpit, press, rostrum, forum, microphone, street corner, classroom, bar, and parlour, these stories descend upon us in an uninterrupted stream.[1]

Ghosts are good for half a column any day the rapists are resting. In the old days you could always know them because they smelled—"sulphurious", Sir Thomas Browne says they were. Of course, up until about a hundred years ago everyone was more or less sulphurious, but spooks gave off enough sulphur and carbon dioxide to make candles burn dim or even go out. Angels

[1] Every item listed in this paragraph has been presented within the past ten years, as a fact, in the newspapers and news magazines.

gave off "ambrosial" odours,[1] and certain ambiguous spirits were difficult to classify because of the undefinable nature of their aromas. John Aubrey tells us that an apparition was seen at Cirencester in 1670 which upon "being demanded, whether a good spirit or a bad? returned no answer, but disappeared with a curious perfume and a most melodious twang".[2]

Naturally they are identified today by more scientific means. In January 1950 the B.B.C. sought to televise Catherine Howard's ghost in the "haunted gallery" of Hampton Court, taking along, for reasons known only to spookologists, a special infra-red spotlight. But the royal apparition did not appear.[3] *Life* had better luck, in May 1953, when it procured for its readers an actual photograph of the ghost of France's Unknown Soldier, "a white, ghostly face" which "slowly formed in the flame" of the eternal light which, according to *Life,* is thriftily rekindled every evening over the grave under the Arc de Triomphe. The close-up view, which the editors supplied, showed something resembling a baboon's skull and raised conjecture as to whether a patriotic simian had not slipped by a lenient draft board.[4]

Sometimes the *lack* of a photograph serves as well as the possession of one. Ectoplasm, a sort of etherealized bubble gum, has often been photographed coming out of the mouths of mediums as proof that the spirit world exists. But sometimes a spirit is revealed by the fact that he does *not* photograph—negative evidence, as it were. Someone encounters a mysterious stranger. He seems normal in all respects and yet there is "something" about him which arouses a little uneasiness. He makes a prophecy which turns out to be true, or it is discovered later that at the time of the meeting he had actually been dead for some time. In the course of the meeting someone had snapped a photograph of the group. It is developed—and lo! the mysterious one simply isn't there.

[1] More, the Cambridge Platonist regarded it as a peculiar mark of divine favour that his urine smelled of violets.
[2] John Aubrey: *Miscellanies,* fifth edition (London: Reeves and Turner; 1890), p. 81.
[3] The *Chicago Sun-Times,* December 28, 1950, p. 4; *Time,* January 8, 1951, p. 50.
[4] *Life,* May 23, 1953, p. 155.

This seems to be the modern or "scientific" form of the old belief that spirits cast no shadow. As they almost always assumed a human guise in their earthly visitations, especially when they were up to no good, it was important to spot them, and this translucence was an absolute giveaway. Dante noticed that he cast a shadow but that Virgil, his guide, did not.

It was one of the infallible tests for the Devil, though few could have applied it; for, despite a great deal of talk about him, actual appearances of Satan have been exceedingly rare, and very little is known about him. Though there are many allusions to him in the Bible, he makes only two personal appearances in its pages, and those not very lengthy. So that the nine-page interview with him which appeared in *Life* early in 1948[1] must not only constitute one of the greatest scoops of all time but must also set some sort of record for the kind of otherwise-unknowable information which that humorous publication bestows so generously upon its readers.

Mr Whittaker Chambers, then an editor of *Time*, had interviewed Satan for *Life* on the preceding New Year's Eve. He had encountered the Devil where any rustic moralist would have expected to find him, in a "swank" New York night club, and had found him—as he had been conceived since the days of the mystery plays, when he was often made to speak upper-class Norman French—an urbane gentleman.[2] The forked tail and

[1] *Life*, February 2, 1948, pp. 76–85. It is interesting to know that the Devil confirmed the proverb by quoting Scripture. Many assume that the assurance that he can do so is a mere figure of speech, a phrase to shrug off the exasperating way that unbelievers often have of being better versed in the Bible than those whose faith has made any close acquaintance with the sacred text unnecessary. But the Devil actually did quote Scripture. When (in Matthew 4: 5–6) he urged Christ to cast Himself down from the pinnacle of the Temple, as proof of His divinity, he was quoting from the Ninety-first Psalm. Christ's answer is a blend of several passages from Deuteronomy. The Devil's quotation is the more strictly accurate, but Christ's slight change may have been an emendation. It is curious that both quote from the Septuagint (Greek) version of the Old Testament rather than from the Hebrew.

[2] "*The prince of darkness is a gentleman!*
    Modo he's called, and Mahu."—*King Lear*, III, iv. 148–9.

Until quite recently Satan was usually pictured in a silk hat and an opera cape. Most villains were wealthy and upper-class, possibly because the rich

the cloven hoof were, as always, discreetly concealed, and his general appearance was simply that of any well-dressed habitué of such a place. The most striking detail was that his eyes were "certainly not the eyes of a Yale man". This is puzzling, and it is to be regretted that Mr Chambers, a Columbia man, did not indicate the significance of the phrase, or at least clear it with Mr William Buckley, Jr. Perhaps Mr Chambers intended it as an oblique compliment to his employer, a Yale man; but, if so, he immediately cleared himself from any possible charge of syco-phancy by having the Devil indicate Rockefeller Centre (where both *Life* and *Time* are published) as his particular province.

Since the Devil so rarely appears to a literate person any more, it is to be regretted that this interview did not produce more original information. It is interesting, however, to learn from Satan's own lips that the moral degradation of the modern world really began with the publication of Newton's *Principia*, that "rationalism, liberalism and universal compulsory education" have been the chief instruments of evil, and that the theory of organic evolution has been one of the Devil's "sublimest strokes".

Not everyone, of course, has Mr Chambers's opportunity of thus confirming the prejudices of the ignorant, and millions who share his basic convictions would still squirm a little at confessing that they had actually seen Lucifer and had a martini with him. *Their* contribution to a muddying of minds is to relate some remarkable instance of clairvoyance or tell of some famous fortune-teller or lost-article finder and, shaking their heads, say that they just don't understand it. They speak solemnly of pro-phecies, tell of those who have seen the Hindu rope trick per-formed, and wonder whether dowsing is, at bottom, radio-activity or merely clairvoyance.

One of the mainstays of the "there might be something to it" crowd is Nostradamus, a sixteenth-century French astrologer who published a volume of ambiguously worded prophecies in 1555. From time to time it is claimed that some event has borne

are a fairly good-humoured minority, possibly because their having money gave them the power to do all the wicked things the poor would like to do.

THE SPOOR OF SPOOKS

15

out one of his prophecies, and there is a great deal of ah-ing and
moo-ing among those who like to ah and moo. "I am not a
spiritualist," Mary Roberts Rinehart wrote in her autobiography,
"but, after all, what about Nostradamus?" And the *Reader's
Digest* reprinted this section of her book under the heading
"Things I Can't Explain".[1]

Well, there are a lot of things that no one can explain, and,
usually, the more you know, the less you can explain, but because
the wise profess to be ignorant the profession of ignorance
doesn't necessarily indicate that one is wise. Some things about
Nostradamus can be explained or at least examined, but such
examinations take months of hard work, and it is easier—and
immensely more profitable—to be mystified. Mr L. Sprague de
Camp, a man of immense knowledge and indefatigable energy,
once took the time to check up on Nostradamus the hard way
and came up with some interesting facts. In the first place, he
found that there were many Nostradamuses—some twenty in all
—the name having become a generic term for prophets. From
their works, as best he could (for their syntax often made it hard
to determine what was intended to be a separate, single prophecy),
he extracted 449 predictions. Of these 18 have definitely proved
to be false. That is, events have turned out the exact opposite of
Nostradamus's predictions in that many instances. Forty-one
have been fulfilled, but most of these were worded in such a way
that they had an even chance of fulfilment anyway. Events
alluded to in the other 390 cannot be identified with anything
that has yet happened. They *may* be verified someday, but for the
first three hundred years Nostradamus's average of success as a
prophet is considerably below what he would have attained by
flipping a coin.[2]

Dixon Wecter, by the way, made a similar analysis of those
"inside" news tips which "confidential news letter" services offer
to credulous tycoons. These were easier to check on because they

[1] The *Reader's Digest*, April 1950, p. 6.
[2] L. Sprague de Camp: "You Too Can Be a Nostradamus", *Esquire*,
December 1942, pp. 306–10.

must refer to something recognizable as a fact and something, if the "service" is to be of any value at all, which presumably will take place within the subscriber's lifetime. In the world of prognosticating, such restrictions are severe impediments and the pundits did what they could with "if's" and "unless's". But to no avail. They, too, were right less than half the time and their subscribers would also have done better to flip a coin. [1]

Predictions, of course, are where you find them, and success as a foreteller is based on a naïve selection of something that has happened from among a mass of things that haven't, the clever interpretation of ambiguities, or a brazen announcement of the inevitable. An amusing mixture of the first and last of these was supplied by the New York *Daily News*'s amazement, when President Truman relieved General MacArthur of his command, in April 1951, at the "almost uncanny accuracy" of their astrologer, Marion Drew, who had boldly predicted, only four months before, that the general would encounter "strong criticism in March or April". It was a fairly safe bet during the whole last ten years of General MacArthur's military career that he would encounter strong criticism any month of the year, and after his defeat at the Yalu River even an astrologer was safe in assuming there would be some grumbling.

It would be beneath rational dignity to discuss whether or not fortune-tellers can foretell the future, were it not that millions insist that they can, and hundreds of thousands, including at least one president of the United States, Prime Ministers of France and Canada, and assorted dictators, have governed their affairs (and, alas, ours) by the advice of clairvoyants. It is a rare social gathering in which someone does not bring up an "irrefutable" instance of prescience and demand that doubters "account for *that*".

There is, of course, one way of accounting for the narrative, if not for the alleged fact; but experience has showed that this explanation has a tendency to disorganize the group, to agitate

[1] Dixon Wecter: "How Much News in the News Letter?" the *Atlantic Monthly*, March 1945, pp. 43–9.

the hostess, and to render further discussion difficult. A less pointed but fairly effective retort is to ask the question that was asked by the few rational men who opposed the persecution of witches. Why, they asked, if these old women were in league with Satan, could command the elements, and even ride over the moon, did they live in such wretchedness, suffer the abuse of petty magistrates and rustic beadles, languish in village prisons, and often die a terrible and shameful death?

Similarly, one may ask why fortune-tellers are poor. For, with the exception of a fortunate few—and, of course, those ensconced in the legitimized branches of supernaturalism—most professional clairvoyants are poor creatures, living in alleys and musty, rented rooms, furtive and harassed. Whereas any human being able to see with certainty as much as five minutes into the future need only hie him to the nearest race track to live in opulence and security.

Events of the past two decades have greatly lessened our admiration for the mysterious wisdom of the Orient, but there are those who still believe in the Hindu rope trick and challenge sceptics to account for it. The trick, as described by those who profess to have seen it performed, is as grim as it is baffling. A man throws a rope up into the air, where it remains vertical and rigid. A small boy then climbs the rope and disappears at the top. The magician, with a knife in his teeth, climbs up after the boy and he too disappears. There are sounds of an altercation, and the boy's body falls from the sky in bloody segments. The magician reappears and descends the rope. He performs some hocus-pocus over the dismembered body, and the boy is reassembled, none the worse.

Such is the story. There have been scores of "eyewitnesses", including Douglas Fairbanks, Sr, and Nina Wilcox Putnam.[1] Many explanations have been offered, some as remarkable as the act itself. It has been claimed that the rope is really a bamboo

[1] Mrs Putnam told Joseph Rinn that she had taken a photograph of it. Rinn offered her $1,000 for a print of the picture, but she never produced it. Joseph F. Rinn: *Sixty Years of Psychical Research* (New York: Truth Seeker Company; 1950), p. 599.

pole—but that explains only a few ludicrous photographs. It has been claimed that the fakir actually hypnotizes the audience, making them victims of "mass suggestion". And it has been claimed that he burns certain mysterious leaves, "something like marihuana", the smoke of which drugs the onlookers into credulity.

Neither hypnosis nor marihuana has been known to have any such effect in the United States, but even if either did, it would be a waste of effort and drug, for the credulous seem quite willing to believe without either. The fact is—though this is utterly unconvincing to those who want to believe—that there simply isn't any authentic account of the trick ever having been performed. When George V, as Prince of Wales, visited India in 1902, Lord Lonsdale offered £10,000 (then an immense fortune) to anyone who could perform the rope trick, but found no takers. Mr G. Huddlestone, writing in *Nature*, said that he had lived in India for thirty years, during which time he had ceaselessly made inquiries regarding the trick, but had never found anyone able or willing to perform it, and did not believe that it could be or ever had been done.[1]

One doesn't hear too much about the rope trick any more, but that doesn't mean that there is any marked diminution in the total stock of credulity. Other mysteries crowd in to take its place, and of these at the moment one of the chief is dowsing, or rhabdomancy, or water-divining, or witch-wiggling, as they call it in Arkansas. Writing on it in 1874, Baring-Gould assumed that it was a *medieval* superstition, lingering on only among outlandish eccentrics. And such, fifty years ago, any intelligent, educated man would have thought it to be. But it is now in full flower. Dowsers are officially employed by many governments. They are incorporated. They have press agents and can, apparently, command fees that would make a surgeon envious. They are consulted by the Southern Baptist Conference *and* the

[1] See *Nature*, February 20, 1919. See also the articles "Rope Trick", *The Standard Dictionary of Folklore*, vol. 2, p. 956; and Lt.-Col. R. H. Elliot: "Indian Conjuring", *Nature*, September 12, 1936, pp. 425–7.

Vatican.[1] They are backed by supporting organizations. In England there is the British Society of Dowsers. In France there is L'Association des Amis de la Radiesthésie, with a special supply house, Maison de la Radiesthésie. In Germany it's the Gesellschaft für Wissenschaftliche Pendelforschung. And from all of them comes an endless account of marvels, wonders, miracles, and inexplicable happenings. Not since Moses smote the rock in Horeb has there been such a clamour over rods and water.

In America the most clamorous voice is that of Mr Kenneth Roberts, the novelist, who has set himself up as the special champion of Henry Gross, a Maine game warden who, in Mr Roberts's opinion, has rhabdomantic powers which, if only recognized and utilized, would flood the earth with life-giving waters and cause the deserts to blossom like the rose. Mr Roberts has set forth these opinions, with supporting theories and proofs, in two books—*Henry Gross and His Dowsing Rod* (1951) and *The Seventh Sense* (1953).[2] In the first of these volumes he included supporting essays by Professor Charles Richet, of the University of Paris, and Miss Evelyn M. Penrose, a famous British dowseress.

Some dowsers dowse only with hazel twigs when the sun is high. Others work around the clock with anything that comes to hand—sticks of any kind, coat hangers, corset stays, grass, or a weight on a string. Some use nothing at all; they just feel vibrations. Pieter Van Jaarsveld, a South African dowser who, like so many wonders of the invisible world, was introduced to the American public by *Life* and *Time*, simply looks down and sees the water. He says the whole thing looks very much like moonshine.[3]

Dowsing is often a strenuous experience. Sometimes the rod writhes in the dowser's hands with such force as to cause blisters or, if he holds it too firmly for that, to break. And there are

[1] For the Baptists, see Kenneth Roberts: *The Seventh Sense* (New York: Doubleday & Company; 1953), p. 275. For the Vatican, see *Life*, March 27, 1950, p. 82.
[2] Both were published by Doubleday & Company, New York.
[3] *Time*, December 1, 1947, p. 40.

psychic strains as well. Aymar, a famous French water witch, always had a rapid pulse and sweated profusely when the power was upon him. Pieter has headaches. Bleton, another Frenchman, fell into convulsions, and Miss Penrose sometimes throws up. Even Henry Gross got tired.

It is plainly a very mysterious force—"pragmatic or telluric", one authority calls it. It seems to be inheritable, though some insist that it goes from "father to daughter and from mother to son" instead of in a direct line. Miss Penrose has a brusque, British, no-nonsense approach to the whole thing. Water, minerals, and oil, she explains, give off electro-magnetic waves to which the dowsers are particularly sensitive. Dowsers, she says, "are merely human radio sets who are tuned in to these wave lengths". She grants, in her jolly way, that this "knocks the romance and mystery" out of the business, but insists that it is "without doubt, the logical and correct explanation". Other thinkers, however, attribute it to "corpuscular effluvia" or "passive perturbatory qualities". Mr Roberts disagrees with them all. He does not know exactly what it is, but he is sure that it has nothing to do with "humidity, nor heat, nor electricity", and that it is "out of the extra-sensory perception class".[1] And Bleton confounded confusion by discovering that if he stood on his head and held the rod between his feet, he felt all the sensations of flowing water but the rod did not dip.[2]

The chief function of the dowsing rod is to indicate the presence of underground water. Some dowsers—"seepage dowsers", Kenneth Roberts scornfully calls them—will find still water; but a really great dowser like Henry Gross responds only to flowing water. Mr Roberts thought, at one time, that the dowser might respond to "running" water, and had so written it, but Henry Gross made him change it to "flowing". There is, apparently, a dowserian distinction here, though lexicographers are unaware of it.

---

[1] Roberts: *Henry Gross and His Dowsing Rod*, pp. 31, 32, 36.
[2] S. Baring-Gould: *Curious Myths of the Middle Ages* (London: Rivingtons; 1874), p. 85.

The common or "seepage" dowser—one is almost tempted to call him a drip—usually has to walk over the hidden water before the mysterious pull is exerted on his rod. But the great ones of the profession have no such limitation. Henry Gross can dowse water eight hundred miles away, Miss Penrose eight thousand. They just take a map and go over it with their rods. They don't need even a map. A simple drawing will do or, in an emergency, just the address. To set all doubts at rest there is a photograph in *Henry Gross and His Dowsing Rod* of Henry with an atlas open before him finding a whole river of water away off under the Sahara Desert. Henry is amazed and is quoted as saying: "By Jingoes!"[1]

One is astonished at his astonishment, for since it has been known for two thousand years that there is underground water in the district his rod indicated, it was, for so versatile a fellow as Henry, a minor feat, a mere bit of long-distance confirmation.[2] Much more remarkable performances have been claimed: the rod, some say, can distinguish bourbon from Scotch, classify canned goods (an invaluable service if the labels have come off), determine blood types, detect spurious paintings, and indicate the sex of as-yet-unborn children.[3] Dowsers have claimed to be able to detect criminals, and at least one unfortunate has been executed on no better evidence than a dowser's say-so. The Abbé Mermet, a renowned Swiss dowser, specialized in finding lost persons. Between 1934 and 1936 he is reputed to have found nineteen,

[1] P. 291.

[2] That there are considerable quantities of water under some parts of the Sahara has been known from antiquity. The Romans put much of it to use, and we are just beginning to understand and renew their great North African irrigation systems. For an interesting and inspiring account of this, see pp. 33–44 of Robert Brittain's *Let There Be Bread* (New York: Simon & Schuster; 1952).

[3] The claims in regard to liquor, canned goods, oil, and at least the Rh negative factor in blood, are made in Roberts: *Henry Gross and His Dowsing Rod*, pp. 30, 35–6, 40, 64–5, 67, 145. Roberts quotes Bernard Berenson (*The Seventh Sense*, p. 11) about the paintings. Henry Gross didn't do so well on the sex of unborn children, and was no good at all at chick-sexing, but other dowsers have claimed more proficiency in these fields. The Nazis are reported to have used dowsers to detect Jewish blood in Aryan-seeming veins. See Claudia de Lys: *A Treasury of American Superstitions* (New York: The Philosophical Library, 1948), p. 397.

all by long-distance dowsing. Most of them were dead, but their bodies were recovered. His most famous find was the body of a six-year-old boy who, the Abbé maintained, had been carried off by a bird of prey. As no known bird of prey can carry over five or six pounds, a six-year-old child who could be carried away by a bird was better off dead; but that in no way lessens the greatness of the Abbé's feat, but rather enhances it, there being so small a body to be located in so vast a space.[1]

One of the most useful, and at the same time most frightening, functions of the rod, as yet not exploited anywhere near so much as its water-finding power, is its ability to indicate whether or not people are at home.[2] This, if developed, would save a great deal of ringing of doorbells and would be an invaluable aid to travelling salesmen. But these benefits would be more than offset by the assistance it would give thieves, and it may be questioned if its use in this way would not violate our constitutional right to cower in darkness while auld acquaintances hammer at the knocker.

Not only has the rod this immense range and scope, but its perceptions are delicate beyond those of any known man-made instrument. Thus Henry Gross's rod was able to detect gold in a rock over which water had flowed that had formerly flowed over gold ore. Not gold ore, not even water that had flowed over gold ore, but rock over which water had flowed that once flowed over gold ore! To appreciate the incredible sensitivity of this performance one must remember that gold is insoluble in water. Chicken-shadow soup—soup made from water on which the shadow of a chicken has been allowed to fall—is veritable gumbo compared to this. Yet Henry spotted it![3]

[1] For the Abbé Mermet, see H. K. Stephenson: "Witching Wands and Doodlebugs", the *Atlantic Monthly*, September 1948, pp. 86-7; and Barney D. Emmart: "All-Purpose Dowsing," the *Atlantic Monthly*, July 1952, p. 91. For results of experiments to determine the lifting power of eagles, with photographs, see *Science Illustrated*, October 1948, pp. 110-11. It was found that an eagle had great difficulty in flying with four pounds, and could not sustain flight with eight. See also David Jacobson: *The Affairs of Dame Rumour* (New York: Rinehart & Company; 1948), pp. 27-31.

[2] See F. and W. Servranx: *Dowsing Applied to Business*, quoted in the *Atlantic Monthly*, July 1952, p. 91.

[3] Roberts: *Henry Gross and His Dowsing Rod*, p. 141.

Such is human obtuseness, however, so malignant the human heart, and so closed the human mind, that many people refuse to believe in the divining rod. And among the unimpressed two groups in particular stand out: scientists, especially water geologists and hydrologists, and most of those who are alleged to have benefited from the dowser's art.

The ingratitude of this last group has to be read of to be believed. Mr Roberts lists page after page of marble-hearted fiends on whose arid lands, he swears, gushing streams of crystalline purity were discovered, but who none the less, out of pure cowardice and fear of being laughed at, brazenly deny the fact or sullenly insist that nothing more was obtained than some seepage in a mudhole.

Upon these craven ingrates Mr Roberts hurls a few thunderbolts of scorn and then leaves them to the reproaches of their consciences. But the scientists receive no such lenient treatment. They are anathema and are consigned, along with well-drillers, to perdition.

The basic fault of the geologists and hydrologists, in Mr Roberts's view, is the pigheaded obstinacy with which they cling to their theories when he has shown them better. It is their contention that water is drawn up from sea and land by evaporation and re-deposited in the form of rain, snow, and dew. Of that which falls upon the land, they aver, part runs off immediately in streams and rivers, and the rest, drawn by gravity, soaks through the overburden and seeps and trickles down to collect in gravel beds and subterranean pools until most of it, eventually, also reaches the sea. Under certain conditions, they grant, there will be some underground streams; but they dismiss Henry Gross's "veins" as a misunderstanding and his "domes" as fantasy. They ascribe what success some dowsers have had to the fact that water, in the quantities that dowsers usually find it, can be found, in most humid regions, almost anywhere. Furthermore they point out that many dowsers have a practical knowledge of the relation of topography to the presence of subsurface water. And they assert that dowsers and their claims have been tested hundreds of times and that a single one of them has yet to locate water "in a place that would have surprised a hydrologist", and that thousands of them have promised water where it has never been found.[1]

To these "droll" arguments Mr Roberts responds with a rattling volley of denunciation: the geologists are wilfully blind; they have a vested interest in their own superstition; men are crying in desperate need for water, yet the hydrologists have signally failed to supply it; and the FBI ought to investigate them.[2] Dowsing "cannot be denied". It is "incontestable". There is "no longer any doubt" of its efficacy. If it "disregards the basic principles of hydraulics, hydrology, meteorology, physics, thermodynamics . . . geology, and even the fundamental laws of gravitation",[3] so much the worse for basic principles. Mr Roberts is through with scientists. He will waste no more of his and Henry Gross's time showing them what they refuse to understand. When they have become more humble, when they have learned "what constitutes sound scientific procedure" and have come to perceive that you cannot possibly investigate a phenomenon without first assuming that it exists, then—and only then —will he again have anything to do with them.[4]

At the last report the scientists were enduring the deprivation pretty stoically.

---

[1] In fairness to Mr Roberts's fairness, it must be said that some of the most telling passages against him are quoted in his own works. See *Henry Gross and His Dowsing Rod*, pp. 52, 70, 198, 242, *et passim*. See also Arthur J. Ellis: *The Divining Rod: A History of Water Witching* (U.S. Geological Survey, Water Supply Paper 416, Government Printing Office; 1938); this booklet contains one of the most complete bibliographies on dowsing known. See also Thomas M. Riddick: "Dowsing is Nonsense", *Harper's*, July 1951, pp. 62-8; and Cecil R. Roseberry: "A Report on Water Dowsing", the *American Mercury*, July 1953, pp. 25-9.

[2] Roberts: *The Seventh Sense*, p. 20.

[3] As Mr Riddick says it does.

[4] Roberts: *The Seventh Sense*, p. 317.

CHAPTER TWO

Psi-ing in the Carolines

W HILE the dowsers have been busy testing whisky and re-affixing the labels on canned peas, a more august group of magi have been labouring to make clairvoyance "scientific".

Time was when faith felt no need for any such props as evidence or reason. Tertullian's *Credo quia absurdum* was not intended as an apology. "Believe or be damned" was good enough for any man, and there was always the heat of the faggot if the light of perception failed. But in an age of lesser credence there is an eager search for assurance, and nothing is so comforting today as to be thought scientific.

Chief among those who have laboured to lend scientific dignity to what had theretofore been considered little better than old wives' tales is Dr Joseph B. Rhine, of Duke University, at Durham, North Carolina, who has discovered, or believes he has discovered, scientific evidence for two remarkable forces: ESP, or Extra-sensory Perception, more commonly known as telepathy and clairvoyance, and PK, or Psychokinesis, whereby the motion of physical objects is affected by the mind. Both forces together are called Psi, and the study of Psi is called parapsychology—from the established word *psychology* and the Greek prefix *para* meaning *beyond, faulty, irregular, abortive,* or *disordered*.

Psi is unconscious. It is independent of time and space. It appears to be hereditary. Those who have it seem to have it in flashes; they can predict the turn of a card, but a tenth of a second later know no more than if they were honest. The power declines through exercise. It can be injured by "unwholesome memories". It has an extraordinary predilection for manifesting itself at Durham and a strange reluctance, shared by many occult phenomena, to show itself in the presence of the sceptical. The lower animals have "much more of this strange gift" than men, who may have lost it, Dr Rhine conjectures, when they developed the power of reasoning.

Its uses stagger the imagination. It permits those who have it to read others' minds, to see through walls and across thousands of miles of space. It reveals the future. It aids the growth of crops. It enables dogs and cats to find their way home and horses to predict the outcome of prizefights. It can project "a firm hand-clasp" from California to Texas and (the Air Force will be delighted to hear) direct the course of falling objects in mid-air. It may eventually "by taking the surprise element out of war . . . enable us to abolish war itself".[1]

In addition to a careful perusal of the Sunday supplements and human-interest stories—the "pitchblende" in which one may find "the radium of truth"[2]—the existence of Psi has chiefly been determined, to the satisfaction of those who believe in it, by the fact that certain people have allegedly at certain times identified certain cards slightly more often than certain other people believe constitutes chance expectancy.

Cards were a particularly unfortunate choice for allaying incredulity, being notoriously manipulatable. Half the terms in the English language that denote trickery and deceit are drawn from cards. It would have been better to have had someone who possessed the power step forward and demonstrate it. In such a manner, up until three hundred years or so ago, sceptics would

---

[1] See J. B. Rhine: *New Frontiers of the Mind* (New York: Farrar & Rinehart; 1937); *New World of the Mind* (New York: William Sloane Associates; 1953); "Things I Can't Explain", *American Magazine*, January 1949; "Can Your Pet Read Your Mind?" *American Magazine*, June 1951; "Mind over Matter", the *American Weekly*, April 20, 1952. For the sports-predicting horse, see *Life*, December 22, 1952, pp. 20–1.

[2] Rhine: "Things I Can't Explain", p. 144. A pretty simile, but there is an old proverb about those who touch pitch.

have been rebuked; but occultism has grown shy and now manifests itself only in darkened rooms and percentages.

"Appalled at the predominance of insecure method and of unverified speculation and assumption in psychology today", and resolved to put the whole thing on a "strictly experimental" basis,[1] Dr Rhine used a pack of twenty-five special cards, in five suits of circles, squares, wavy lines, plus signs, and stars. A variety of tests was made with these, but the most common one was for the subject to attempt to name the cards as the observer drew them from the pack and held them face down. Because there are five kinds of cards, it was argued, the subject would have a one-in-five chance of making a correct guess each time, and Dr Rhine assumed that if anyone did better than this he did so by means of extrasensory perception and his doing so proved the existence of Psi.

Objections have been raised to the nature of the procedures employed, the validity of the data obtained, and the soundness of the assumptions drawn.

In the first place, despite a ceaseless, almost jabbering, lip-service to science, the atmosphere of the investigations has been, to put it mildly, unscientific. Dr Rhine has never been a detached or impartial observer. Inclined in his youth to enter the ministry, he has, from the beginning, been resolved to find "scientific" proof of "a transcendent self that is not entirely mortal". He seems far more interested in "whether" than in "whether or not". Anything that confirms his hypothesis is "encouraging" or "exhilarating"; adverse findings are "fruitless".

Scepticism, the questioning spirit that leads true scientists to challenge their own findings and to be most on their guard when they most want to believe, appears to be alien to his mind. He has repeatedly rejected the suggestion that, unknown to the subject, blank cards be interspersed through one of his packs, his objection being that this would be a form of deception and that deception would disturb the poise of the subjects.[2]

---

[1] Rhine: *New Frontiers of the Mind*, pp. 55, 175.
[2] See Joseph Jastrow: "ESP, House of Cards", the *American Scholar*, Winter 1938-9, p. 19.

The atmosphere in which the ESP investigations were carried on was certainly more chummy than chilly. For his investigators Dr Rhine sought out "good sports", men and women willing to "play the game" and lay aside constricting doubts. He preferred those who were avowedly interested in getting "good" results (*i.e.*, in proving that ESP does exist), filled with a "missionary spirit", and willing to wring their hands in despair when the evidence did not support the theory. The very worst kind of investigator, he found, was the intellectual academic, the doubting type that checks and re-checks and has a cold, inhuman interest in facts.[1]

He urges whoever would prove ESP to have nothing to do with such people. Let him rather find investigators who have the magic charm of "salesmanship" and can encourage the subjects like a cheerleader, removing any suggestion of a "critical" attitude. It is highly important that a jolly atmosphere prevail. Undergraduates are best, both as subjects and observers, because they are such a friendly lot. The parapsychological laboratories at Duke, as Dr Rhine describes them, must have been very gay: the subjects were "stirred by teasing and high tension" as they challenged each other "to see who could be the most intuitive".[2]

[1] Rhine: *New Frontiers of the Mind*, pp. 83, 108, 110, 111, 156–7. Scepticism is fatal to ESP. Under even so mild a doubt as Dr Rhine's, Lady Wonder, the talking horse, "lost her telepathic ability" and came to depend on visual signals ("Can Your Pet Read Your Mind?" p. 136). Lady Wonder answered three questions for a dollar, a moderate fee considering that she could foretell the outcome of prizefights. Her greatest feat was answering "Pittsfield Water Wheel" when asked where the body of four-year-old Danny Matson, missing for two years from his home in Quincy, Massachusetts, could be found. Water wheels were found at Pittsfield, Mass., but no body. Then William Ferazzi, Quincy's Acting Police Chief, had a telepathic communication that came to him "just like a boot in the rear end". He decided that "Pittsfield Water Wheel" had been an equino-psychic blunder or horsegraphical error for "Field and Wilde's water pit", an abandoned quarry not far from the child's home, a place where one not gifted with telepathy would have thought the police might have looked in the first place. There the body was found! The event filled hundreds of newspaper columns in December 1952. See *Time*, December 15, 1952, p. 21.

[2] Rhine: *New Frontiers of the Mind*, p. 101. Since ESP in college students is not correlated with high grades, some have wondered why those possessing the power do not read the professor's mind during an examination. A number of explanations have been offered: (1) ESP is correlated with

It was undoubtedly great fun, but—especially with the questioning spirit ruled out—it must have created an atmosphere which would not elsewhere have been regarded as conducive to strict objectivity. In some sour, suspicious minds it would be enough to invalidate all the findings.

An illustration of the prevailing spirit and of Dr Rhine's generous broad-mindedness is supplied by a remarkable demonstration of telepathy made by a Miss Turner and checked by a Miss Ownbey, Dr Rhine's "most gifted assistant", a young woman fully convinced of the reality of ESP and eager to demonstrate it, though unfortunately "easily disturbed by observation". On one occasion she was testing Miss Turner, who was two hundred and sixty miles away. There was no observation to disturb them, and Miss Turner scored an average of seventeen correct impressions out of a possible twenty-five.

Dr Rhine was ecstatic. "Nothing," he says, "has been offered by anyone" to explain this feat away, "unless conceivably there was some collusion." And that, he hastily interjects, could not have been, because Miss Ownbey was "trusted" and Miss Turner "beyond reproach". It is true that Miss Turner mistook her instructions and mailed her report directly to Miss Ownbey instead of to Dr Rhine. But Miss Ownbey brought the letters "straight from the Post Office". They were in Miss Turner's handwriting, and as both young ladies were Southern gentlewomen, no one but a cad would refuse to accept the results. [1]

To all suggestions that there may have been conscious or unconscious collaboration between some of his subjects and their observers and to complaints of disqualifying carelessness, Dr Rhine's answer is that he has complete confidence in the integrity of his assistants. He admits that he did not himself oversee most

[1] Rhine: *New Frontiers of the Mind*, pp. 168–9.

a high ethical sense that forbids those who have it to use it in any way to their own advantage. This also explains why they don't get rich. (2) ESP is a flighty power, and is driven out of the student by the emotional pressure of examinations. This is Dr Rhine's explanation. (3) A full knowledge of the average professor's mind is of little value even in one of his own examinations.

of the experiments upon which his conclusions are based, but he "knows" that those who carried them out were honest and careful.

None the less, as the subjects have not been able to repeat their more spectacular performances, he must know that his results are open to a strong suspicion of error of record. He does not claim that his best performers can demonstrate ESP at will, but only that they have demonstrated it .36 or .23 "above chance"; and he must surely know that, under the circumstances that he describes, truly scientific experimenters would make an allowance of that much or more for error of record.[1]

Assuming, however, that the record is impeccable, that all the camaraderie, the favourable bias, and the exclusion of doubt had no effect whatever on the findings, there remains an even more serious criticism of Dr Rhine's procedure. And that is the objection, raised from the beginning, to his selecting only the favourable showings of his subjects to demonstrate the existence of the powers he claims they have.

The theory being that only some people have ESP, it is fair enough to disregard those who show no sign of it in preliminary trials. But once those who presumably have it have been selected, their entire record should constitute the test, for the chance allowance is based on that condition. But under Dr Rhine's peculiar system a subject is used only when favourable and discarded as soon as he ceases to confirm the existence of extrasensory perception.

Anyone who was more eager to examine the problem than to demonstrate a definite conclusion would have begun by establishing a norm—that is, by giving the tests to a large number of people. A norm so established would give a spread or distribution, an essential control in such a study because without it it would be

<hr>

[1] See Jastrow: "ESP, House of Cards", p. 17. See a special study of these effects in this very field, conducted at Yale (*Science News Letter*, April 5, 1952, p. 217). And see the experiments of Professor R. H. Gundlach, of Seattle, reported in *Science News Letter*, November 6, 1951, p. 298. The Bureau of Internal Revenue has found that most errors in addition in income-tax returns are in the returnee's favour.

easy to think a score exceptional that actually comes within the normal range. Dr Rhine simply assumed that his theoretical norm of one-in-five and the actual norm were the same, and that the difference between them, were an actual norm established, would probably be very small—but then the variation upon which those who believe in Psi base their belief is also very small.[1]

When a norm had been established, the exceptional person should then be tested with a sufficiently long run. That is, he should be tested until the results are stable, no longer altered by additional experiments. Then, and then only, can the tester be sure that he has established a difference between this individual and the group. And it is exactly this that Dr Rhine did *not* do. Again and again when his "promising" subject started to "decline", when, in Dr Rhine's quaint phrase, he began to do "worse than chance", when, that is, he began to show results which, when averaged out, would perhaps nullify his earlier positive achievement, the experiment was broken off and it was said that his ESP was "tired". None the less, the fragmentary positive findings were kept as "evidence".

Everybody knows that the way to win money shooting craps (if you can find anybody who will play with you on such terms) is to stop when you are winning. It would be even easier if you didn't have to play for keeps until you started to win and were allowed to ignore some of your bad runs because they weren't up to normal! You may get by with this at Durham, but don't try it at Las Vegas.

Even if a variation from "chance expectancy" could be established, however, it would not necessarily justify a belief in the supernatural or extra-sensory.

Perhaps the confusion, which is fairly widespread, is semantic. The "laws" of nature are merely expectations based on

[1] Some mathematicians agree that the one-in-five is all right. Some maintain that the same odds would not hold all through the deck. Some have objected that while five (out of twenty-five) may be the most likely score on one run through the deck, it might not be the average over a large number of runs because possible scores may extend on one side down to zero but no lower, while in the other direction possible scores may range twenty points above the most likely score.

observation; yet many people regard them as supernatural legis-
lative enactments with Nature as the Policeman. And as anyone
who can disregard civic ordinances with impunity must be above
the law, so any happening which does not meet the observer's
expectation must indicate a power above the natural law.

The "laws" of chance are even farther removed from the naïve
conception of law than the laws of nature, and a misunderstanding of what is meant by the term has been a rich source of confusion. The odds against anything having happened just the
way it did can be shown to be enormous, but that does not justify
the assumption that any one particular act is out of the order of
nature.[1] One could make a great to-do, if one were so inclined,
over the fact that the only two sets of quintuplets to survive in
the whole history of the human race were born within a few
years of each other, and in the same hemisphere. Or of the fact
that during World War II a German rocket came down through
the exact hole in the roof of the British Museum which a previous rocket had made, and that neither rocket exploded. The odds
against such things happening are fantastic, yet happen they did,
and millions of other things, equally improbable, happen every day.

The supposititious monkey that was to reproduce all the books
in the British Museum may again be pressed into service. Some
late nineteenth-century wit said that if a monkey were set to

---

[1] Dr Horace Levinson, in *The Science of Chance* (New York: Rinehart &
Company; 1950), p. 29, attempts to drive home this fact by commenting
on a prudent midshipman in Marryat's *Peter Simple* who stuck his head
through a hole made in the ship by a cannonball, on the assumption that
the odds were overwhelmingly against another ball hitting that exact spot.
Says Dr Levinson of the resourceful lad's reasoning:

"He was of course correct in believing that the chance that two balls
would hit the ship at the same point is very small, but he was entirely
mistaken in his belief that *after* a ball had hit, the chance that a second
one would hit the same spot is smaller than the chance that it would hit
any other spot *designated in advance*.

"Before the engagement began, the betting odds were enormously
against the two balls landing on the same spot . . . but once half the
"miracle" had been accomplished, the betting odds were immediately
reduced to the odds that any indicated spot would not be hit."

During World War I, soldiers liked to take refuge in a *fresh* shell hole,
reasoning that that spot was less likely than others to be hit again immediately.

strumming aimlessly upon a typewriter it would, given time enough, reproduce all the books in the Museum Library. It may be. The assertion does not lend itself to verification, and was doubtless intended more as a dramatic illustration of the nature of infinity than as a practical suggestion to the trustees of the library.

But some light is thrown on the monkey's task by a passage from Professor George Gamow's *One Two Three . . . Infinity* (New York: The Macmillan Company; 1947; pp. 11–12), in which the number of possible arrangements of the fifty letters, signs, and other typographical symbols that constitute the standard keyboard, within the sixty-five spaces of the average line, is estimated to be $10^{11°}$. This is a number so immense, says Professor Gamow, that if every atom in the universe were a printing press and all these presses had been printing ten billion lines every second since the Creation, they would not yet have exhausted the possibilities of combinations in that one line.

This being so, the trifling half-million or so words in the English language sink to such statistical insignificance that by "chance expectancy" the monkey would not produce one word in a million years. Yet what more likely than that it should hit an *i* before a *t* or an *a* before an *s* or an *e* after an *m* or an *h*—and that within the first ten minutes of its strumming? And then should repeat the performance within an hour? Statistically, it would take googols to express the unlikelihood of it, and whole mountains of monkey metaphysics could be reared on it by those so inclined. But what would it prove? That some monkeys have supernatural powers? Or that chance expectancy is a meaningless concept when applied to any specific random act?

Even if Dr Rhine's findings are valid, even if some people can, sometimes, for a short while, guess the order of cards in a pack slightly above chance expectancy, it still does not necessarily prove that they possess ESP. It doesn't *prove* anything except that on certain occasions they so guessed. Dr Rhine is at liberty to assume that this verifies his belief in extra-sensory perception; that is his privilege under the Constitution. But others are equally

B

at liberty to make other assumptions, equally justified. Those who believe in divine communications can say that a god whispered in the subject's ear. Those who believe in bi-location can say that it proves the subject was also, at the same time, standing beside the one who was drawing the cards. The logic that proves the existence of ESP could prove either of these claims and a hundred more.

Still more misleading is the argument, which runs through all of Dr Rhine's writings, that the immense odds against a "successful" series are, when such a series occurs, immense odds in favour of ESP. That, as Professor Jastrow remarked, "is throwing mathematical dust in the reader's eyes".[1]

Furthermore, in his zeal for the occult, Dr Rhine has cut the ground from under himself. For if the evidence for the existence of extra-sensory perception is the guessing of cards something beyond "chance expectancy", then psychokinesis, Dr Rhine's later finding, nullifies it by ruling out chance. Any test of statistical significance, as G. Spencer Brown has pointed out,[2] depends on "the randomization of the set of observations". That is, the cards must be truly randomized by shuffling. Because if the shuffler can influence the cards, the statistical significance of the results is worthless. But now Dr Rhine claims that through psychokinesis the shuffler's thoughts *can* affect the cards. And if they can, there is no randomization; and if there is no randomization, there is no chance expectancy. That is, Dr Rhine's conclusions from his ESP experiments "depend solely on a test of significance" which is valid only if the results which he claims from his psychokinesis experiments do *not* occur. And as the evidence for psychokinesis is also drawn from "chance expectancy", this time in the rolling of dice, but as here, too, it makes impossible the randomization upon which the chance expectancy must be based, psychokinesis not only swallows ESP, but, at the same time, like the squidgicumsquee, swallows itself.

[1] Jastrow: "ESP, House of Cards", p. 15.
[2] G. Spencer Brown: "Statistical Significance in Psychical Research", *Nature*, July 25, 1953, pp. 154–6.

Dr Rhine insists that his findings have been widely confirmed and that all but a stubborn minority of scientists now accept Psi as proved. But, to put it as kindly as possible, there is a difference of opinion on this. The majority of those who have attempted to repeat his experiments have not achieved his results. At Stanford University, at the University of Glasgow, at Southern Methodist, Colgate, and the University of Chicago, hundreds of thousands of tests have been made with his own cards without finding anyone who could guess them more accurately than chance expectancy would indicate.[1] Of the three hundred and sixty Fellows of the American Psychological Association who answered a questionnaire addressed to them by Dr C. C. Clark and Dr Lucian Warner, only five stated that they were favourably impressed by ESP.[2] Jastrow addressed a similar question to two hundred psychologists in our leading universities and found them "overwhelmingly opposed" to Dr Rhine's conclusions.[3]

The test to which Dr Rhine has called most attention, as a confirmation of his findings, is that made by Professor S. G. Soal, of London University. Over a period of five years Professor Soal tested one hundred and sixty subjects, recording one hundred and twenty-eight thousand guesses, but could find no one who could demonstrate ESP by using Dr Rhine's cards; he therefore concluded, though reluctantly, that ESP did not exist and that the experiments at Duke University had been conducted in a manner that could not be duplicated. However, re-checking his records in 1939, at the insistence of Mr Whately Carrington, he found that two of his subjects, while they had not demonstrated ESP, had demonstrated clairvoyance. That is, there was in their records a "beyond-chance expectancy" naming of cards that were *to be* turned up. This has been hailed as one of the great events in the history of Psi, and Dr Rhine's kissing of Dr Soal's rod is one of the more risible humilities of our time. But in the general exchange of forgivenesses and pardons it

[1] Jastrow: "ESP, House of Cards".
[2] The *Journal of Parapsychology*, December 1938, pp. 296–301.
[3] See a letter from Jastrow to Joseph Rinn, quoted in Rinn: *Sixty Years of Psychical Research*, p. 595.

is overlooked that, while "precognition" was discovered, clairvoyance was discredited.

And even precognition brings a train of difficulties in its wake. For those who believe that the future can be foretold must, of necessity, believe that there is a future to be foretold, a definite and fixed arrangement of things to come, even to such details as the order of cards in a shuffled pack. And once *that* is accepted, the whole avalanche of Foreordination, Foreknowledge, Necessity, Conditional Necessity, Divine Omniscience, Moral Responsibility, and Freedom of the Will comes tumbling about our ears.

They are themes of perpetual fascination, but only simplicity would hail their discovery as a *new* frontier. The beliefs that Dr Rhine and those who agree with him seek to establish are among the oldest *barriers* of the mind. Paranormal communications, ghosts, oracles, and the power of some minds to influence external objects——these things have been dear to the illiterate, the ignorant, the untrained, and the unbalanced since the dawn of time. The *new* frontier of the mind, and a very new one it is, is the material, limited one that Dr Rhine thinks he has passed.

Those who believe in Psi magnify their few and faint successes and ignore their many and overwhelming failures. They forget the prophecies that don't come true, the premonitions that prove groundless, the clairvoyances that do not correspond with the facts. The ultimate test of the validity of any experiment is that those who repeat it will get the same results. Dr Rhine's insistence that Psi is "incredibly elusive" and cannot be demonstrated in the presence of the sceptical simply means that, despite his protests, it can never be an established fact. For that which is undemonstrable must remain undemonstrated, and that which is undemonstrated must remain unaccepted.

Dr Rhine is fond of comparing himself with great scientists of the past whose discoveries were at first greeted with scorn. But merely being laughed at doesn't make you right. *Their* demonstrations worked just as well in the presence of sceptics as of believers. The solemnest ptolemist who ever feared a fact has to admit when once he puts his eye to a telescope, any telescope, anywhere, in any one's presence, that—despite anathemas, Dominicans, doctors, dungeons, and edicts—Jupiter has the satellites that Galileo said it had. And it is just this sort of demonstration that those who believe in Psi won't—and can't—give.

Their claims are so contrary to the view of the world worked out with painstaking care by scientists over the past three hundred years that to accept them would mean rejecting almost everything upon which modern thought depends. If we must, of course, we must; but one does not jump overboard in mid-ocean merely because someone says that someone else in whom he has the utmost confidence says that he just saw a sea serpent off the port bow. Not even if he insists that he saw it .23 beyond chance expectancy.

CHAPTER THREE

The Dark Rearward and Abyss

NEVER has a generation contributed so much to, and been so uninterested in, history. The past is of no importance. The popular mind is fascinated by the future and greets the Golden Age with each year's new models. It is particularly appropriate that it should have been Henry Ford who enunciated the principle that history is bunk.

One hears, of course, that "history repeats itself" any time there is a similarity of events. But the expression is not expected, at most utterances, to be taken literally, and, indeed, it requires very little reflection to perceive that it could not be. The elements in any historical situation are always different: climates alter, empires dissolve, religions fade and merge, and new knowledge, new techniques, and new sources of power change the old equation. The world of steam and electricity is not the world of the slave and the water wheel. The aeroplane and the wireless have shrunk the globe and obliterated terra incognita. The control of infectious diseases has removed some of the most powerful forces that formerly shaped men's destinies. Nuclear fission has introduced "riddles of death Thebes never knew". Things cannot be the same again.

Yet, under much verbiage, some of our greatest oracles have no sounder basis for their predictions than that history repeats itself and human events move in predictable cycles. Spengler and, more recently, Toynbee have reaped rich harvests of renown from prophetic foresights resting on this fallacious foundation.

The common man, of course, has scarcely an awareness that such philosophizings exist. His knowledge of even the larger facts of one small segment of the past is, at the best, confused and fragmentary. The movies have made him acquainted with the Romans, brawny and statuesque, to a man infatuated with Christian damsels. They got their come-uppance, and history passed into the Dark Ages, when there was little learning, but perfect faith. After that there was the Renaissance, distinguished by sinister Italian nobles and a great deal of poisoning. The masses throughout these years were downtrodden wretches ruled over by profligate kings who brazenly flaunted their wickedness and claimed to act by Divine Right. And in any popular discussion of the broader aspects of history someone is certain, sooner or later, to imagine how amazed the men of the past would be if they could return to life and see all of our wonderful inventions.

As for the Romans, no great injustice is done them, probably, by leaving them to Hollywood. Certainly they would love themselves in CinemaScope.

The "Dark Ages", however, is a fighting term. Some insist that it shows a limited, parochial outlook. They grant that the culture of Rome may have been almost extinguished in the interminable wars that followed in Europe upon the collapse of the Empire. But meanwhile, they point out, a brilliant civilization was flourishing in the Moslem world. In astronomy, medicine, mathematics, physics, and chemistry, the Arabs developed the ideas they had learned from the Byzantine Greeks and "rose to as high an intellectual level as any people has ever reached".[1] The rebirth of the European mind, they maintain, did not come from those remnants of Latin culture which the monasteries had saved, but from contact with Greek thought as perpetuated and developed by the Arabs.

[1] Professor George Sarton, *Science News Letter*, March 10, 1934, p. 151.

Others take opposite umbrage at the description of the period from the fall of Rome to the beginnings of the modern era as the Dark Ages because, they say, this was the great age of faith and hence of spiritual enlightenment rather than of darkness. They prefer "The Middle Ages", which, with the help of G. K. Chesterton and Hilaire Belloc, they envisage as mankind's last great period of sanity and serenity.

And certainly if there ever was a period of universal and unified religious faith in Europe, it would have had to be then. Antiquity, whatever else it was, was not Christian. The greatness of the early Christians was that they testified, often with their lives, to their faith in the midst of heathens. Had they not been a minority, there would have been no glory in what they did. And from the early sixteenth century on, Christendom was split by the Reformation and then shaken by the Enlightenment, by materialism, secularism, modernism, indifferentism, and all the other -isms that are still so fiercely inveighed against.

So that if there ever was unity in Christendom, it must have been somewhere between the fourth and the sixteenth centuries in an area extending from the Adriatic west to northern Spain and from the Mediterranean north to the vague and fluctuating line of "Slavic heathendom".

Even among the faithful of that time and place, however, there were serious schisms and heresies. The Arians, the Manichees, the Albigenses, and a score of other misguided groups of unfortunates had to be hunted down and extirpated, and no sooner were they dealt with than error sprouted elsewhere as Wycliffism, Lollardy, or plain, diabolic atheism.

It is the astonishing amount of this last condition which raises serious doubts about the accuracy of the term "the Age of Faith". It is true that this was the age of the cathedral-builders. It was the time of the founding of the monastic orders. It was a time of a certain sort of learning within the Church and a time of great saintliness of some of its members. But it was also a time of astonishingly widespread and active scepticism.

Pope Gregory the Great speaks of many, even within the

Church itself, who did not believe in the soul.[1] Chaucer's Pardoner flippantly suggested that the soul went blackberrying after death, and Chaucer himself (a devout man) had to confess that no man *knew* anything about the hereafter, that it was all hearsay and speculation based on "olde bokes".

Almost every moral writer in the "Age of Faith" inveighs against those who laugh openly at the Bible and hold the sacraments in contempt. A homily is not a sociological treatise, but there must surely have been some fire to justify all this fulmination. The charges brought against Pope Boniface VIII have been dismissed as slander; but the very fact that they could be brought shows that it was at least thought that something close to freethinking was possible even in a pope.[2] Certainly it was possible in an emperor, or else Frederick II has been much maligned by pious chroniclers. Dante says that thousands among the upper classes of Florence were complete materialists and utterly contemptuous of Christian beliefs.

Nor was disbelief confined to the rich and powerful. Bernardino of Siena insisted that "the many" believed in nothing "higher than the roofs of their own houses" and laughed at the Scriptures. Indeed, unless the religious and secular writings of the times are to be discounted entirely, there was an extent and degree of hostility between the clergy and the common people inconceivable today. Chaucer's Host, who is said to be an arbiter of social behaviour, is deferential to the Prioress and the Monk, not (as he would be today) because they are a nun and a monk, but because they are of "high degree". He suspects the Good

[1] *Dialogorum . . . de Æternitate Animæ.* English trans. 1608. Ed. E. G. Gardner (London; 1911). Vol. 3, p. 38.

[2] See J. A. MacCulloch: *Medieval Faith and Fable* (London: George G. Harrap & Co.; 1932), p. 232. The *Encyclopædia Britannica* says that it is "probable, though not quite certain, that Boniface privately held certain Averroistic tenets, such as the denial of the immortality of the soul" (fourteenth edition, vol. 3, p. 850; the eleventh edition is much stronger). The *Cambridge Medieval History* says "the evidence seems conclusive that he was doctrinally a sceptic" (vol. 7, p. 5). Dante puts him in Hell, just to be on the safe side (*Inferno*, canto XIX, lines 52–7); though it is curious that he places Averroës, the fountainhead of this infidelity, among the good heathen in limbo.

Parson of heresy (because he objects to swearing), is jocular with
the Nun's Priest, and openly disdainful of the other clerics.[1]

The clergy, then as now, belaboured the unbelievers, but to
the twentieth century the astonishing thing is the open frankness
with which the attacks were returned. Hostility to religion was
more outspoken then than would be tolerated now or even conceived. Langland says that the table talk of men of wealth was
openly blasphemous,[2] and Thomas of Walsingham thought that
the public scorn of Christianity among the barons was one of the
causes of the Peasants' Rebellion. In the *Roman du Renart*, one
of the most popular poems of the Middle Ages, the sacraments
and rituals of the Church are openly mocked; and the humour
of the goliards, which was immensely popular, consisted in large
part of burlesque and parodies of the most sacred things—of the
prayers, the creed, and even of the Mass itself.[3]

All of this does not mean that the times were universally god-
less. But it can hardly be maintained, in the face of it, that they
were universally pious. Indeed, there is probably more faith in
the world today than there was in the Dark Ages, and there is
certainly less open jesting and scurrility at the expense of Christianity now than there was then.

[1] Of all figures of English life, the clergy have been most consistently
satirized in English literature. Before the Reformation the parish priest,
"Sir John", was the butt of a great deal of aggressive wit in popular
literature; and after the Reformation "parson" took his place and held it
down to very recent times. Only in the past two decades have the bishop,
the vicar, and the curate ceased to be stock absurdities in *Punch*. Charlie
Chaplin's *The Pilgrim* was probably the last popular presentation in America
which dared to have fun at the expense of the clergy. *The New Yorker*
will sometimes have a clergyman in a joke (such as the worldly rector of
an obviously prosperous parish telling a new curate that he will get on all
right in the community if he just lets controversial matters, such as "politics
and religion", alone) but *The New Yorker* has a select group of readers and
the jokes are always good-natured.

Physicians also are coming in for more respect. An examination of the
doctor as shown in American movies, published in the *Lancet* in 1953,
showed that while the doctor is a common figure in movies (237 portrayals
in 428 films in 1950), he is handled very gently. In only 25 of the portrayals
was the doctor anything but admirable, and in only 2 was he humorous.

Even lawyers are not publicly ridiculed any more! If the professions are,
in Shaw's phrase, "conspiracies against the laity", they never had it so good.

[2] *Piers Plowman* (Oxford; 1886), I, 289, 292.

[3] MacCulloch: *Medieval Faith and Fable*, p. 280.

A trifling but tenacious item in the popular conception of medieval religious activities—worth, perhaps, a passing mention —is that the schoolmen argued about the number of angels that could dance on the point of a pin. It is continually adduced as the ultimate in frivolous pedantry.

Actually, there is no evidence that this topic was ever discussed by medieval philosophers, and it doesn't quite ring true as an example. It sounds like a mid-nineteenth-century Protestant sneer, but it is faint and timid. Some of the propositions that *were* discussed are far more bizarre: What do angels do with material bodies that they used on some mission, but no longer require? Do angels defecate? If a cannibal family has for generations eaten nothing but human beings, so that the entire substance of their bodies is made up of the absorbed bodies of others, what will they do at the Resurrection for bodies of their own wherewith to suffer in Hell?

There are scores of such questions, far more suitable for satire, one would have thought, than the angels on the pin, which really were debated, at great length and with tremendous earnestness. But in making fun of actual problems the satirist may well have found himself laughing at things that *he* thought were serious— and then uneasily have backed away.

But if popular fancy has overestimated the piety of the Middle Ages, it has sought to make amends by equally overestimating the villainy of the Renaissance. This, in vulgar imagination, was the heyday of subtle murder—the deft thrust of the stiletto through the arras, the fawning tender of the envenomed chalice, or the fatal handclasp of the poisoned ring.

No doubt, during the Renaissance as today, certain unhappy persons were done in, but it may be doubted if the homicide rate was anything like what it is in the United States. In the first place, murder was not as easy then as it is now. There was very little privacy. Cities were small and densely populated, and most men and women were rarely alone at any time in their lives. The whole plot of many stories and plays of the time hinges on the efforts of lovers to be alone for a few moments. Only the greatest personages had a room to themselves, and such rooms were usually guarded. When they went abroad, they were attended by a train of servants, and even the most naïve was wary of ambush. [1]

Machiavelli, in the eighth chapter of *The Prince*, relates an incident that shows the elaborate preparations necessary to catch even a benevolently inclined uncle off guard. Olivorotto da Fermo, an orphan lad of parts, after serving an apprenticeship with the famous *condottieri* the Vitelli brothers, felt that the time had come for him to make his mark in the world. He therefore paid a visit of state to his uncle, Giovani Fogliani, who had reared him, and excused his bringing a hundred armed retainers with him on the ground that they served to mark his greatness and hence redounded to his uncle's credit also. The good uncle, overjoyed, gave a banquet for the dignitaries of the town. Olivorotto was vastly ingratiating, and at the conclusion of the meal began to talk of matters deep and dangerous and to hint of still more fascinating intrigue and scandal to come. When he saw that the elders' ears were wagging with sufficient curiosity, he urged them to step into an inner room where he might communicate certain facts to them of so weighty and ticklish a nature that they could not be divulged in a dining-room. He had his bravos behind the hangings of the inner room, and when the gullible guests were lured within their reach they were—uncle and all—strangled. [2]

This very inaccessibility of potential victims led, no doubt, to a great deal of speculation about poison. A sure, easily administered potion would save all the bother and danger of ambuscades, and the ideal poison was as avidly sought as the philosopher's stone. But though poisoning was talked about a great deal in Renaissance times, though there were thought to be venoms whose very touch would produce instant death, there is serious doubt that anything particularly potent was at hand.

[1] Cellini remarks that as a matter of simple hygiene he always "walked wide" at corners.
[2] Success went to Olivorotto's head. He grew too big for his breeches. Not long after, he tried to ambush Cesare Borgia at Sinigaglia and departed this life.

The Ten at Venice were thought to have especially malignant poisons and poisoners at their disposal, but the recipes which have been found in their secret "Cabinet of Poisons" do not seem to us either practical or powerful. They had arsenic, antimony, some mercurial compounds, henbane, aconite, and the like; but prussic acid, strychnine, curare, snake venoms, beryllium, radio-active salts, and the toxins of various bacilli, which would fill such a cabinet today, were unknown to them.

Their "mysteries" consisted of endless stewing and stirring, which in all probability vitiated what materials they had to begin with. One of the best recipes in the Cabinet of the Ten is a mixture of silver sublimate, arsenic, ammonia, hartshorn, and verdigris, endlessly boiled, decanted, infused, and slopped to-gether. A preposterous touch of common sense intrudes at the end when the administrator of the poison is warned not to let the victim drink more than two glasses of wine infused with it lest he vomit and undo the good work so far accomplished.[1]

Poison rings—hollow rings that had on the under side short hollow needles through which poison might be injected—are occasionally exhibited, and may be genuine. But it is hard to believe that they were ever effective. The hearty, modern hand-squeeze was not, in those happier times, in use. Men may have clasped hands occasionally, but for the most part they knelt or bowed to their superiors and embraced their equals. A deter-mined poisoner might hang on to his victim in an embrace and gouge his ring through several layers of clothing, but it would be absurdly unsubtle and, worst of all, not very likely to succeed.

For the people of the Renaissance simply didn't know any poisons so deadly that a scratch moistened with them would be fatal. It would take perhaps an ounce of their worst poisons to kill a man for sure, and anyone wearing a ring that could hold an ounce would, one assumes, find his overtures of friendship met with distant acknowledgments. Then it is hard to see how such a

[1] See D. Erskine Muir: *Machiavelli and His Times* (New York: E. P. Dutton & Company; 1936), pp. 54-5; and Frederick Baron Corvo (Fred-erick Rolfe): *The History of the Borgias* (New York: Carlton House; n.d.), pp. 241-70.

quantity of liquid could be conveyed through rings before the development of rubber. There were no bulbs to squeeze. The poisoner would have to depend on gravity, osmosis, or blowing into one end of the ring; the first two would convey only minute amounts of the poison and the third would certainly convey a warning to the victim!

Everybody in the Renaissance seems to have thought that everybody else had terrible and mysterious poisons, and, of course, such fears would not lack for supposed confirmation. Almost every ailment that produced sudden and violent intestinal pain and terminated rapidly in death would be thought to be the effect of poison. Appendicitis, perforated ulcers, some cancers and stoppages of the bowel, and various infections could all be so regarded. Then there were thought to be still more subtle poisons that produced lingering death through slow wasting—and to these could be attributed diabetes, miliary tuberculosis, and a host of other misfortunes. As late as 1791 even so intelligent a man as Mozart could, apparently, believe that he had been poisoned when actually he was dying of typhoid.

Of course those who could afford the care of a physician *were* poisoned—just as soon as he could get his purges, clysters, and soporifics into them. Not always fatally, but enough to add the symptoms of poisoning to the original disease. And only the rich, who could afford a physician, were thought to have been poisoned. No one cared what the poor died of.

When they were not poisoning each other, rulers of the past were occupied, in folk history, with sin and open dalliance. Formerly there was a strong element of disapproval in the popular estimate of this conduct, but today, if one may judge from recent historical novels, there is a good deal of envy, and the better-behaved kings of these latter days are more despised than admired. Thus, at the abdication of Edward VIII many who longed to see him keep both the crown and the lady felt that it would have been otherwise in the good old days, and that Charles II or Louis XIV would have taken no nonsense from Mrs Grundy or the Archbishop.

But, despite romantic fiction, the kings of old were rarely open in their profligacy. Royal mistresses were either concealed completely or attached to the court as ladies in waiting, and the most elaborate mummery was gone through to preserve the fiction of their status. When we say that "everybody" knew about it, and that it was "openly acknowledged", we are speaking from the safe distance of several centuries, equipped usually with knowledge gained from the closely guarded and posthumously published memoirs of gossipy courtiers. No such talk was allowed at the time. The important thing about Henry VIII's six wives is not the *six*, but the *wives*; he was a man of indefatigable morality. Voltaire got into serious trouble for even mentioning Louis XV and Mme de Pompadour in the same poem. And when the King was taken ill at Metz and was thought to be dying, the Bishop of Soissons refused to administer the sacrament when he learned that the Duchess de Châteauroux and her sister were in the town. Louis was forced to send her back to Paris, and on the way her coach was stoned by an indignant populace.[1]

The doctrine of Divine Right, in which some kings certainly believed, was not the mere brazen assertion of their own superiority which some staunch democrats seem to think it was. Many who dismiss it with derision might be uneasy if they realized what their derision included. For Divine Right was attested by one of the most thoroughly authenticated miracles on record.

The famous doctrine seems to have grown up in England and France as a sort of "me too" answer to the claims of political absolutism advanced by some of the more vigorous popes. These popes claimed that they were God's vicegerents upon earth, and that the kings ruled solely as their representatives, but some kings—especially the French and English kings—insisted that they had a direct commission from the Deity. Such a claim required proof, and the proof they offered was that they could work a highly specialized miracle: they could cure scrofula (tuberculosis of the skin) merely by stroking the ulcers.

[1] See Georg Brandes: *Voltaire* (New York: A. & C. Boni; 1930), vol. 1, p. 321.

So strongly was this power impressed on the popular mind that the disease was known as "the King's evil", and so dependent was the king's authority on the esteem his curative touch elicited [1] that, though the performance was vastly repugnant, no monarch dared to omit frequent public demonstrations of it. Charles II (who hated "the ugly office") touched almost one hundred thousand persons during his reign. There was an established ceremonial. The churches throughout the realm announced in advance when one of the touchings was to take place. The king was always attended by ecclesiastics, and the Book of Common Prayer contained a special liturgy for the occasion. An official record of every cure was kept by a surgeon appointed for that purpose, and these records are extant. The efficacy of the Royal Touch was attested by Catholic and Protestant bishops alike, with no dissenting voice. It was officially confirmed by the University of Oxford and, needless to say, enthusiastically endorsed by the ulcerated populace. Few human claims to supernatural performance have been as thoroughly examined and as unhesitatingly affirmed by the most unimpeachable witnesses, over an immense period of time, as this of the Royal Touch. [2]

---

[1] Down through the Stuarts, that is. The power of all English kings since has rested so obviously on the consent of the governing that there was no need of Divine legation. Edward the Confessor was canonized, in part, for possessing this power. Shakespeare seems to have believed in its efficacy. Dr Johnson was touched, when a child, by Queen Anne. It didn't heal him, but he was loyal to the Stuarts. Queen Elizabeth's Roman Catholic subjects were shaken when she demonstrated this power even after she had been excommunicated.

[2] See Raymond Crawfurd: *The King's Evil* (Oxford: The Clarendon Press; 1911); W. E. H. Lecky: *History of Morals* (New York: D. Appleton & Company; 1927), vol. 1, pp. 363–5; Thomas Babington Macaulay: *History of England* (New York: Harper & Brothers; 1849–61), chapter 14; *Macbeth*, IV, iii, 149–55, notes in the Furness Variorum edition. The belief does not seem wholly to have died out. The Duke of Windsor in his memoirs (*Life*, May 22, 1950, p. 124) mentions "the touching mania" as one of the "most remarkable" and unpleasant things that he had to endure when, as Prince of Wales, he travelled about the empire. He writes: "Whenever I entered a crowd it would close around me. . . . I can still hear the shrill, excited cry, 'I touched him!' If I were out of reach a blow on my head with a folded newspaper appeared to satisfy the impulse. My staff and I bore stoically the daily share of knocks and bruises."

In rejecting the divinity of kings, then, one is affirming, in effect, that great churchmen are willing to deny the evidence of their own senses, year after year, in order to flatter those in power; that the testimony of millions of eyewitnesses, and even the direct assertions of thousands who professed to have been healed, are worthless; that scientific records, carefully kept, can be rubbish if the one who keeps them is committed in advance to any particular interpretation of the phenomena he is observing; that mighty universities, speaking in solemn conclave, can dish out pernicious twaddle; that rulers, supported by august dignitaries, can go through the most ridiculous ceremonies, knowing in their hearts that the whole thing is a disgusting lie, but not caring so long as it helps to keep them in power.

It may all be so, but it is a somewhat larger order of scepticism than the common man usually likes to cut out for himself.

Not that it would be likely to bother him here. His general reflections on history are far too vague to be concerned with the King's Evil or the implications of its cure. He is more concerned with "progress", by which he means the increase of mechanical devices and material comforts, and one of his favourite speculations, as has been said, is the awe with which such improvements would strike our ancestors could they but see them.

Pride in our mechanical, material civilization is certainly justified. No other has ever done one tenth as much for one thousandth as many. But its blessings are not yet universal, and much of mankind was better off in the past. In almost every material sense Egypt, for example, is probably worse off today than she was under the Pharaohs. You could get a better drink of water in Spain or Italy two thousand years ago than you can in most parts of those countries today. The great ruined aqueducts of the Romans cast their shattered shadows over a thousand contaminated modern wells. Pompeii seems to have been more livable than most of contemporary Naples. So with India: excavations reveal civilizations there which three thousand years ago surpassed modern India in comfort and hygiene. The Incas had better transportation, better communications, and better methods

of farming than their wretched descendants of today. The deso-
lation of northern Africa was the *granary* of antiquity! Spain has
never risen to the level of the Moorish civilization she so exul-
tingly destroyed. And it would be hard to imagine a more striking
contrast than between the Arab world of the eleventh and
twelfth centuries and its squalid modern remnants.

The assumption that someone from the past (or a modern
savage; they are often equated in the popular mind) would be
overwhelmed if shown an aeroplane, a gum-vending machine,
or any other of the marvels we take for granted, and the corollary
assumption that anyone possessed of modern knowledge would
have had the world in his grasp had he lived in the past, both
overestimate gadgets and underestimate people.

It is probably true that many things to which we have become
accustomed (though most of us no more understand them than
Methuselah) would seem magical to our ancestors. But they
might not be so amazed by them as we would expect them to be
because *they* were accustomed to magic. Luther relates that he
was alarmed when he heard a strange sound one night until he
perceived that it was *only the Devil*, and so went back to sleep.
Dillon Ripley, in his ornithological expedition into Nepal, was
interested to learn that the Chini Lama, a saintly man at Boddh-
nath, "had been causing no end of trouble to the municipal
electric power authorities" by tapping the power lines before his
meter so that he could get extra power free. Mr Ripley tactfully
forbore from making any comment on the Lama's morals, but
could not restrain an exclamation of astonishment at his unexpected technical proficiency. Nepal is one of the remotest
countries in the world, and electricity could scarcely have been
introduced there more than a few years earlier. But the Nepali
who had informed him of the incident was unimpressed. "After
all," he said, "the Lama is a very holy man."[1]

When Alexander Kirk, the first American minister to Saudi
Arabia, flew to Riad, an engineer was sent ahead to prepare a

[1] Dillon Ripley: *Search for the Spiny Babbler* (Boston: Houghton Mifflin
Company; 1952), pp. 77–8.

landing-field, no plane having ever been there before. As the engineer sat beside his radio waiting for the plane to come in, he told a curious Bedouin that a djinni in the box had informed him that in an hour and a half a huge bird would appear, bearing men in its belly. The Bedouin thought that this would be worth waiting to see, and the engineer prepared to enjoy the Arab's amazement when the plane should arrive. But when it did arrive, half an hour late, *he* was the one to be amazed; for the Bedouin merely remarked, with contempt, that the djinni had failed to estimate the time of the bird's arrival correctly.

Instead of being astonished at our accomplishments, the ancients might be more astonished that we had not done more. For they, too, had imagination and, like us, expected vast things of posterity. We are proud of our conquest of the air and delighted that our children dream of flying to the moon. But three hundred years ago it was taken for granted that these things would be, and we might not be so much admired for finally having done a part of them as reproached for not having done all of them and sooner. "I doubt not," Joseph Glanvill wrote, in 1661, "but . . . some Ages hence a voyage to the Moon will not be more strange than one to America. To them that come after us, it may be as ordinary to buy a pair of wings to fly into remotest regions: as now a pair of boots to ride a Journey."[1]

Or, perhaps, the visiting primitive or the revived ancestor might be more impressed with the price we pay for some of our marvels than with the marvels themselves. Instead of gasping at an automatic bread-slicer, he might gasp at the inferior quality of the bread being sliced, and gasp even more at our apparent unawareness of it. Montaigne tells of the three American Indians who were "at Rouen at the time that the late King Charles IX was there" who, having been shown all the wonders of a sixteenth-century metropolis, were asked "what of all the things they had seen, they found most to be admired" and answered, disconcertingly, "the docility of the poor". For they thought it

---

[1] In his *The Vanity of Dogmatising*, in which work, by the way, he also discusses the possibility of the electric telegraph.

strange that so many suffering so dreadfully amid such luxury "did not take the others by the throats, or set fire to their houses".[1]

In a like manner, were one of our simple-minded forebears to be revived, the ingenuity with which we enrich canned dog food with vitamins, for example, might not astonish him as much as the fact of our doing it at all. And when we tried to stun him with a display of modern furniture, we might find him a few doors down the street grinning into the window of an antique shop at the prices we are willing to pay for some of the things *he* made!

The other illusion—that a man with modern knowledge would have the world in his grasp if he were miraculously transported into the past or thrown among savages—has furnished a score of comic strips and provided the basis for some good novels. Mark Twain, Kipling, and H. Rider Haggard have all used it and thereby contributed many happy hours to millions of boys. But it's a boy's dream. Wholly apart from ignoring the necessity of having the myriad skills, devices, and materials without which the knowledge would be useless, these imaginings overestimate our power of persuasion and underestimate the others' obduracy.

For we are not the first generation to hug ignorance to its bosom. Stupidity was upheld in the past with the same loving care we bestow on it. Then as now it was interlocked with solemnity and respectability, and stoutly defended. As G. B. Shaw opined, if Mr Pickwick's physician had advised him to throw away his bed curtains and open his window at night, Mr Pickwick would have changed not his habits, but his physician.[2] To have protested against phlebotomy or to have doubted the theory of the four humours when that practice and theory were current would have earned not gratitude, but detestation from mankind.

[1] "Of the Caniballes", *The Essayes of Montaigne* (Modern Library edition, pp. 170-1).
[2] As Mr Shaw would most likely have changed *his* physician if he had advised him *not* to open his windows.

We are inclined to smile, for instance, when we think of the various "giants" that were imagined out of mastodons' bones in the seventeenth and eighteenth centuries, and we see ourselves, in our mind's eye, like one of Steig's "dreams of glory", explaining the facts of paleontology to awe-struck savants.

But we forget that giants were then taken for granted; whereas mastodons were not only inconceivable, but probably inexplicable, as any attempt to explain them would have contravened Holy Writ as then understood and would have led directly to the stake. It may have been startling to dig up Goliath's tooth, but it would have been nowhere near so startling as to have been told that it was the tooth of a woolly elephant that proved, by its existence, that what passed as sacred truth was mythology, that what was being taught as history was nonsense, and that all the learned great ones of the day were ignoramuses.

Orthodoxy always has the advantage of possession. In reading history, one is often moved to shout advice back down the vistas of time. A man feels, for example, that if he had been living during the witchcraft persecutions he would have spoken sense and that that particular instalment in the serial calamity of humanity would never have been. But a moment's reflection is enough to show that this is a hallucination of hindsight. The Bible says that there are witches and that they are to be put to death, and the sceptic would simply have been hustled out to the pyre himself, one more witch so far as the public knew.

No and alas! What evidence there is suggests that our fathers were much like us, credulous and incredulous at the wrong times, enamoured of their own ignorance, learning the simplest things only through repeated disasters and reserving their admiration chiefly for themselves.

CHAPTER FOUR

Alms for Oblivion

THE COMMON man's history is largely a collection of anecdotes, and most of these anecdotes have an element of
fiction in them. In antiquity there are Diogenes with his
tub and lantern and Horatius at the bridge. The knowing tell you
that Cæsar was born of a Cæsarean; the romantic sigh over
Cleopatra's love for Antony and her death at the adder's fang;
the unco' guid still glower at Nero for fiddling while Rome
burned.

That Diogenes lived in a tub seems to be founded on nothing
more solid than Seneca's statement, three hundred years after
Diogenes' death, that he was so surly he *ought* to have lived in a
tub. And as for the lantern, what cynic would bother to look for
an honest man, day or night, with or without a light?

It rather hurts to see brave Horatius fade from the Sublician
Bridge. There he has stood, for generations now, where
Macaulay placed him, a thin smile of contempt on his heroic
face, while Lars Porsena scowls with baffled fury and the Consul
begs him to run back while there is yet time.

But, apparently, he must go. His undignified last name was
his undoing. Horatius Cocles!—it has a Dickensian levity,
wholly unsuited to so resolute a figure, and the iconoclasts got to
him. Ihne, Pais, and others have shown that he is one of the
Cyclops and his heroic stand a confused fragment of the legend of
Vulcan. It's all very sad, but at least it clears the city fathers: they
weren't quite such fools as to let an irresistible army get within

two miles of their walls before starting to destroy the bridges. And Lars Porsena's men weren't such dreadful poltroons after all. Still, these advantages are dearly bought at the cost of the dauntless three!

Despite the etymological suggestion, the evidence is against Julius Cæsar having been "from his mother's womb untimely ripp'd". We know that his mother, Aurelia, survived his birth to become, Tacitus tells us, the model of a stern Roman mother and to receive a number of respectful letters from her son. It was required by Roman law that all women dying in an advanced state of pregnancy should be cut open in an effort to save the child, but there is no record of the operation being performed on a living woman until about A.D. 1500, and there are very few records of any woman surviving it until the introduction of modern surgical methods.

It is possible, of course, that some earlier member of the family had been named Cæsar (from *cædere*, to cut) because he was so born, but this is highly conjectural and lacks any support but Pliny's guess.[1]

A secret admiration for the misbehaviour of "the ne'er lust-wearied Antony" has led the less virile to cherish the memory of his revelries with the tawny serpent of Old Nile[2] for two thousand years. Among their mythical misdeeds none is more famed or more persistent than Cleopatra's taking a large pearl from one of her earrings and dissolving it in a cup of wine to drink Antony's health. Pearls were regarded as aphrodisiacs, but as the Cleopatra

---

[1] Cæsar's reputation has had a strange history. Associated as his name was with the grandeur of Rome, he came, in medieval legend, to be considered a dignitary of the Roman Catholic Church, and in popular lore was made a bishop. In other stories he was the flower of chivalry and brought into the Arthurian cycle as the lover of Morgan le Fay, upon whom he fathered Oberon, the king of the fairies. His sexual prowess, which was regarded as unusual even in his own time (See Gérard Walter: *Cæsar*, New York: Charles Scribner's Sons; 1952, pp. 15–16, 23, 49, 421–2, 515), became tremendous; Rabelais lists him as chief among "the fabulous fornicators of antiquity".

[2] Despite Shakespeare's adjective and Michelangelo's free use of burnt ochre in her portrait, Cleopatra was not an Egyptian; she was a Greek.

of legend stood in no need of any such stimulus,[1] the act has been interpreted as a sheer gesture of prodigal luxury and has become a symbol of amorous recklessness, a challenge to the extravagant, and a reproach to the penurious.[2]

Experiments by the curious (and wealthy!) have shown, however, that it takes several days to dissolve out the mineral constituents of a large pearl in the strongest vinegar and that even then the organic matrix remains.[3]

The story that Cleopatra killed herself by applying an asp to her bosom is derived from Plutarch's account of her death, but Plutarch does not give it as a fact. He says that "some relate" that such was the manner of her suicide, and he gives several other conjectures. It is true that the statue of her carried by Octavius in his triumph had an asp on it, but the asp was the emblem of Egyptian royalty—and that fact alone may be the basis for the whole story.

The persecution of the Christians under Nero led to his exaltation in the Middle Ages to the position of the baddest man that ever was. There is hardly any wickedness imaginable—and as imaginers of wickedness the chroniclers were unsurpassed—which was not ascribed to him and depicted in vivid detail. In time the propaganda overdid itself, and he became funny. Even today there is an aura of comedy about him.

Not content with the crimes he did commit, his detractors loaded him with the most ingenious horrors. It was said that he ripped open his mother's womb merely to gratify a whimsical curiosity about the place of his origin. A question arising as to whether rest or exercise was the more healthful after eating, he

[1] Emily Hahn classifies Antony and Cleopatra as "Very Unpleasant Characters". She says that Antony was a poltroon and that there was no love lost between the famous couple. See pp. 37–57 of her *Love Conquers Nothing* (New York: Doubleday & Company; 1952).

[2] There are some, apparently, who still feel this to be a culinary custom among the affluent decadent. Thus a Mr Spicely, a chef, speaking on a radio programme called *Speak Your Mind* (WGN, Chicago, June 17, 1948), spoke out strongly against this expensive and foolish practice, which he seemed to feel was a European custom, expressing his personal preference for the unjewelled victuals of the U.S.A.

[3] See *Notes and Queries*, March 4, 1916, p. 198.

commanded two slaves to be fed, had the one rest and the other exercise, and then had both eviscerated to see which had digested his meal the better.[1] And so on.

Of all these delightful anecdotes all that remains today is the belief that he fiddled, in fiendish exultation or callous indifference, while Rome burned. Some, aware that fiddles were not known in ancient Rome, say that he played the lyre or lute.

Tacitus, now regarded as the soundest authority, states emphatically that at the time of the conflagration Nero was at his villa at Antium, fifty miles from Rome. He hurried back to the city, took every measure possible to check and control the fire, and set up shelters and public-relief measures for the victims. And after the fire he rebuilt the city in an intelligent and much-improved way. Nero's life was dissolute and dreadful, but his conduct in relation to the fire (except in accusing the Christians of having started it) seems to have been the brightest spot in it.

It is interesting that the Roman populace revered his memory as that of a munificent protector and that the Greek populace, for a century after his death, honoured him as a great patron of literature and art. Like King Arthur and Friedrich Barbarossa, he was thought to be immortal, and it was believed by all that he would return. The Christians identified him with Antichrist and thought he would return in time for Armageddon, but the Romans thought he would come back as a saviour.

The historical figures upon whom some such fictionalization has been imposed, or who have been created out of whole cloth, would fill a whole biographical dictionary—indeed, probably *do* fill most biographical dictionaries. A half-dozen or so are worth a brief notice.

[1] That modern Nero, Joseph Stalin, was said, in his latter days, to keep "a group of 40 carefully selected Georgians" closely resembling himself in "general physical make-up" upon whom his physicians tested various health régimes and certain mysterious "life-prolonging serums" (*Time*, October 6, 1952, p. 30). See also "Laboratory of the 30 Stalins", pp. 11–15 of *Science Digest*, April 1953. This was the issue that ran a special caption on the cover: "Why Stalin May Live to Be 100". It appeared on the newsstands the day he died.

The story of Lady Godiva is improbable, but not impossible. The thought of some Saxon Lady Chatterley exhibiting herself to the lower orders under the pretence of lowering the taxes is appealing—though she did well to reap her fame before Dr Freud arrived on the scene. A slender thread of validation for the story is that she is always called "Lady", though her husband was an earl. The title "countess" for an earl's wife was introduced by the Normans in 1066, and the retention of the older title suggests that the legend antedates the conquest. Peeping Tom came into the story much later, and the assertion that he was struck blind for his voyeurism later still.

William Tell seems unassailable because his legend is so detailed and specific. It was on November 18, 1307, that the intrepid mountaineer refused to do obeisance to the hated Gessler and was condemned to shoot the apple from his son's head. Of his marksmanship, of the second bolt intended for Gessler had the first killed the boy, of the hero's bold defiance, his arrest, escape, killing of the tyrant, and firing the desire for freedom that established Switzerland, the whole world knows in song, story, opera, painting, and sculpture. The very rock on which he leaped ashore is pointed out to tourists, and several boys are injured every year when their friends attempt to emulate the famous shot.

But alas, for all the exactness of time, name, and place, the story is a myth. It was told in Norway, in several forms, in the eleventh century. There are Danish and Icelandic versions, and by the twelfth century it appeared in Persian. In no contemporary Swiss or Austrian record is there any mention of either Tell or Gessler. Sixty years ago the Canton of Schuyz ordered the story to be expunged from its schoolbooks.

Those who feel that removal of these heroes lessens the world's very limited supply of noble examples must comfort themselves with the reflection that it also lessens the supply of villainous examples, for every hero must have an opposing villain. If we take Horatius from the bridge, we also take Sextus from the bridgehead. If Tell's particular heroism is banished from credence, so is Gessler's particular inhumanity.

Among the moral monsters that scepticism has dissipated is Lucrezia Borgia. The incestuous murderess seems wholly a creation of prurience and malice. Although the actual Lucrezia was married four times before she reached the age of twenty-two, and one of her husbands, the Duke of Bisceglie, was murdered, she does not appear to have been more than a pawn in the hands of her ambitious father and unscrupulous brother. Discouraging as it may be to romantic conceptions of her wickedness, Lucrezia's fault was an insipid, almost bovine, good nature. She was famed in her own time for a sort of lady-bountiful piety, and Dr Erskine Muir says that the only time in her life when she was known to show the least force of character was when on her wedding journey to Ferrara she insisted on holding up the progress while she washed her hair.[1]

Of our own American heroes the most shadowy is probably Henry Hudson, who is so universally believed to have been a Dutchman that his name is often spelled Henrik. But he was an Englishman. He was certainly a great navigator, but it so happens that he did not discover the river, the straits, or the bay that bear his name.

For one who occupies more space on maps than all but two or three men who ever lived, he is an extraordinarily vague figure. The exact circumstances of his birth and his death are unknown. He appears on the stage of history for only four years—and even then is largely an offstage voice, for he was at sea most of that time. He is first mentioned in 1607, when, appointed master of the *Hopeful* by the Muscovy Company, he attempted unsuccessfully to sail from England to China by way of the North Pole. In 1608 he attempted, again unsuccessfully, to find a Northeast Passage. In 1609 he entered the service of the Dutch East India Company and, as master of the now famous *Half Moon*, again attempted to find a passage to the Orient by sailing east along the north coast of Russia. It was on this voyage that he made his trip up the Hudson. That would seem to be somewhat out of the way of his intended course, but his crew had mutinied off the coast of

[1] Muir: *Machiavelli and His Times*, p. 61.

Nova Zembla, and as he was thus prevented from continuing his search for the Northeast Passage, he had decided to have a go at the North*west* Passage, and had simply turned around, sailed across the Atlantic, explored the coasts of North America, and gone up the great river that is named after him to a point (about the present site of Albany) where it became clear beyond doubt that it was not a passage.

His next and last voyage was again in the service of the English. He was a man of headstrong will and, apparently, of a morose and suspicious nature. After a winter of incredible hardships and bitter quarrelling, his crew mutinied and set him, his son, and seven other men ashore on the edge of the bay that bears his name and probably his bones. In school-book illustrations the son is sometimes depicted as a little boy. He was between twenty and twenty-two and, it would appear, was very much his father's son. [1]

If Hudson is a real figure dimly seen, Betsy Ross is an unreal figure fixed in the popular mind with detailed clarity. For all the facts that her house is preserved in Philadelphia and visited as a shrine and that a special stamp was issued in 1952 to commemorate the two-hundredth anniversary of her birth, the legend that she sewed the first American flag in accordance with a design which George Washington submitted to her seems to be a myth. The red and white stripes, with the union jack where we now have white stars on a blue ground, was in use in the British navy long before the Revolutionary War, and the substitution of the starred jack would appear to have been an adaptation of the flag of Rhode Island. The story of Betsy Ross was first promulgated by her grandson in 1870, and is utterly lacking in any contemporary support. None the less, the chances are that she is in history to stay. [2]

[1] G. M. Asher: *Henry Hudson the Navigator* (London: Printed for the Hakluyt Society; 1860) brings together all known original documents relative to Henry Hudson. From them emerges a moving suggestion of an extraordinary, demonic, driven, unhappy man.

[2] See *The New Yorker*, July 1, 1950, p. 17; *Time*, January 7, 1952, p. 32; *Life*, February 18, 1952, pp. 57–9; the *New York Times*, December 26, 1952, p. 17C.

As firmly established is John Montague, fourth Earl of Sandwich. The story is that his lordship, an inveterate gambler, could not tear himself away from the gaming table even to eat and had the inspiration to order a servant to bring him a piece of meat between two slices of bread. And lo, the sandwich was born!

That the sandwich was named in honour of the Earl there can be little doubt, but that he invented it is preposterous. Men had been eating meat and bread for a long time—indeed, in the Middle Ages a slice of stale bread was the customary plate for the poor—and it is hard to believe that humanity had to wait until five a.m., August 6, 1762,[1] for someone to think of putting the meat between the bread. As a matter of fact, we know that they didn't, because the Romans had a word for it: *offula*.

A grimmer legend, cherished for its irony, that "Dr Guillotine who invented the guillotine was himself guillotined by the guillotine"[2] has even less foundation in fact.

Dr Joseph Ignace Guillotin, in the first place, did not invent the guillotine. He merely urged the adoption of some sort of mechanical decapitator in the Constituent Assembly—on the democratic grounds that the aristocrats were not entitled to the exclusive privilege of being beheaded. There were also humanitarian advantages (and we must never forget that the French Revolution made a great *profession* of being humane): the condemned person, Dr Guillotin assured the Assembly, would feel only "a slight freshness on the neck".[3]

Influenced by these moving, if undemonstrable, considerations, the Assembly a few years later had such a machine constructed under the direction of Dr Antoine Louis, Secretary of the

[1] This exact date is given by Joseph T. Shipley in his *Dictionary of Word Origins* (New York: Philosophical Library; 1945). Mr Shipley does not accept the legend. If the modern pronunciation continues, future folksetymologists will discover one Sam Widge to have been the inventor and identify him, perhaps, as a rough democratic fellow who scorned patrician plates and effete forks.

[2] Senator Tom Connally, so quoted in *Time*, May 22, 1944, p. 19. "Was not good Dr Guillotine executed by his own neat invention?" asked Thackeray.

[3] Peter Quennell: *Singular Preference* (London: William Collins Sons & Co.; 1952), pp. 192–3. Mr Quennell is paraphrasing Sanson's memoirs.

Academy of Surgeons. For a while it was called the *louisette*, after Dr Louis, but the fickle populace (which at first had resented the contrivance because it cheated them of the spectacle of the more protracted agonies that hanging afforded) transferred the honour back to him who had originally suggested the improvement, and *guillotine* it became.

Even Dr Louis, however, had not invented the device. He merely improved on an Italian model. The Scotch had been using a thrifty, rope-saving contraption much like the guillotine for centuries, under the affectionate name "the Maiden". The Regent Morton was executed in Edinburgh by such a machine in 1581. A German woodcut, dated 1539, shows St Matthew being guillotined.[1]

Dr Louis died a natural death in 1792, a few weeks after his invention had its first official use. Dr Guillotin was imprisoned during the Terror, and must have had some apprehensions of feeling a slight freshness on his own neck, but he was released and died in bed in 1814.

The unveiling, in 1950, at the Spaarndam Lock in Holland, of a statue of the little Dutch boy who held his finger in a hole in the dyke and so saved the town of Haarlem was a remarkable triumph of stubborn fiction over yielding fact. The boy, who is nameless in the story, first appeared in an interpolated episode in Mary Mapes Dodge's *Hans Brinker, or the Silver Skates*, in 1865. Mrs Dodge, who was editor of *St Nicholas*, a magazine for children, obviously knew very little about dykes but, equally obviously, a great deal about the common reader. The story was immensely popular, and within a generation was generally assumed to have been a historical fact. The Dutch, who had a vast and painfully acquired knowledge of real dykes and actual inundations, were exasperated by the demand of Americans to be shown the spot where the heroic lad had "with a chuckle of boyish delight" "put his chubby little finger" in the hole and held

[1] This woodcut is reproduced in the *Encyclopædia Britannica*, fourteenth edition, Vol. 10, p. 971. The representation probably has very little bearing on the manner of the Saint's demise, but it has a great deal of bearing on the date of the guillotine.

it there. For almost a century they did everything they could to dissipate Mrs Dodge's preposterous fantasy, but at last apparently decided that this was a flood they could not stop—or perhaps that tourists were as much a source of wealth as dykes—and put up a statue of the boy. Queen Juliana, who attended the unveiling, sought to pacify the more rational of her subjects by insisting that she was there solely as the mother of four children.

The citizens of Spaarndam, according to all accounts, are pleased with the statue. It draws tourists and gives the inhabitants something to talk to them about—namely, that it never happened. [1]

[1] "The Hero of Haarlem", Chapter 14 in Mary Mapes Dodge: *Hans Brinker, or the Silver Skates* (New York: O'Kane; 1866). See the *New York Times*, June 8, 1950, p. 5; August 20, 1950, pt. 2, p. 21. And see *Time*, June 19, 1950, p. 35.

CHAPTER FIVE

Through a Glass, Darkly

SAYINGS are more often ascribed to those who, in the popular estimate, *ought* to have made them than to those who did. It does no good to insist that it was Charles Dudley Warner who said: "Everybody talks about the weather, but nobody does anything about it." The epigram has been transferred to Mark Twain, and there it will remain. Horace Greeley repeatedly and publicly disclaimed having said: "Go west, young man, go west." He even reprinted the article, by John L. Soule of the *Terre Haute Express*, in which the phrase had first appeared. But the phrase is stuck to Greeley, and Greeley is stuck with the phrase.

Louis XIV often longed, no doubt, to say "*L'État, c'est moi!*" but it is highly unlikely that he ever did. Not in public, anyway.[1] He was far from being the absolute ruler he would have liked to be. At the height of his power he could not even get *Tartuffe* played openly. Also, the phrase expresses his arrogance and self-esteem too neatly. It has more style to it than one would expect from a king. It reflects too patly the enlightened eighteenth century's idea of the Grand Monarch, and was probably made up by Voltaire.

But if Louis XIV's most famous phrase was made up by Voltaire, Voltaire's was made up by S. C. Tallentyre in the twentieth century.[2] Voltaire's actual witticisms are still too bold

---

[1] J. A. Dulaure: *History of Paris* (Paris; Furné et Cᵉ; 1863), p. 387, says that Louis uttered the famous phrase at the age of seventeen, interrupting the President of the French Parliament.

[2] *Voltaire in His Letters* (London: John Murray; 1919), p. 65.

to be popular, but "I disapprove of what you say, but I will defend to the death your right to say it" has just enough exaggeration to be striking and enough paradox to seem vaguely witty. And as Voltaire was a passionate champion of freedom of speech, it is "in keeping".

In reality, however, Voltaire clung to his life with great zest and was not prepared to give it up to defend any piece of senseless babble. What he actually said in his "Essay on Tolerance", the words that Miss Tallentyre "paraphrased" into the rather pompous utterance so often attributed to him, was "Think for yourselves and let others enjoy the privilege to do so too."[1] That is something different.

Successful propaganda passes as news in the present tense and history in the past and, as the best lies are those that least depart from the truth, the most effective colouring of the past often consists of nothing more than the change of a single word or the transferring of a remark from one context to another or even from one person to another.

The famous "Let 'em eat cake" appeared first in the sixth book of Rousseau's *Confessions*, where it is attributed to "a great princess". The date of composition of the *Confessions* is uncertain, but 1766 is commonly accepted for at least this part of it. This was four years before Marie Antoinette, then a child of eleven, came to France. And from the context it is plain that Rousseau had heard the saying by 1740, eleven years before her birth. "Cake", by the way, is an improvement on the original, which was "*brioche*".

The remark that the English were "a nation of shopkeepers" is invariably ascribed to Napoleon, and he may well have uttered the comment. But if he did he was simply quoting Adam Smith, who had first used the phrase in his *Wealth of Nations*.

That "God is always on the side of the big battalions" has also come to rest to Napoleon's credit, or discredit; though remarks of

[1] See *Modern Language Notes*, November 1943; Christopher Morley and Louella D. Everett, eds.: *Bartlett's Familiar Quotations*, twelfth edition (Boston: Little, Brown and Company; 1951), p. 1168n; the *Saturday Review of Literature*, June 28, 1947, p. 36.

C

a similar nature have been expressed by various authors clear back to Tacitus. Its earliest dated appearance in its present form is in a letter of Voltaire's written in 1770. The same wording, however, is used in an undated letter of Frederick the Great's which most authorities think was written ten years before Voltaire's, and as Frederick wanted so badly to be a writer, it would be a shame to deprive him of any epigram to which he has a reasonable claim.

Few soldiers have uttered as many quotable (and unquotable) sayings as the Duke of Wellington, and it is a pity that so great a stylist and so uncompromising a realist should have foisted upon him the snobbish, inaccurate, and absurd remark that the Battle of Waterloo was "won on the playing fields of Eton".[1]

It is true that the Duke attended Eton as a boy, but, according to his great-grandson, the seventh duke, his career there was "short and inglorious", and he never had any particular affection for the place. Indeed, affection for your college is a fairly modern product, largely the work of American alumni secretaries, and the belief that college athletics foster "those qualities in men that make good soldiers" is more recent still. When Wellington was at Eton there were fields and the young gentlemen played in them, but there were no playing fields in the modern sense of the term and no organized sports, no teamwork, no stiff upper lip.

Two of the most famous quotations of modern times already need a little exegesis.

Neville Chamberlain's pathetic assurance that he brought "peace in our time" back from Munich is often quoted as if he were a cynical brute who didn't give a damn so long as the shooting didn't start while he was still living.

Such an assumption is as erroneous as the one it derides. To give even the most bewildered poor devil his due, Neville Chamberlain was not a cynic. It was his misfortune at Munich to believe in Hitler's good intentions, and his misfortune, on returning to England, to quote in sincere piety from the Book of

[1] H. Allen Smith's quip, that the Battle of Yorktown was lost there, has more substance.

Common Prayer to a generation that had little piety of any kind and practically no knowledge whatever of the Book of Common Prayer, but which was soon to have a thorough knowledge of Hitler's intentions.

When he jubilantly announced that the Munich agreement assured "peace in our time", he did not mean that he and his hearers could count on whole skins and let their children stop the bullets. He did not mean, as is generally inferred, that he had merely put off the evil day. He probably assumed, in quoting the Order for Daily Evening Prayer, that a grateful people would recognize an allusion to the passage in which God is besought to save the State, endue Ministers with Righteousness, and save the People and make them dwell joyfully in safety. It was a poetical way of saying that he had brought back peace and humbly thanked God for it.

But he thereby worked his own historical damnation in contradistinction to his great successor, whose "blood, toil, tears and sweat" was also a quotation.

The rhetorical combination of these three of the four liquid exudates of the body in one phrase had, apparently, first been made by John Donne, and it is probable that some echo of that divine was in Churchill's mind; for it is hardly likely that he would have used it as he did had he remembered that Byron had also used it, but had used it to describe what the Tories wrung out of others by their wars.[1]

History is usually written by the victors. Of necessity it must be written by the literate, and until very recently the literate were part of a small, dominant group through the glass of whose unconscious prejudices we see the past darkly.

Consider the brothers, the English kings Richard I and John. Richard, "the Lion-Hearted", is a national idol, the pattern of kingly virtue, one of the greatest of English heroes; while John is a rat and a wretched rascal, a villain and a knave. Yet few of

---

[1] Churchill's use was in his first statement as Prime Minister, in the House of Commons, May 13, 1940. Donne's use is in his *An Anatomy of the World* (1611), I, 430–1; Byron's in *The Age of Bronze* (1823), line 621.

her kings have done England as much harm and as little good as Richard. He never spoke English. He was in the country less than one year, all told. He bled the land white to finance the Crusades, in which he sought chiefly his own glory, and to pay the ransom that was, eventually, the price of his own ill temper and overbearing disposition. He was a bad son and a faithless husband, and his habit of prevaricating led him to be called, by those who knew him, not the Lion-Hearted but Richard Yea-and-Nay. John seems to have been every bit as reprehensible as his brother, and much less attractive personally. But at least he stayed in the country he ruled, and his endless conflicts with the barons and the papacy were, one would have assumed, to the advantage of the common people. Magna Carta was extorted from him by the barons and thereby, as everyone knows, the bases of English liberties were secured; but the barons *thought* they were getting a confirmation of special privilege. And, at any rate, as the grantor, John ought to be honoured. But he isn't; he is execrated. And in part this must be attributed to the fact that John opposed, while Richard supported, the group that was to write the histories.

Two events in more recent history illustrate the manner in which various kinds of propaganda colour history. Few facts are generally thought to be more incontrovertible than that Napoleon's Grand Army was destroyed by the "invincible" Russian winter in 1812, and that, a generation or so earlier, a great number of people had been smothered in the Black Hole of Calcutta. But the popular conception of both events needs modification.

Armchair strategists who speak knowingly of the severity of the Russian climate usually cap their remarks by some reference to the loss of Napoleon's army, the majority of whose members, they seem to think, froze like the mythical Russians in Finland in 1940, in the very act of taking a step.

Their chief source of knowledge, though they are probably unaware of it, is most likely some reproduction of Vereschagin's "1812" paintings, a series executed in 1893 as avowed pacifist propaganda. For, actually, the winter of 1812 in Russia—at least the part of it that concerned the Grand Army—was unusually mild. The retreat from Moscow began on October 19, and the first frost did not appear until October 27. On November 8 the fine weather moderated and the nights became sharply, but not intensely, cold. It could not have been too far below freezing much of the time because part of the horror of the crossing of the Beresina on November 26 was that that shallow, sluggish stream was *not* frozen. After Napoleon left the army at Smorgoni on December 5, the temperature fell into the twenties—cold enough, certainly, to kill the miserable thousands of sick and wounded who fell helplessly by the way, but certainly not cold enough to have demoralized any disciplined and properly provided-for body of troops.

The chief factor in the destruction of the Grand Army seems to have been sickness. The soldiers were ravaged by typhus, diphtheria, and dysentery, and the mobility of the entire army was seriously restricted by colic among its horses long before it reached Moscow. The campaign had begun, with the passage of the Niemen, on June 24, in a prolonged hot spell. There were hundreds of casualties from sunstroke, and then thousands more from disease. The army, thus weakened at the outset, proceeded through accumulating disasters to its ruin. But it might well be argued that more were lost through heat than cold. Perhaps the fear of the cold, the myth of the Russian winter (as active then as now, and supported by fantastic tales—many dating back to Charles XII's campaigns in Russia a century before—of birds freezing on the wing and voices being frozen into silence), may have contributed to the panic that, by destroying discipline, completed the rout.

The common conception of Napoleon's own feelings about the disaster is expressed in the famous historical painting that shows him on a white horse in the midst of a frozen, wind-swept plain. His staff huddles uneasily behind him, while the Emperor's sunken head and dejected mien express overwhelming despair and pity for his men.

This attitude, however, is at variance with what General de Caulaincourt, who accompanied him from Smorgoni to Paris, records: the Emperor appeared to regard the débâcle almost as a lark and seemed chiefly concerned with politics at home and with the amazement the passing peasants would have felt had they only known who he was.[1]

Few "facts" of history are more solidly fixed in the minds of English-speaking people than "the Black Hole of Calcutta". It is safe to assume that thousands know it for every one who has heard, say, of Amritsar. The phrase has become a household term, tingling with horror. The ordinary user might be hard put to give any very clear account of the historical event it names, but he would know that it was one of history's supreme atrocities, that it took place in India some time in the past, and that it consisted of a great many white people being smothered by Hindus in a dungeon.

Those who wished to be more accurately informed would find the incident set forth as an unquestioned fact in almost every standard work of reference. Macaulay recounts it with full horror. James Mill expressed a faint doubt, but was severely castigated for it and consigned to oblivion. Lecky had no scepticism here. The *Encyclopædia Britannica* repeats the story in four separate places.

At the capture of Calcutta by the troops of Suraj-ud-Dowlah, the fanatical young Nawab of Bengal, in 1756, they say, one hundred and forty-six persons were forced, on the night of June 20, into an ill-ventilated room, approximately eighteen by fifteen feet, and confined there in dreadful heat all night. When they were released the next morning, only twenty-three were still alive.

There are minor variations. Some say that one hundred and fifty-six were incarcerated. Some say that only ten survived. And there are half a dozen different estimates of the size of the room. None says that the imprisonment was a deliberate act of cruelty;

---

[1] See General de Caulaincourt, Duke of Vicenza; *With Napoleon in Russia* (New York: William Morrow & Company; 1935).

yet they manage to infer it, even while admitting that the survivors were released early in the morning as soon as their plight
was made known to those in power.

Whatever the facts, there can be no doubt of the propaganda
value of the phrase "the Black Hole of Calcutta". The occupation of India, unlike that of America or Australia, could not
be regarded as the planting of colonies in an empty or thinly
populated savage land. India was densely populated and highly
civilized (at least at the top—which is as much as could be said
for Europe at that time), and the whites made no pretence of
colonizing. It was a military occupation, for commercial exploitation, at the best; and in practice, in the early years, there was a
great deal of just plain robbery.

Now, men are not content merely to rob and murder. They
desire earnestly that such actions be graced with some compli-
mentary terms, or at least justified as retribution or justice. The
English conscience had been aroused by Puritanism at the very
time when her colonial expansion began. There was much
searching for justifications of what was going on, and the story of
the Black Hole served as one of the strongest. It suggested that
the Hindus were indifferent to normal human considerations
and that it was an act of Christian duty to move in and take
over.

The very name "the Black Hole" carries creepy connotations,
and it comes as a mild surprise to learn that it was an *English* jail,
not a Hindu, and that the term "Black Hole" was applied to it
before the incident that made it famous. It was not then *the* Black
Hole, but *a* Black Hole, the phrase being the common designation of an English military prison until the middle of the nineteenth century, as "the brig" is the designation of an American
naval prison today.

The story is worth tracing. All accounts of the incident derive,
ultimately, from "A Genuine Narrative of the Deplorable
Deaths of the English Gentlemen and Others, who were Suffo-
cated in the Black-Hole in Fort-William at Calcutta, in the
Kingdom of Bengal; in the night succeeding the Twentieth Day

of June, 1756. In a Letter to a Friend. By J. Z. Holwell, Esq. London . . . 1757".[1]

Holwell, at that time a minor magistrate, had remained behind at Fort William, in command of a rear guard of from one hundred and eighty to two hundred men, when the governor and many of the senior officers had withdrawn down the river. His wisdom in electing to remain had been questioned. There had been contention and recriminations and, for years after, there were accusations and exculpations. When the senior officers withdrew, a curtain came down over the scene, and when it was raised, with the recapture of Calcutta by Clive, there was only Holwell's account of what had happened. His narrative had the conviction that minute details give, and the gloss of dignity was added to the seal of authenticity by his later becoming, for a brief period, governor of Bengal. His story has been accepted by all English-speaking peoples and rejected by all Hindus. He himself returned to England, with the customary fortune amassed by early officers of the East India Company, and lived out a long life in comfortable leisure. Among his philanthropies was a monument at Calcutta to his fellow sufferers in the Black Hole.

In his account of the event, Holwell states that he was among the first to be thrust into the Black Hole, "a cube of about 18 feet" with two windows opening on a veranda. With a rather charming frankness that does compel a certain amount of credence, he says that he at once "got possession of the window nearest the door" and hung on to it. Many of those crammed into the room, he says, had been wounded in the fighting, and their thirst and suffering soon grew intense. Those who tried to sit down "were instantly trod to death" and still others died standing, "unable to fall by the throng and equal pressure round". The guards allowed water to be brought, and it was drunk from hats passed through the bars, though in the struggles to get it

---

[1] A copy is in the Widener Library at Harvard. All materials relevant to this examination were collected by Professor George W. Hartmann, of Harvard and Columbia, and published in the *Journal of Social Psychology*, February 1948, pp. 17-35. In this article Professor Hartmann brought together all previous investigations.

still others were trampled to death. Curiously enough, he insists that the water afforded no relief from the thirst and the sufferers began, *by preference*, to lick their own perspiration and to wring out their soaking garments into their mouths, finding this "more soft and pleasant" than the best water imaginable. On the last page of his pamphlet, Holwell gives a list of the dead, exclusive of sixty-nine Dutch, Portuguese, and natives whose names he did not know.

As this is the sole eyewitness account of the event, it has to be scrutinized carefully, and such a scrutiny raises at least two minor doubts.

Accepting Holwell's figures, we find approximately 2.2 square feet of standing room and approximately thirty cubic feet of air per person. This isn't much standing room—though it is more than fifty per cent *more* than is allotted to standees in the New York subway trains during rush hours[1]—but it is still enough to let the dead slump to the floor.

This may seem—as it did to Lord Curzon—callous and contemptible quibbling. After all, Holwell was in no position to measure the floor to the inch, and the victims presumably did not stand at attention, each on his allotted space. They were defeated, frightened people, exhausted, many of them wounded, and most of them, apparently, hysterical and panicky. But the very excited milling around that this would cause, the struggling to get to the windows and the tramplings, make it all the harder to believe that the dead remained upright, unable to fall. Yet Holwell goes out of his way, in a special footnote, to stress this detail.

The business about the perspiration is even more peculiar. The amount of liquid that one could get by licking his own or anyone else's body or squeezing out sweaty garments would be small, and if the victims of the Black Hole *did* find stale sweat more refreshing than water, they are the only people who ever have so found it. It is true that they would get a little salt this

---

[1] From a letter written by Mr Jerome Daly, Secretary of the Board of Transportation of New York, to Professor Hartmann. The *Journal of Social Psychology*, February 1948, p. 21.

way, and that those prostrated by the heat are often helped by
salt, but they wouldn't get much, and it is unlikely that they
would have known it would be helpful. The whole thing sounds
like someone straining to be gruesome.

Doubts aroused by these exaggerations are strengthened by the
fact that there is no mention of the event in the records of the
East India Company at the time or immediately following,
though matters of far less moment are recorded.

Two other almost contemporary accounts have been found.
They both seem to be by the same man, a Captain Alexander
Grant, who had deserted his post the day before Fort William
fell, was subsequently cashiered, and was anxious to vindicate
himself. As he was not one of those captured and incarcerated in
the Black Hole, his knowledge must have been hearsay; but as
his account was written before Holwell's "Genuine Narrative",
it is of great importance. His dates, facts, and figures all differ
from Holwell's. He says that the fort was taken on June 30. He
sets the number of those captured at "about 200". He describes
the Hole as "a place of 16 foot square" and affirms that water was
"absolutely denied" and that there were "not above ten" survivors.

If this account be accepted as corroborating Holwell's narrative, however, it completely destroys the most vital part of it; for
it lists one hundred and three English names as those of men
killed or missing at the taking of the fort, but lists only five, one
of whom is Holwell, as "Prisoners". And in several other
accounts, such as the inscription on the monument that was paid
for and unveiled by Lord Curzon in 1902, there seems to be a
confusion, bordering on the disingenuous, between the number
of those killed at the taking of the fort and those who died in the
Black Hole.

In 1915 a blow was dealt to Holwell's reliability as a witness
by the publication of a monograph by J. H. Little in which it was
demonstrated that Holwell had forged at least three documents.[1]

---

[1] "The Black Hole—The Question of Holwell's Veracity", *Bengal, Past
and Present* (the official journal of the Calcutta Historical Society), 1915,
Serial Number 21, pp. 75-104.

One of them was a speech he had foisted upon the Nawab Alavardi Khan. One was a whole book presented as a translation of ancient Hindu scriptures. And the third was a charge brought against the Nawab Mir Jaffa, accusing him of killing certain persons who were later shown to be alive. *The Cambridge History of India*, though it defends the traditional account of the Black Hole, confesses that Holwell "was not a virtuous man".[1]

Just what happened in that fateful room in the English military prison at Calcutta on the night of June 20, 1756, will probably never be known. But surely there is enough evidence to make one hesitate to accept uncritically Holwell's account. He was a notorious liar. He had much to gain by exaggerating his sufferings. There are some patent absurdities in his narrative. There is no mention of this extraordinary event in the contemporary records of the East India Company. And what evidence there is other than Holwell's makes it uncertain whether those who died were killed at the fort or smothered in the prison. Surely, in the face of all this, doubt is something more than the "preposterous fabric of perverted ingenuity and casuistical manipulation" that Lord Curzon labelled it.

[1] Volume 5, p. 156. By Professor H. H. Dodwell.

CHAPTER SIX

Superman

I F THE Hero is the great figure of the past, the leader is the great figure of the present. The world has never had more leaders. There used to be a pretence that leadership grew out of merit, that the most capable men put aside their personal interests and, for the common good, assumed the burden of directing affairs. There is no such nonsense any more. Leadership is now regarded as a trade to which any brisk lad, unsuited to other occupations, may be apprenticed. It's a poor college that doesn't offer at least half a dozen courses in the training of executives. Entrance blanks always ask if the applicant is a "leader" or a "follower", and leave no doubt that the former is desirable.

It may be doubted, however, that it is. There is no necessary connection between the desire to lead and the ability to lead, and even less between the ability to lead and the ability to lead somewhere that will be to the advantage of those led. "A craving for public attention," as has been pointed out, "is not in any sense a qualification for public responsibility." Leadership is more likely to be assumed by the aggressive than by the able, and those who scramble to the top are more often motivated by their own inner torments than by any demand for their guidance. The urge to leadership, says Dr C. S. Bluemel, in his study of nervous and mental diseases, "is a psychopathic trait that seldom associates itself with judgment or wisdom". Dr Bluemel found that the broadcasts of the national political conventions disrupted the decorum of his insane asylum, and felt it necessary to silence the radio during the elections in order to protect his patients.[1]

And, once in power, the vociferous will be heard above the informed; the restless will start more than the staid can stop; and the energetic will always get the better of the thoughtful. Decisions of lasting consequence often hinge upon considerations apart from the issue. Justice, Mencken once observed, in commenting on the jury system, is the opinion of the man who smokes the worst cigars. Under the cherished filibuster, law, in the United States, may be no more than the prejudice of the man with the biggest bladder[2]

Certainly our acceptance of "leadership" as a profession in itself, the "managerial revolution", as it has been called, has had some alarming effects and portends worse. Legislators who are of even average intelligence stand out among their colleagues. Many governors and senators have to be seen to be believed. A cultured college president has become as much a rarity as a literate newspaper publisher. A financier interested in economics is as exceptional as a labour leader interested in the labour movement. For the most part, our leaders are merely following out in front; they do but marshal us the way that we were going.

There is thought to be an ability called "leadership", apart from a particular eminence or power of guidance, which enables those who have it to direct anything. And it is felt that the demonstration of this power in any activity is assurance that it can be exercised in all activities. It does not seem to be recognized that the qualities making for leadership under one set of circumstances might be impediments to even average performance under another. Military success, in particular, is achieved under conditions so different from those of civilian life that it is extremely

---

[1] C. S. Bluemel: *War, Politics, and Insanity* (Denver: World Press; 1948), p. 105.

[2] Or, possibly, of the man with the most skilful tailor. The suits of those who undertake to filibuster are, reportedly, equipped to meet the exigencies of the situation—though Senator Wayne Morse, who in his record filibuster of 22 hours drank a dozen cups of various liquids, insisted (on *Meet the Press*, NBC, May 10, 1953) that it was merely a matter of being "blessed with great powers of self control". And see *Time*, May 4, 1953, p. 23.

dangerous to assume that a great military leader will make a great civil leader. Psychological studies of soldiers during World War II, particularly of aviators, suggested that many of the traits that made a good leader in combat might be definitely undesirable in civil life, and, conversely, that one who had been a failure in civil life might, for the very reasons that made him a failure, make a successful military leader. Cromwell, Grant, and Hitler were all failures until war or its aftermath gave their genius its chance. It was not for nothing that the officer's trench coat became the symbol of the malcontent between World Wars I and II.[1]

When the brass of mediocrity becomes apparent through the electroplate of adulation, as it did, say, with Coolidge, those who believe in the greatness of leaders *qua* leaders sometimes seek to mitigate the effects of the revelation by insisting that a mediocre man often compensates for his own lack of ability by building "a strong organization" around him.

That this is often done is, however, questionable. Assuming that a mediocre man could recognize superiority in his assistants, which is highly doubtful, it is not likely that he would willingly

---

[1] All authoritarian political systems offer "leadership", and those who support them argue that they are at least efficient. They get things done!

This is untrue. The publication of Hitler's private conversations shows him to have been semi-literate, confused, and ignorant. The Nazi régime was riddled with corruption, cynicism, and inefficiency. Refugees got past his border guards by the thousands. Spies were set ashore in America in a ludicrously ill-contrived way. German invasion maps of England, when captured, turned out to be common Ordnance Survey maps, purchasable at any stationer's for a few pence, and twenty years out of date, lacking new highways, bridges, bypaths, and vital targets. A map of Oxford, for instance, marks the University as a single building in New College Lane!

The myth of fascist efficiency is fossilized in the endlessly repeated assurance that Mussolini "made the trains run on time", a phrase that implies that, whatever minor inconveniences the fascist régime may have caused the Italians, it at least brought order.

It didn't; it brought disaster and reduced the Italian people to beggary for generations to come. And the trains did *not* run on time! The author was employed as a courier by the Franco-Belgique Tours Company in the summer of 1930, Mussolini's heyday, when a fascist guard rode on every train, and is willing to make an affidavit to the effect that *most* Italian trains on which he travelled were not on schedule—or near it. There must be thousands who can support this attestation. It's a trifle, but it's worth nailing down.

endure the humiliation of the comparisons that their presence would bring.

Confirmation of this view is supplied by the work of Dr Elliott D. Chapple of Harvard and his associates, who conducted investigations, extending over many years and covering thousands of cases, into the correlation of ability and position in business. Dr Chapple found that people who have the power to choose their subordinates see to it that those under them really are their inferiors. Where he found an inferior foreman, he found an inferior crew.[1] Had he wanted historical examples, our presidents and their cabinets would have furnished them for him.

The hero, the great leader, is always endowed with supernatural powers. In the old days he slew dragons and giants, descended into the underworld, rescued and/or ravished innumerable damsels, and, when finally overcome by incredible combinations of villainy and force, did not die but withdrew to Avalon or the Kyffhäuser, whence in the hour of need he will return.[2]

It is claimed for many leaders that they have prophetic foresight. They get on, it is said, with little or no sleep. We are told that they exhaust whole retinues of secretaries and underlings. They "never forget a face" and will greet by name someone they happened to pass in a washroom door thirty years before. To those with intellectual pretensions is often attributed a "camera eye" which permits them to read an entire book before a college professor could have followed his finger to the second page.

In whisky advertisements, at banquets and commencements, and in certain sumptuously printed magazines, nothing is more stressed than the fact that our leaders are seers, "men of vision" who "look ahead" and "plan for the future", which lesser men are incapable of imagining.

It has been found, however, in the course of testing a large number of executives, that, as a class, they are not highly

---

[1] See *Nation's Business*, April 1947.
[2] As the world shrinks, the hero is compelled to hibernate farther afield. Hitler was last seen in the vicinity of Tierra del Fuego.

imaginative. What they have is a large vocabulary. This does not necessarily mean that they have talked themselves into their jobs (by referring to their superiors as "men of vision"), but that they have an unusual amount of factual knowledge, clearly defined. An executive's function is to make decisions, and successful decisions must be based on knowledge and concisely conveyed to those who have to carry them out. Executives are highly paid not because they are supermen, but because (it is hoped) their decisions will make money for those who pay them. That—and the fact that more and more they have the key to the till.

One of the illusions concerning leadership which the leaders themselves often share is that they are continually on the lookout for "new blood" and new ideas. Men who have never entertained a thought that postdated the fourteenth century will solemnly and sincerely assure graduating classes that they and the world are eagerly awaiting correction and instruction. Only the intimidating presence of the deans prevents the faculty members from rolling in the aisles.

What the world really welcomes is a new gimmick, a new "twist" or "angle" to make the old ideas acceptable. But to really new ideas, it has always been hostile. The old ideas—most of which were once new and had to fight their way slowly to acceptance—have become the foundations of institutions and the warp of whole systems of thought, and men's livelihoods and reputations depend on their maintenance. Those who struggle for power are more marked by the noble hue of resolution than by the pale cast of thought, and by the time they gain positions of influence they are usually past middle age, conservative, closed to conviction. Their future is increasing weakness, and their estate stands on them to defend, not to debate. The hope of the World is not that men in power may be persuaded, but that they will be replaced. The great symbol of progress is dead men's shoes.

Mendel's findings in genetics lay forgotten for forty years. The sulpha drugs were known twenty years before they were used. DDT was known sixty years before it was used. Modern trade and commerce would be utterly impossible without the use of

Arabic numerals; yet their adoption was strenuously opposed by the Florentine merchants, the great businessmen of the Middle Ages. Nor can we comfort ourselves with the illusion that such things happened only in the benighted past. It is impossible, seemingly, to get the metrical system adopted in our weights and measures. Linguists estimate that phonetic spelling would save two years of every child's schooling, a boon in terms of human life that reduces the beneficent promises of atomic energy to comparative insignificance, but no one needs to be told that there isn't the slightest chance of getting our spelling reformed.[1]

Even mechanical devices whose advantages are plainly demonstrable meet with stubborn resistance. It has been almost four hundred years since an incubator was first used to save a premature baby; yet the general use of incubators in hospitals is quite recent.[2] Microfilming was used during the siege of Paris in 1870; yet one would have thought, from the hubbub made over it in the 1940's, that it was invented then.[3] Commodore Vanderbilt, a "leader" if ever there was one, dismissed the Westinghouse air brake, without which modern railroads could not function, as folly. The telephone was regarded as a "toy", the electric light as "a failure". The zipper was patented in 1893, but did not come into general use until the 1930's. The list could be extended indefinitely.[4] S. C. Gilfillan analysed nineteen inventions that came into important use between 1888 and 1913, finding that one hundred and seventy-six years had elapsed, on the average, between the inception of the idea and the making of a working model, that another twenty-four years passed before the device

[1] See Robert A. Hall, Jr: *Leave Your Language Alone* (Ithaca, N.Y.: Linguistica; 1950), p. 198.

[2] Licetus (1577–1657) was a premature baby. His father, an ingenious physician, devised an incubator for him. The child survived and lived to be eighty.

[3] Minute copies of the agony column of *The Times* of London were photographed and sent into the beleaguered city by carrier pigeon. They could be read only under a microscope.

[4] See Roger Burlingame: "Bottlenecks of Invention," *Nation's Business*, January 1951; and Georg Mann: "The Tragedy of Wasted Knowledge", *Science Digest*, August 1947, pp. 9–15.

came into practical use, and fourteen more before it was a financial success.

So much for foresight. In addition to possessing this magic power, it is often claimed for the hero that he needs far less sleep than his sluggish inferiors. The ordinary mortal, who finds getting out of bed even after eight hours' sleep like disengaging so much Scotch tape from the sheets, sighs with humiliation at the thought of the brisk superman's briefer somnolence. Some supermen don't wait to have it claimed for them, but advance the claim themselves. John Wesley said that he found five hours completely restful. Napoleon boasted that four were enough for him, and Edison professed to get on with even less.

But the common man would do well to save his admiration for other aspects of these heroes' careers. They were all colossal egoists who affected singularity, and whose word, in this one respect, is open to question. Wesley's greatness did not lie in the field of scientific observation; he was a firm believer in ghosts, poltergeists, and witches. Napoleon so wore himself out bragging every morning how little he had slept the night before that he usually dozed off in the afternoon. Indeed, in this particular, it is a matter of satisfaction to remember that he fell asleep during a most critical period of the Battle of Waterloo, while Wellington, who professed no superhuman powers of sleeplessness, remained wide awake. And Harvey Firestone, who knew Edison as well as any man then living, said that he had a good laugh every time he heard how little Edison slept. To be sure, the Wizard of Menlo Park allowed himself only a comparatively short period for sleep at night, but he took cat naps throughout the day which brought his total to the average.

Some people insist that they do not sleep at all. Every year or so, during a dull period in the news, we read of these indormants. Thus in the 1920's Paul Kern, of Budapest, disclosed to the press that he had not slept in twenty-two years. In 1936 Rai Badahur Ramijidas Bajòria offered one hundred thousand dollars to anyone who could cure him of permanent insomnia. Just before he died in 1947, Mr Alfred E. Herpin, of New Jersey, nonchalantly revealed that he had not slept for ninety-four years. Few men can have looked forward to death with more eagerness! Dr Ferdinando Pavoni, of Almenno San Salvatore in northern Italy, was reported in the *American Weekly* to have jogged on for sixty years without sleep. He made a virtue of necessity and specialized in night calls.

These things may be. Of those who have submitted to scientific observation, however, no one, though subject to ceaseless goad-ing, has been able to remain awake more than four days and nights. From what is known of the physiology of sleep and wake-fulness, it is not likely that anyone ever will.

One of the most ludicrous of the many indications of super-human powers in the leader that are advanced by sycophantic admirers is that he can "wear out" a dozen secretaries and whole cadres of assistants. In the telling, it is implied that the Great One pits himself against a horde of subordinates and vanquishes them—thinks more thoughts than they can comprehend, dictates more than they can transcribe, and exudes more energy than they can cope with.

This, of course, is sheer nonsense. The really great men of the world have produced their thoughts without one millionth of the clatter with which empty men conceal their total lack of thought. Plato, St Paul, Shakespeare, Newton, and Einstein together, in their whole lives, probably didn't use one half as much secretarial assistance as a fourth vice-president needs on an off day. Anyone of a fussy and self-important nature who has power over others and can compel them to suit their time to his whims can wear them out, but his doing so is a mark of his greatness only in his own estimation.[1]

It is claimed as a mark of superiority that some men "know thousands of people by their first names", and in the advertising of courses for improving the memory, much is made of the gratification felt by such obscure folk as Mr Addison Sims, of

[1] In the days when the bellows of church organs were pumped by hand there was a story of a muscular rustic who boasted that he had pumped a tune that a famous visiting musician had been unable to play.

Seattle, when addressed by name. And certainly it is a humiliation on the one side and an annoyance on the other not to know a name that one is expected to know. Politicians are elaborately briefed before they greet any delegation of visiting firemen. But that they know "thousands" is more than doubtful.[1] If they do, it may explain why their memories are exhausted when it comes to recollecting favours done them or promises they have made to others.

Mr James A. Farley is the popular prototype. Some insist that he knows twenty thousand people by their first names. Others set the figure at eighty thousand. Either number may be confidently asserted, for neither could be checked. To ask Mr Farley to set down a list of the thousands that his admirers claim he knows, to get in touch with these people, to bring each one before him in the presence of witnesses, mingled, as in a police line-up, with others, would take years and cost millions. It's much easier to believe it than to test it.

It is interesting, however, to speculate how many people a man might really be able to know. "Knowing", at a minimum, would surely have to consist of recognizing a face, being able to attach the right name to it, and having some knowledge, however slight, of the personality and the history of the person recognized and named.

Sir Francis Wylie, the Oxford Secretary of the Rhodes Trust during the first twenty-five years of its operation, is an interesting man to consider in this connection. Gifted with extraordinary talents of amiability, he devoted himself assiduously to knowing the young men in his charge. It was to their advantage to impress themselves upon his attention, and they were presumably, by the very fact of their having won out in sharply contested elections to their scholarships, able to do so. He, on his side, had a pretty complete record of every Rhodes scholar who came into residence. He followed each man's career at Oxford with close

---

[1] Governor William G. Stratton of Illinois was quoted in *Time* (July 13, 1953, p. 24) as saying that he thought he knew more than 250,000 people in Illinois.

attention for three years, and was provided with special funds in order to entertain them freely. Every Rhodes scholar who was at Oxford during Sir Francis's tenure of the secretaryship must have seen "Uncle Frank" in his office a dozen times, dined with him three or four times, and had tea with him six or seven times. In addition, Sir Francis must have discussed every man several times with the authorities of the man's college.

Yet one of the reasons that he gave for his retirement in 1930 was that "he could not remember any more Rhodes scholars". That this was in no way due to a failure of his faculties is proved by the fact that he lived more than twenty years longer in full intellectual vigour, as hundreds who visited him at Boar's Hill and received birthday letters from him every year can attest. He who had made a career of knowing people had, apparently, simply reached the saturation point. Now, at the time of his retirement approximately fifteen hundred Rhodes scholars had attended Oxford. Assuming that he knew five hundred other people,[1] this would give him two thousand "known" acquaintances, and it is hard to conceive of circumstances more favourable to forming acquaintances than those he had.

In the intervals of greeting thousands of friends, the modern superman reads thousands of books. We are told of Lord Acton, whose "vast knowledge bordered on omniscience", that he "read, annotated, and virtually memorized" an average of two books a day.[2] T. E. Lawrence is said to have read "most" of the forty thousand books in his college library when he was at Oxford. Thomas Wolfe reputedly ready twenty thousand books in his college days. Hitler was reputedly one of these gargantuan readers, and so was Mussolini.

[1] See the *American Oxonian*, April 1953, p. 65. The author, who has lived in several countries and for twenty-five years taught a very large university class (who has had, that is, unusual opportunities to know a large number of people) and who believes that he has at least a normal memory, has never been able to list more than 300 people, living and dead, whose names he could connect to a face.

[2] See Herman Ausubel: "The Cult of Acton", the *Saturday Review*, March 14, 1953, p. 22.

In Lord Acton's case, we are not told what the books were—anyone can read two comic books a day; millions, alas, apparently do!—nor are we given a glimpse of the annotations. And what is it to "virtually" memorize something? And for how many days did this process continue? And, most important of all, what good came of it at last?

"How tiresome all this is," Van Wyck Brooks says of these claims, "and how untrue." As one who has read six or seven hours a day for twenty years, Mr Brooks finds it hard to be patient with such glib assertions. He estimates that in that twenty years he himself has read "less than six thousand, less than a book a day".[1]

Those who make such claims for others (they are made far more often *for* people than *by* them) explain the mystery by saying that the superman can read "at sight", can "grasp the meaning" of an entire page or even of an entire book by "photographing" it with a glance.[2] The standard version of the myth is often assigned to Theodore Roosevelt: a friend brings him a book and asks his opinion of it. The president accepts the book and seems to be fingering it idly while they chat for a few minutes. The friend, on taking his leave, says that he will be interested to know Mr Roosevelt's estimate of the book when he has read it. "I have already read it," says Mr Roosevelt (who, by the way, had been retarded as a reader when a child because of poor eyesight), "while we were talking." And, sure enough, to his visitor's amazement, he shows a detailed knowledge of the book!

The possession of this talent has been ascribed to almost every distinguished figure in the modern world except Helen Keller. George Ade, Wendell Willkie, Robert Maynard Hutchins,

[1] Van Wyck Brooks: "From a Writer's Notebook", the *Nation*, November 14, 1953, p. 400.
[2] Mr Alva Johnston, writing in *The New Yorker* (August 20, 1949, p. 52), referred to Mr Clifton Fadiman as a "camera-eye reader", one of those persons who has "the faculty of photostating a whole page in their minds in a very few seconds". Yet Mr Fadiman, in a letter to the author, states that he reads "most modern novels . . . at a speed of about 100–125 pages an hour", and adds: "The better a book is, the more slowly I read it."

Clifton Fadiman, and Morris Fishbein have all had it foisted upon them by admirers. "Specialists" in reading have even gone so far as to urge this as the only desirable way of reading and to warn the beginner (who, unfortunately, can't read their books) that the "old-fashioned" way of reading will lead to mental paralysis. Thus Mr W. E. Schutt, in his *Reading for Self-Education*, urges the neophyte "to read with the eye alone" since it is "fatal to proper reading" to make "mental images of the sound of words" as one reads.

But what else can one do? Letters are only symbols for sounds, and while some people can translate them into sounds and the sounds into meanings faster than other people can, all must go through the same process. Words are words. How does one "get the meaning at a glance"? Words can be understood only in their contexts. The implications of voice, mood, tense, punctuation, and, above all, associations must be considered. Where a word has various meanings, several must be tested and weighed. He who understands at a glance what he reads, reads only what he can understand at a glance. Anyone whose reading goes beyond a primer is continually encountering strange words, or familiar words in strange senses. And all of this cannot be comprehended automatically. It is not the beginner, but the adept reader, who keeps several dictionaries within reach and repeatedly goes back over a passage to make sure that he has understood it. Reading is an exercise of one's whole experience and capacities, not just a registering on the optic nerve.

When superman is not reading "at sight", he still manages to save time by "skipping". Mr Norman Lewis, in his *How to Get More Out of Your Reading*, says that "up to seventy-five per cent" of the time normally spent in reading a book can be saved by "expert skipping".

But how does the expert skipper know what to skip without reading it first? One wonders if Mr Lewis and those who share his view have not—innocent, apparently, of the whole process of reading—mistaken expert skipping for skipping by an expert? They are not the same thing.

It is true that someone deeply read in a special subject can sometimes form an opinion of a new book on that subject by merely turning a few leaves and reading here and there. And this tentative opinion may prove to be a sound one, one that a careful reading will corroborate. But no magical performance has taken place. The expert has probably turned to one or two crucial passages to judge the extent of the new author's knowledge or the bent of his attitudes. A single word is often enough to reveal a point of view and a whole set of values behind that point of view, and the expert knows that, given those values and that point of view, this or that interpretation must follow. But only the expert is equipped to form such a judgment—and he can do so not because he reads lightly but because he has read thoroughly.

CHAPTER SEVEN

The Chameleon's Dish

MOST supernatural feats are assigned by folklore to men. It seems immodest, apparently, or perhaps unbefitting their lower natural station, for women to perform them.

An exception is made in one field, however: almost all people who have lived without eating have been women. There have been a few men, but very few. Perhaps it is a tribute to women's ethereal natures. Extreme sensitivity and delicacy—as in the fairy story of the princess whose royalty was revealed by her ability to detect a pea under twenty mattresses—are often thought to indicate an innate superiority.[1] And what could possibly be more delicate than not to eat at all?

From the beginning there have been accounts of people who have subsisted without eating. Pliny described a whole race whose mouths were too small to enable them to eat, and who existed, perforce, on the smell of flowers. Sir John Mandeville actually saw them.

[1] George Orwell believed that the assumed susceptibility of the white race to sunstroke was a superstition that served to mark their delicacy and hence their superiority. It used to be asserted that a white man could not safely walk in tropical sunshine without a pith helmet. During World War II, however, whole armies manœuvred in the tropics without pith helmets, and the belief was quietly dropped. With the weakening of the white man's grip on the coloured peoples, it probably wasn't wise to call attention to any supposed physical delicacy, but rather (as was done) by tremendous feats of exertion and endurance to show that he was a tough customer. See George Orwell: *Such, Such Were the Joys* (New York: Harcourt, Brace & Company; 1953), p, 89 and note.

In later times the power was claimed not for an odd race but for particular members of our own. Often they are no more distinct than "a young lady of Bern", "a nun at Leicester", "the Norwich woman", or "one that lived forty years upon meer aire". But some achieved local habitations and names and had a few supporting details added. One Margaret Weiss went without food, we are told, for three years, and Katharine Binder, of the Palatinate, went nine. Liduine of Schiedam lived from 1395 to 1414 on beer and apple-peelings, but—quite understandably—lost interest in eating altogether, and simply did without food from 1414 to 1428.

Most of the early non-eaters were non-excreters too—as a proof of their veracity; though modern non-eaters are inclined to excrete normally—as a proof of their unusualness. Katerin Cooper, of Schmidweiler, for nine years "ate not, slept not, and voyded not". Veitken Johans, a non-eater of Glabbitch, after four years found himself freed from any urge towards those "necessary works of nature which every creature is forced to". And while modern non-eaters make a great point of their abounding vigour and too, too solid flesh, the earlier ones were sere and withered. A physician who examined Jane Balan after she had not eaten for three years found "all the muscles, intestines, bowels, other parts of her belly . . . withdrawn and annihilated" for want of food, there remaining of her "fleshie substance" nothing but "lappings and filaments". Her "passages were shut", she did not excrete—she didn't even sweat, and her head was not "charged with dandriffe".[1]

Eve Fliegen, "the maid of Brabant", lived, if we may trust contemporary accounts, from 1597 to 1611 solely on the smell of a rose. It is said that, a poor swineherd, she had prayed to God, in 1594, to relieve her of the pains of hunger and that her prayer

[1] See Hyder Rollins: "Some English Accounts of Miraculous Fasts", the *Journal of American Folk-Lore* October–December 1921, pp. 357–76; Eric John Dingwall: *Some Human Oddities* (London: Home & Van Thal; 1947), p. 33; William A. Hammond: *Fasting Girls* (New York: G. P. Putnam's Sons; 1879), pp. 2–8. Dandruff, by the way, was long regarded as a form of excrement. It was felt that the brains sort of dried up and fluffed off.

was granted by the unexpected method of allowing her to live without eating at all. Even with divine help, however, the deep-rooted habit of eating had been hard to overcome, and it had taken her three years to break it. And there was one relapse: in 1599 she was persuaded by the Countess of Meurs to eat a cherry. But she suffered such indigestion in consequence of this overindulgence that she remained thereafter a complete abstainer. A wax effigy of her was exhibited in Amsterdam (where it was seen by Sir William Brereton in 1634), so lifelike that it, too, ate nothing.

Then there was a woman at Kendal in Westmorland who in the mid-seventeenth century went for fourteen years without eating anything except "two or three spoonfuls of milk each day before twelve o'clock". Dr John Worthington examined her in May 1660, and reported that she did not evacuate and gave out an unpleasing smell "yet not so bad as might be expected".

Non-eating has always been regarded as a mark of sanctity, and Protestants and Catholics had at various times insisted that only abstinents of their own faith were genuine. The Catholics had been able to produce more inediants than their opponents, and the Kendal woman was triumphantly claimed by the Protestants. But the Catholics retorted that she was "a mere corps kept in its form by the power of the Devil" and likely to remain so till doomsday.[1]

The first scientific investigation of one of these claimants was that of Ann Moore, "the fasting woman of Tutbury", in 1813. Ann had the distinction of having given up eating on purely æsthetic grounds. She said that she just couldn't bear the sight of food, gave it up, and noticed no ill effects. She ate a few black currants on July 17, 1807, and "gradually diminished her liquids" during the ensuing month. After that, nothing at all.

[1] Rollins: "Some English Accounts of Miraculous Fasts", pp. 371–2, 359. Catholic abstinents do not, of course, abstain from the Eucharist, and Protestants have jeered at this as cheating. But the Catholic answer is that whereas ordinary food is assimilated by a man into his natural life, the Eucharist assimilates the man into supernatural life.

A number of pamphlets were published about her, and she became the object of considerable speculation. Some were of the opinion that she lived on air, others that she was a miraculous presage of famine in France. A few surly folk went so far as to doubt that she was telling the truth,[1] and in September 1808 a succession of four-hour watches, composed of the most worshipful persons of the neighbourhood, was established and maintained for sixteen days. At the end of that time she seemed to be in even better health than she had been at the beginning, and the committee decided that her claims were beyond question.

For the next four years she attracted crowds, and the donations of her admirers, who were as much impressed by her piety as her inedia, amounted to an impressive income.

There were still a few doubters, but Mrs Moore, who had in two or three years banked four hundred pounds, was willing to let them carp. Her followers, however, took them more seriously and when, in the summer of 1812, Alexander Henderson, physician to the Westminster General Dispensary, wrote an unfavourable *Examination* of her case, they goaded her (though most reluctantly and against her better judgment) into submitting to a second observation.

But the fame which had proved so lucrative now proved her undoing. The committee that undertook to conduct the second watching contained men of a much higher level of education and scientific knowledge than the first. It included Sir Oswald Mosley, the Reverend Legh Richmond, a Dr Fox, and his son. They met on April 20, 1813, and fixed a month as a fair period for the test, arranging for one of them to be in her room at all times. At the suggestion of Dr. Fox's son, the bed, with Mrs Moore in it, was placed on a weighing machine, and it was soon apparent that under constant surveillance she was losing weight steadily. After nine days of strict watching she began to sink, and was warned that she must assume the responsibility for her own death if she continued to refuse food. Frightened, she confessed that she had "taken sustenance" during the years in which she

[1] They were probably Communists.

professed to have been fasting. Out of pity or amusement, the committee allowed her to insert "occasionally" before "taken"; after all, three times a day is still "occasionally". The credulousness of the first set of watchers was revealed in her admission that during the whole sixteen days of her first observation she had been fed by her daughter while the watchers were in the room. The younger woman had soaked towels in milk and broth and wrung them into her mother's mouth while washing her face. She had also conveyed food from her mouth to her mother's while kissing her.[1]

In fairness, it must be confessed that some non-eaters have had physicians support their claims. Five doctors of medicine upheld Louise Lateau's insistence that she had not eaten, drunk, slept, urinated, or defecated for four years. The claim shook Europe in the middle of the nineteenth century. Five other doctors of medicine published works attesting their disbelief.

Miss Lateau, like most recent inediants, was possessed of many remarkable powers. She was subject to paroxysms of ecstasy in the course of which she would remain, totally unsupported, in mid-air about a foot above her bed. At these times she was rigid and motionless, except that a light smile was sometimes seen to play over her face.

Dr Warlomont, an uncouth and discourteous fellow who was sent to investigate her claims by the Belgian Royal Academy of Medicine, unexpectedly wrenching open a cupboard in her room, found a cache of food, and got Miss Lateau to admit that, while she never slept, she was subject to nocturnal periods of forgetfulness.[2]

Among those who supported Miss Lateau was the celebrated Dr Imbert-Gourbeyre, who seems to have made a practice of gifted non-eaters. Among his patients was also Palma d'Oria, who professed to have eaten nothing for seven years, though a "divine fire" which raised her body temperature to 212° F.

---

[1] Hammond: *Fasting Girls*, pp. 11-12. See also the *Monthly Magazine*, October 1811; the *Gentleman's Magazine*, 1813, I, 479; Alexander Henderson: *An Examination of the Imposture of Ann Moore* (London; 1813); and *A Full Exposure of Ann Moore,* third edition (1813).

[2] Hammond: *Fasting Girls*, p. 41 *n.*

compelled her to drink a great deal of fluid. Dr Imbert-Gourbeyre solemnly records that she drank two carafes of water in his
presence and vomited the water boiling. Sometimes she vomited
oil, a procedure that must have been dangerous when the divine
fire within her reached—as it did, at times—the point at which it
set fire to her underwear.[1]

Mollie Fancher, of Brooklyn, who died in 1916, was another
famous non-eater who was vouched for by physicians. She, too,
was extraordinarily accomplished. She could read without using
her eyes at all, becoming instantly aware of the contents of a
book without bothering to open it. In 1864 she gave up breathing, but—perhaps finding it uncomfortable or perhaps feeling
that it was a little too ostentatious—resumed respiration after
only ten weeks of abstention. All of this is formally attested to by
her doctors, Dr Ormiston and Dr Samuel Fleet Speir, who had
the further support of certain unspecified "distinguished scientists". Dr Speir's parting information, that his patient had not
eaten for fourteen years, seems hardly worth mentioning.[2]

The grimmest of all the medical investigations was that of
Sarah Jacob, "the Welsh Fasting Girl", who, according to her
parents, took no nourishment whatever for two years, two
months, and one week.

The one week is certain, though its termination leaves some
doubt about the preceding two years and two months.

The child—she was only twelve years old—was the daughter
of an uneducated farm couple in Wales. At the age of ten she had
convulsions of some kind and some seeming paralysis with an
accompanying pain in the stomach. To relieve the pain she
stopped eating, and found—according to her account and that of
her parents—that she could live without food. The assertion
aroused the usual doubts. The usual group of watchers undertook to test the claims and, after the usual dozings at the bedside,
brought in the usual confirmation of the "miracle".

[1] Hammond: *Fasting Girls*, pp. 36, 39–40.
[2] Hammond: *Fasting Girls*, p. 49; the *New York Herald*, October 20, 1878;
and R. Dewitt Miller: *Forgotten Mysteries*, p. 126.

However, the vicar of the parish, the Reverend Evans Jones, B.D., decided there was an imposture and called on the parents to cease and desist. They not only stuck to their story, but also converted him. They said that the girl was under the care of "Doctor Mawr" (i.e., "the Big Doctor", i.e., God), and the vicar could not believe that any such touching simplicity was consistent with deception.

Indeed, fired with a convert's zeal, he became Sarah Jacob's press agent and spread her fame, as an instance of Dr Mawr's power, throughout the land. Visitors flocked to see the wonder, leaving small sums of money as tokens of their awe. There was a brisk local trade in supplying the pilgrims with tea, beer, and other necessities. Enterprising little boys bore placards at the railway station, offering themselves as guides to Llethernoryadd-ucha, where the sceptical might with their own eyes see Sarah not eat.

On February 19, 1869, the vicar, to make atonement for his former doubts, published a description of the marvel in the *Welshman*, asserted his own faith in its supernaturalness, and challenged medical sceptics to investigate.

Unfortunately for the child, they did. A group of physicians, under the leadship of a Dr Robert Fowler,[1] came down from London, bringing with them a number of nurses from Guy's Hospital, better trained observers than the local watchers, and less addicted, it turned out, to sleep and whisky. The nurses were instructed to care for the girl, to give her food whenever she asked for it, and in no way to interfere if food was offered her by others. Dr Fowler examined the child and found her in good health. In percussing the region of the stomach he noted a certain amount of rumbling which suggested something more substantial within than could have been obtained from the fortnightly moistening of her lips which the parents claimed to be her sole contact with food or drink.

The nurses established their watch and soon reported that, whether or not the child ate or drank, she certainly evacuated and

---

[1] It is from his *A Complete History of the Welsh Fasting Girl* (London: Renshaw; 1871) that the fullest account of this incident is drawn.

passed urine. Under their vigilance this grew less, however, and within a week she began to decline so alarmingly that they notified Dr Fowler and the vicar. Face to face with the consequences of his credulity, the Reverend Jones was de-converted, and begged the parents to allow their daughter to be fed. They sullenly insisted, though, that the symptoms of debility could have nothing to do with a need for food, as she didn't eat. Sarah herself, it must be said, never asked for food and, on December 17, died.

There was, of course, intense feeling *against the doctors*, and they were indicted along with the parents on a charge of conspiracy. At the preliminary inquiry, however, the magistrate threw out the indictment against the physicians: they had merely stood by in an advisory capacity, and their advice had never been asked. The parents were charged with manslaughter, arraigned, and convicted, the father being sentenced to twelve months hard labour, the mother to six.

The most famous of contemporary non-eaters is Miss Theresa Neumann, of Konnersreuth in Bavaria. She may, indeed, be the most famous of them all. The number of ecclesiastical and medical dignitaries who have vouched for the truth of her claims is impressive. Pilgrims by the tens of thousands have flocked to gaze upon her. She is the subject of half a dozen books and hundreds of articles. The least event that concerns her is headline news in the American Roman Catholic press. It is no exaggeration to say that millions of sober, sensible people believe beyond doubt that this woman does not eat or drink.

She herself professes to see nothing remarkable in the fact that only the Eucharist has passed her lips since 1927. "I do not fast," she told the Reverend Father Bernard Weigl, O.S.B. "Anyone who fasts becomes hungry. I am not hungry. For more than twenty years I have not taken any nourishment except by way of Holy Communion."

Despite an extraordinary series of physical misfortunes—she suffers from kidney trouble; for six years she was bedridden with a paralysis of the spine; for four years she was blind; in 1950 she had a heavy fall in which a broken rib punctured a lung, subjecting her to several weeks of acute discomfort—she seems to be in vigorous health. All who describe her stress her glowing cheeks and sturdy body, and the few who have been privileged to witness her ecstasies (she is a stigmatic, and about twenty-five times a year used to repeat in her person the agonies of the Crucifixion) have been amazed at her strength and her powers of recuperation. During her visions (in which, by the way, she sometimes speaks Aramaic) she loses blood copiously, and her weight will fall five or six pounds; yet she regains full strength and weight within a day or two.

The Roman Catholic Church has never, officially, recognized her claims as true, and there are many, even within the faith, who are inclined to be sceptical. A few thinkers, such as Dr Hilda Graef, of Oxford, have sought some "natural" explanation of the phenomena, but they have gained little but scorn for their pains. Most believe that Miss Neumann is either a saint or a fraud.

To an outsider it would seem an easy question to settle. Miss Neumann could be placed under observation for a fraction of the cost of the paper and ink already expended in disputing about her. Early in her non-eating career she was under the observation of four Mallersdorfer sisters, members of a nursing order, who watched over her for a two-week period and who testified that she had gone without food or drink. But doubters have not been content with the duration or thoroughness of that test, and have long insisted that she submit herself to another test. For years Miss Neumann resisted such demands on the grounds that they were repugnant to her father, who would turn her out of doors if she submitted to them. She has pointed out that she did not accept a ration card in World War II, and feels that that fact ought to silence all but the malevolent or the perverse. Such people are hard to silence, however, and with the increasing insistence of the ecclesiastical authorities of her own diocese over the past sixteen years (these things move rather slowly), she has, in the past decade, shown more willingness to submit again to observation.

D

It is to be hoped that sometime within the century a proper, scientific test will be made. If Miss Neumann can show, beyond any question of doubt, that she does not eat or drink—and if she does not, it ought to be easy to show—surely the benefit to the Church of which she is so ardent a member would be enormous. The jeering voice of doubt would be stunned into silence. Millions would be converted, and materialism would be dealt the severest blow it has sustained since the publication of *Three Dialogues Between Hylas and Philonus*.

Even if she should prove to be a fraud, the gains would be considerable. The Catholic Church, by demonstrating that it does not countenance dishonesty of this kind, would increase immeasurably the degree of respect in which it is held by the educated of other sects and faiths.[1]

Actually, even from Miss Neumann's point of view, little time is to be lost; for other claimants for these empty honours already throng upon the stage. In 1948 a Chinese girl, Yang Mei, professed not to have eaten for nine years, but, being detected in an unguarded moment picking her teeth, was discredited. In 1949 Joseph McAllister, of Hammond, Indiana, heeded what he said was a divine call to stop eating. But either the call was spurious or the fast was not, for one hundred and four days later he died.[2]

India, which has always figured prominently in the supernatural news, produced a non-eater in 1953, Dhanalakshmi

[1] For a favourable account of Thérèsa Neumann, see Albert Paul Schimberg: *The Story of Thérèse Neumann* (Milwaukee, Wis.: Bruce Publishing Company; 1947). For expressions of doubt from Roman Catholics, see Hilda C. Graef: *The Case of Thérèse Neumann* (Westminster, Md.: Newman Press; 1951); the Reverend Paul Siwek, S.J.: *Une Stigmatisée de Nos Jours* (Paris: Lethielleux; 1950).

For an account of Miss Neumann's illnesses, her ecstasies, her gift of tongues, her attitude toward demands that she submit to observation, and for a general exploitation of the supernatural aspects of her career, see the *Register* (Denver), September 24, 1950, p. 1; June 24, 1951, p. 2; August 19, 1951, p. 1; January 20, 1952, p. 6; February 17, 1952, p. 1; April 27, 1952, p. 1; June 17, 1952, p. 6; *et passim*. See also Patrick Mahony: *Out of the Silence, A Book of Factual Fantasies* (New York: Storm Publishers; 1948) pp. 178–80.

[2] The *Chicago Sun-Times*, June 2, 1949, p. 4; July 22, 1949, p. 6.

Aiyanna, a eighteen-year-old girl of Coorg. News of her accomplishment spread, and the devout began making pilgrimages. The usual number of physicians declared her case to be genuine, and the usual number of mystical philosophers explained it all to the lower orders. The commonest explanation was that she derived nourishment from the air. Judge Panchapakesa Ayyar, of the Madras high court, identified the feat as an ancient yoga mystery —"*Vayu Bhakshina*" or "air food".

Moved by fear or stupidity, however, the young woman allowed herself to be placed under observation by the Ministry of Health in the Victoria Hospital at Bangalore. India's food problem is acute and *Vayu Bhakshina* would have been an incredibly wonderful solution if it would only work. But after only two days of careful watching, the girl asked for food and confessed that her performance had been something even older than yoga —hokum.[1]

[1] *Time*, November 30, 1953, p. 41.

CHAPTER EIGHT

Some Homely Fallacies

HOUSEKEEPING is such an empirical process that it doesn't provide a fertile soil for fallacies. None the less, there are enough old superstitions lurking in the house and enough new doubts and confusions coming in with the new gadgets to be worth looking at.

On the introduction of aluminium cooking utensils, it will be remembered, there was a widespread belief that aluminium was poisonous—so widespread that there may have been a definite campaign by commercial rivals to discredit the new metal—but one does not hear this any more. All sorts of authoritative bodies, such as the United States Public Health Service and the American Medical Association, have said that there is nothing to it.[1] When canned foods began first to be used, there was a belief that they were poisonous if left in the can, and many women made a point of getting the food from the can to a dish within a few seconds. But that, too, has been discredited. The United States Department of Agriculture says that it's quite safe to keep food in the can in which it came if the can is kept cool and covered.

Home freezers seem to have a number of fallacies connected with their use. Cornell University has conducted experiments to show that freezing meat doesn't make it more tender. The rate of freezing doesn't affect the degree of tenderness, either, though many housewives say it does. Nor does freezing have much effect

[1] See *Nature*, March 25, 1933, p. 432.

on vitamins, at least for the first six months of storage—though vitamin content will decrease if meat is kept frozen too long.

Few men or women today are in any way concerned about distinguishing a mushroom from a toadstool, but until a couple of generations ago, when mushrooms began to be cultivated for the popular market, this was a serious concern. Every household had its amateur mycetologist who was convinced that he had an infallible way to distinguish between them, and the other members had to take fearful risks to soothe him. In country towns and on farms the problem lingers on, as every year's vital statistics grimly affirm.

To the expert, the very terms are meaningless: "A mushroom," one authority has said, "is an edible toadstool or a toadstool is a poisonous mushroom, whichever way one may wish to put it."[1] One of the commonest tests is to put a silver coin in with the mushrooms while they are cooking. If the coin turns black, the mushrooms are poisonous.[2] But the U.S. Department of Agriculture says this is a fallacy, and their words are echoed in the winds sighing over a score of graves. The best way to recognize edible mushrooms is by the word "mushroom" printed on the box in which you buy them at the store.

A stubborn domestic illusion is that cane sugar is sweeter than beet sugar. Many assert this positively, though in doing so they are merely echoing a bit of advertising for cane sugar which is now more than a hundred years old. But it is untrue: both sugars are sucrose, $C_{12} H_{22} O_{11}$, and there is no difference between them. Some of the beet sugar is coarser grained, but that is a matter of packaging and has no bearing on the taste or composition.

Brown sugar is cane sugar that has been only partly refined. Because of certain impurities, beet sugar has to be completely

[1] Dr Fred J. Seaver, Curator of the New York Botanical Garden, quoted in *Science News Letter*, June 4, 1932, p. 356.
[2] "Then Scalise found mushrooms and boiled them. Custer was sure they were poisonous, but Scalise dropped a silver coin into the brew and when it stayed shiny, instead of turning black, Custer was satisfied."—*Time*, October 4, 1948. p. 35. Custer was lucky, too.

refined; so there is no brown sugar made from beet sugar. The sweetest of all common sugars is levulose, found in honey. Maple sugar, many people are astonished to learn, is identical with beet and cane sugar. If completely refined, it is indistinguishable. Its characteristic taste is due to certain substances which are not refined out.

The ease with which "suds" can be made to rhyme in radio and television commercials has helped to rivet the illusion that bubbles, of themselves, indicate the presence of cleansing powers. But it all depends. If soap is being used, the presence of suds indicates that there is some chemical activity left for washing purposes. But in many detergents now used in dishpans and sinks the presence of bubbles has nothing to do with the detergent action. Some detergents don't foam at all, but because housewives, jingled into it, wanted copious suds, the manufacturers just added a foaming agent. This may have cheered the dishwasher, but it has caused a great deal of trouble and expense in municipal sewage-disposal plants, where the lather sometimes buries the plant, clogs the pipes, and interferes with the purification process.[1] If a dry cleaner, by the way, gets any suds, he begins to worry.

One of the most expensive delusions of housekeeping—and one that seems to be held from Maine to California—is that coffee grounds "cut" grease and therefore should be dumped in the sink.

Speaking for his profession, Mr John Cahill, Chicago Master Plumber, condemns this belief in vigorous language. Grounds mix with the grease to clog the drain, he says. Most of the time the ensuing mulch will be washed on down, but if there is any obstruction the drain will be blocked. It is particularly harmful, he adds, in summer when families leave a last deposit of coffee grounds and bacon grease in the pipes before they set out on a vacation. During their absence this often hardens into a compound so impenetrable that it can't be rodded out, and the pipes have to be taken apart. As physicians now come considerably

[1] See *Scientific American*, July 1953, p. 48.

cheaper than plumbers, it would be more economical to swallow the grounds.

Almost every housewife has some theory about "deodorizing" her house. It used to be believed that lighting a few kitchen matches would remove unpleasant smells, and many a house reeked of sulphur in order not to reek of onions.

Many mechanical deodorizers have been sold that offer to "ozonize" the air. This is vague, but impressive. Ozone is commonly thought of as a sort of concentrated oxygen, possessing the virtues of fresh air to a magical degree. Heroes of western tales expel the fetid atmosphere of cities from their lungs and draw in "draughts" of "pure ozone" among the pines, inhalations that make them finer, better men.

But were the ozone so inhaled created by any process more real than nature-writers' imaginations, the heroes would soon be corpses. For ozone in anything more than infinitesimal concentrations is a poison more deadly than carbon monoxide, as the Federal Trade Commission has on occasion had to point out to certain gentlemen who were attempting to persuade their fellow-men to sniff it in. As a deodorizer it seems to work not so much by removing the offensive odour as by deadening the sense of smell. Some will insist that, the effect being the same, it is a mere quibble to argue by what means it is achieved; but others are not yet convinced that anæsthesia is the answer to a stink.

A quaint domestic fallacy that may still linger on in a few places, though it is never heard in cities any more, is that fruit stains cannot be removed from a cloth until the fruit that made them is out of season. Because it takes a little time to get a cloth to the laundry and often longer to get it back, and as the season of many fruits is short, the belief might well have seemed demonstrable. But it is pure sympathetic magic, a survival of one of mankind's deepest-rooted beliefs, that "dead things retain yet an occult relation to life".

Whenever wine is spilled, someone is sure to urge that salt be poured on it at once because "salt prevents wine from staining a tablecloth". The advice is good, but the reasons offered to justify it are often wrong. Salt is always at hand, and if dumped on spilled wine soon enough will soak up some of the wine and so prevent it from spreading. But a sponge or a blotter or a piece of tissue paper would do it as well or better. No specific chemical property in salt, that is, makes it particularly valuable in this respect. Salt does have a great affinity for moisture, however, and so may keep the stain moist until the cloth is laundered.

A number of domestic illusions concern glassware. Some bartenders insist that beer glasses are ruined if gasoline or even milk is put in them because the glass "absorbs" the flavour of these substances. But as glass is completely non-porous, it is hard to see how this could be. Pottery mugs, unglazed, might retain some taints, but glasses, properly washed, should not.

Of course, casks will preserve a flavour with which they are impregnated, and old-fashioned bottles, which were made of leather, unquestionably did. These were the "old bottles" of the Bible which would burst with the fermentation of new wine, but glass bottles (the two words are almost redundant now) would not be affected.

One is often told that if a metal spoon is placed in a glass, it will prevent the glass from cracking when hot liquid is poured into it. Some insist that it must be a silver spoon "because silver is a good conductor of heat". The theory seems to be that the spoon will absorb enough of the heat to reduce the liquid to a temperature at which it will not crack the glass. But much would depend on the size and thickness of the spoon, the amount of liquid to be poured in, and the thickness of the glass. Where it is required that the spoon be put in the glass before the liquid is poured in, and that the liquid be poured over the spoon, the belief might justify itself—in that the care needed to see that the liquid fell first on the spoon might ensure a slow enough filling of the glass to permit an even expansion.

Many cheap restaurants seem to labour under the delusion that tumblers of unusual thickness will last longer than ordinary drinking glasses. They will, of course, stand moderate knocks better than delicate wineglasses; but they will shatter if dropped and, because glass is a poor conductor of heat and expands un-evenly, they will break even more quickly than lighter glassware if plunged into hot water.

Still, the restaurateur, gazing in dismay at the month's bill for breakage, probably thinks: "How much worse it would have been but for those thick tumblers!" and continues his besharded descent into the Avernus of bankruptcy.

Watches and clocks have their special lore and fallacies. In a desperate search for distinction, some aver that they can't carry a watch, that no watch will run near their bodies. When ques-tioned, they usually retreat into a confused mumble about "electricity".

The claim may certainly be challenged. All human tempera-tures are so nearly alike that significant variations of heat or cold may be ruled out of consideration. Some people perspire more than others, but the cheapest watch is waterproof enough to keep out sweat. Those who work around generators and transformers often have to have special watches, but there are in the human body no electrical impulses strong enough to have the slightest effect on a watch.

There is a deep-rooted belief that it damages a clock or watch to turn the hands backward, and millions of citizens, especially at the end of September in those areas that have daylight-saving time, laboriously advance their timepieces eleven hours rather than turn them back one. Their concern and labour are un-necessary. It does no harm to the ordinary, non-striking watch or clock to turn the hands backward, for the wheels immediately connected with the hands are connected to the rest of the train of wheels only by friction. When the hands are set forward, the amplitude of the swing of the balance wheels is slightly increased temporarily; when they are set backward, it is decreased.

There are two exceptions. If striking clocks are turned back, the correlation of the number of strokes with the hour may be destroyed, and individual electric clocks connected by a synchro-nizing mechanism with a master clock cannot be turned back.[1]

[1] See *The New Yorker*, September 29, 1951, pp. 22-4.

That the owner's clock would stop at the moment of his death was once widely believed, and was even used to support some sonorous reputations. Thus it is said that Swedenborg, asked to demonstrate his prescience, predicted that a certain Olof Olofsohn would die at 4.45 the next morning and, lo and behold, the said Olofsohn was found dead in bed the next morning and a clock in the house had stopped at 4.45.[1]

Clocks and watches are far too common today for any such magic sympathy to be ascribed to them, though their stoppage at the moment of death is still a convenient literary device. In murder mysteries the moment of the crime is frequently established by a stopped wrist watch, but it is always made plain that the "force of the blow" or the "impact" was the cause.

The old belief was probably not lacking in "proof" because when clocks were few and valuable the head of the house (and it was only on *his* demise that the clock stopped) always took the care of *the* clock upon himself. The weekly winding was a solemn rite performed by him alone, and just the sort of thing that would be neglected in the confusion attendant upon his death. Afterward it would be noticed that the clock had stopped, and awe, ignorance, inaccuracy, and the zeal of gullibility would have little difficulty in believing that the stoppage had occurred at the exact moment of death.

In many places it was believed that the clock *should* be stopped. In New York and New Hampshire it was felt that it would bring bad luck to allow a clock to run on after a death in the family, and the same belief existed in England and Germany. When General Grant died, the attending physician, Dr Douglas, stopped the clock on the mantel. Perhaps it was a way of marking a solemn moment, a symbolic way of saying that this is the end of all things. Or—as some have suggested—it may have been an attempt to limit the power of death by introducing a wholly new period of time.[2]

[1] See E. J. Dingwall: *Very Peculiar People* (London: Rider & Company: 1950), p. 52.
[2] The *Journal of American Folk-Lore*, vol. 2 (1889), p. 12. For Dr Douglas's act, see *Life*, March 26, 1951, p. 98.

A generation or so ago, when large dummy clocks were a common sign of a jeweller's store, one often heard it said that the hands on such clocks were fixed at the hour Lincoln died—as though the whole nation had agreed to stop its clocks and let time be no more after that dreadful moment. But the facts don't fit. Lincoln was shot a little after ten in the evening on April 14, 1865, and died at seven-twenty the next morning. The hands on jewellers' clocks were usually painted at eight seventeen—in order to allow as much space as possible for whatever the jeweller wanted on the face as an advertisement.

The laws of physics usually operate in the house, as they do outside, without any theorizing on the part of the householder. But there are at least two minor points on which there is sometimes some mistaken conjecturing. Many people, assuming, apparently, that a lightning rod attracts lightning, feel that such rods should be insulated from the house. And the knowing will sometimes tell you that the swirls in washbowls and toilet bowls invariably rotate in one direction north of the equator and in the opposite direction south of the equator.

Franklin, the inventor of the lightning rod, said that a lightning rod could be fastened to a house with staples of iron, adding that: "The lightning will not leave the rod to pass into the wall through these staples." Rather, he said, if there were any electricity in the wall, it would "pass out into the rod, to get more readily by that conductor into the earth".

Yet many who are willing to trust Franklin in the main and put the rods up will decide, apparently, that he didn't know what he was talking about in the details, and will go to the unnecessary expense of adding insulators.

Of course if the rod is improperly grounded and one of the iron staples should happen to be in contact with something metal in the house that *was* grounded, then the rod would "draw" lightning. But that's another matter.

The deflecting force that the earth's rotation exerts, turning all moving objects to the right in the Northern Hemisphere and to the left in the Southern, can be seen in great vortices, such as turbine intakes. But small swirls are subject to too many other forces: the impulse of the left- or right-hand faucet, whichever happens to be turned on first, the shape of the toilet bowl or, in washbowls, the action of the hands—any one of these things can overcome the effect of the coriolis force in small bodies of water.[1]

Perhaps related to this, but more likely simply a relic of magic, is the common belief that a cake must be stirred in one direction only. It doesn't matter whether it is clockwise or counterclockwise, so long as the direction in which the stirring is started is kept to the end. There seems to be nothing to it, however, if we may trust the experience of Miss Gerda Oberg, of Mexico City, who boldly risked a cake in the cause of science. "In spite of having been stirred carefully half-and-half in both directions," she writes,[2] "the cake came out perfectly all right."

Vermin seem to breed fallacies, along with dirt and resentment. Flies in particular. Two hundred years ago it was possible to be sympathetic with "the little, gilded fly". My Uncle Toby (in *Tristram Shandy*) was greatly admired for the tenderness which led him to carry a captured fly to the window and let it go, saying: "There is room in the world for me and thee," and William Oldys's poem "Busy, thirsty, curious fly" was much declaimed by children. But the hygienists have changed all that; outside of his own species, the fly hasn't a friend left in the world.

The screen and the covered garbage can and DDT have made him almost a rarity in comfortable, middle-class homes, and a rarity is easily the subject of fallacies. Thus it is widely believed that flies grow. Not that the average person gives much thought to the subject at all, but, if questioned, he will usually confess that he had always assumed that small flies were baby flies that would, in time, grow to be those bumbling monsters that buzz between blinds and panes.

---

[1] See Rachel L. Carson: *The Sea Around Us* (New York: Oxford University Press; 1951), pp. 135–6; James E. McDonald: "The Coriolis Effect", *Scientific American*, May 1952, pp. 72–8; and a report on vortices by Professor Andrade, F.R.S., in the *Proceedings of the Royal Institution*, No. 137, pp. 320–38, and No. 138, p. 345.

[2] In a letter to the author, dated June 11, 1947.

Actually, however, flies, like bees, wasps, and butterflies, emerge full-grown from the chrysalis. That some of the smaller species often appear early in the summer supports the mistake. Bluebottles, which also appear early, are sometimes thought to be veteran leftovers from the last season, though they are generally perceived to be members of a different species.

One still hears, occasionally, that flies are enabled to walk upside down on ceilings and other surfaces because they have "suckers" on their feet, but this is now known to be untrue. A fly's feet are equipped with hooks and hairy pads. Some believe that the hairs secrete a sticky substance. Others aver that the secretion is merely a liquid to establish the capillary adhesion necessary to overcome the slight gravitational pull that so light a creature experiences. When a fly is "washing" itself, by the way, it is cleaning its feet.

In 1945 E. D. Eyles, of the Kodak Research Laboratories in England, managed to take high-speed photographs of flies taking off and landing. Among other interesting things, he discovered that flies start off with a backward leap—which may explain why so many of us miss our swat.

G. B. Shaw once remarked that there seemed to be a law of conservation of credulity: the dispelling of one illusion seems to create a vacuum which draws in another. Several years ago the idea that a fluff of cotton tied on the screen door would keep flies away spread like wildfire through Ohio, Kentucky, Indiana, and parts of Illinois, and hundreds of thousands of screens in the Middle West were adorned with little white blobs. It died down after a couple of seasons and then flared up anew in the Chicago area in the summer of 1953 after a television "home adviser" (somewhat in the rearward of even the sillier fashions) had recommended the practice.

When questioned, the users usually state vehemently that it "works" and toss the justification for it back to the questioner; though after it has fallen into disuse, the same users are at a loss to explain why they have abandoned so cheap and salutary a practice. At the height of the vogue many explanations were offered: it worked "because cotton looks like a spider's web and that frightens them away"; "it moves when the door opens and flies are afraid of things that move"; "it looks like snow and maybe they think it's winter".[1]

Vance Randolph says that when bananas first began to appear in village stores in the Ozarks, folks got the idea somehow that a banana stalk hung up in the chicken house would rid the whole place of chicken lice, and that one still occasionally finds one of these stalks hanging in an outbuilding.[2]

One fact of nature which many a harassed housewife is to be excused for rejecting with scorn is that cockroaches are delicate creatures, most difficult to keep alive. Yet those who raise them (and there are such; not Charles Addamsish fiends, but scientists and experimental exterminators) find cockroaches extraordinarily difficult to rear. They are finicky in their diet, fatally susceptible to the mildest changes in weather, helpless before a host of foes, and altogether easily discouraged and signally lacking in *élan vital*. Several years ago *Nature* lamented the decline of this fragile species. For experimental purposes they are now being replaced by locusts.[3]

The assurance, in the New Testament, that there are no moths in heaven is a powerful incentive to piety in housewives. No creature is more loathed, more furiously pursued, and more relentlessly squashed by angry women than the moth. But, aside from the emotional catharsis it provides, the attack rarely does any good. For the fact is that moths don't eat clothes: their larvæ do the damage. It may do good to kill the moth that one sometimes catches a glimpse of on a garment, scuttling speedily for the protection of a fold, because such a moth may not yet have laid her eggs. But the free-fluttering moth, the kind upon which indignant women most often ease their resentment, has already

---

[1] The matter was discussed by Erminie W. Voegelin in the *American Anthropologist*. See also "Dawn of a New Superstition", *Science Digest*, April 1947.

[2] Vance Randolph: *Ozark Superstitions* (New York: Columbia University Press; 1947), p. 42.

[3] *Nature*, February 12, 1949; *Science News Letter*, April 16, 1949, p. 252.

laid her eggs. She has done her worst, and can die beneath the blow with a sneer of triumph.

It doesn't do any good to sprinkle mothballs in a closet, either. If the clothes are thoroughly seeded with mothballs and then wrapped tightly in paper, they will probably be protected, but mothballs scattered loose have little effect.

Cedar chests are pleasant, but equally inefficacious. Dr C. H. Curran, of the Department of Insects and Spiders of the American Museum of Natural History, writing in *Natural History*, says: "We know that some insects do not like certain odours, but it has never been proved that the clothes moth does not like cedar."[1]

None the less, cedar closets with their wholesome, piny fragrance will continue to be built into houses by those fortunate enough to be able to afford them, while poorer folk will go on lining their closets with paper that has been impregnated with the smell of cedar. Some of this wallpaper is made to resemble cedar panelling, but, of course, that won't do any good unless the light is left on so that the moths can see it. Some people have such faith in the insect-repellent powers of cedar that they insist that spiders will not spin their webs on a cedar-shingled roof.

Next to moths come mice, and the best-known thing about mice is that they love cheese, a fact so established in folklore, so rooted in jokes and cartoons, that anyone who doubted it would be accused of deliberate perversity. Yet professional exterminators do not bait their mousetraps with cheese. It is true that hungry mice will eat cheese—they will also eat shoes, suitcases, and each other—but, when given a choice, they seem to prefer sweets. Mr Edward Batzner, a Milwaukee exterminator who professes to use the most scientific methods, uses gumdrops. They have the lure of sweetness, he points out, plus an adhesiveness that detains the luckless mouse for a fatal half-second. Of all gumdrops he has found lemon the most effective, though he is inclined to attribute this more to the colour than to the flavour.

[1] For a report on mothballs, see *Nature*, October 27, 1923, p. 622. For the inefficacy of cedar, see *Natural History*, September 1949.

Another bait that Mr Batzner recommends is even more surprising: cotton batting. The mice want it for building their nests. [1]

Unnecessary care is often taken in handling mousetraps and rat-traps on the assumption that mice and rats have an "instinctive" aversion to the smell of human beings, recognizing therein a "natural" enemy. Many use gloves when handling traps (unaware, it would seem, that the gloves would have the odour too). And some go so far as to sandpaper each trap after every catch to remove the added odour of "death"—though mice and rats eat carrion with relish and have no objection to cannibalism.

The idea of a special fear of man is a piece of human egotism; in the natural state, man would rank low in the long list of a rat's or a mouse's enemies. And, anyway, the whole point of a trap is that it will not be perceived as a natural danger. The subject was investigated, with experiments, a generation ago in connection with the Rat Exhibition held in the London Zoo in 1919. The conclusion was that "it was superfluous to avoid handling traps on the assumption that rats are detracted by the odour of man". [2]

A number of domestic illusions have to do with acts, manners, and customs. Some have an element of rationality in them. Others appear to be confused justifications or downright superstitions.

The practical objections to opening an umbrella in the house, for example, are many and obvious: it's an awkward thing in a confined space; it obscures the vision of anyone doing it; and the ferrule might easily break ornaments, put out an eye, or otherwise bring disaster. Yet the feeling against it, which is often strong, is not based on rational grounds. It's just "bad luck" to do it. There seems to be a conviction that God intended umbrellas to be used out of doors and will punish those who flout His intentions.

Two other dreaded domestic accidents—breaking a mirror and passing under a ladder—have also their rational justifications. The one leaves dangerous splinters of glass, and the other exposes

[1] See the *Milwaukee Journal*, October 31, 1949, p. 20.
[2] *Nature*, October 2, 1919, p. 98.

the passer to the chance of having various things dropped on him. But the real feeling here is also, basically, irrational: the shattering of the image will, by sympathetic magic, injure the person whose reflection the image was; walking through the triangle established by the ladder and its support violates a magic enclosure. It is interesting that the proper protection for one who must walk under a ladder is not to shield his head but to cross his fingers.

There is a strong feeling against crossing the knife and fork on the plate after eating, though if the fork is laid with the points of the tines up and the knife blade is placed across the hollow of the fork, this would seem a sensible way of disposing of them. Custom, however, dictates that they shall be laid parallel on the right side of the plate. Where the person who is picking up the dishes is stacking them as they are picked up, this probably does make the task easier, but no consideration could be further from polite concern. In defence of the custom it is sometimes alleged to be "bad manners" to "make the sign of the cross" with menial utensils—though, if we may trust Browning, others have considered it an act of piety to cross them.

The actual reason is probably utilitarian. If the fork is laid with the points of the tines down and the knife is laid across the raised handle of the fork, there is an increased chance of both slipping from the plate while it is being removed from the table.

It is an article of plebeian faith that the domestic customs of the rich, particularly their elaborate table settings and certain ways of eating, have no practical value, but are devised solely to confuse and thus unmask interlopers. A bewildering array of eating utensils is set beside the plates, not to facilitate eating—what more could anyone want than knife, fork, and spoon?—but to test the social proficiency of any Jiggs whose ambitious Maggie has dragged him above their social level.

Actually, snail clamps, asparagus forks, salad forks, butter knives, fish knives, steak knives, coffee spoons, dessert spoons, and soup spoons are highly efficient, each designed for a special purpose. They are not efficient, of course, in the ordinary small household of limited budget and plain meals, where their cost and care would outweigh their usefulness. But if you can afford to serve meals elaborate enough to need them and to hire some-one to wash them and put them away, they serve their purpose better than ordinary tableware.

The æsthetic values of their use, the ones most loudly scorned by those who can't afford them, may, perhaps, have the most "practical" value of all. Dr W. B. Cannon has pointed out that the niceties of a delicately served meal conduce to better digestion, and that better digestion conduces to health and longevity. The poor may get what comfort they can from laughing at this or that detail in the lives of the rich; but the last laugh, a long, senile cackle, is with the rich, who, as a score of needless surveys have showed, enjoy better health and live longer than the poor.

CHAPTER NINE

The Moan of Hormones

IN CONSIDERING a few illusions that cluster around love and courtship, it might be well to dispose first of all of the jolly bachelor.

The jollity of the bachelor—if we distinguish bachelors, as we should, from young married-men-to-be who just haven't signed up yet—is a fantasy of the gloom of the married man. Statistics show the bachelor to be much worse off than the married man. He goes mad three times as often. His suicide rate is much higher. He is more prone to accidents, and he is twice as susceptible to almost every disease known.[1] So that if he *is* jolly, he must live more in delusion than delight.

It is likely, of course, that bachelorhood is as much the effect as the cause of these misfortunes, but that does not change the conclusion.[2]

One need not dwell, however, upon the pains and penalties of the single state, for most of those who are able are all too quiveringly eager to abandon it. Time was that parents and guardians managed, or at least assisted, in arranging for the marriages of

[1]See Louis I. Dublin: "These Are the Single", in Hilda Holland (comp.): *Why Are You Single?* (New York: Farrar, Straus & Young; 1949), pp. 78–81.
[2] "Though marriage has many pains, celibacy has no pleasures. The unmarried are outlaws of human nature. They are peevish at home and malevolent abroad. They dream away their time without friendship or fondness and are driven by boredom to childish amusements or vicious delights. To live without feeling or exciting sympathy, to be fortunate without adding to the felicity of others . . . is a state more gloomy than solitude: it is not retreat but exclusion from mankind "—Samuel Johnson, in *Rasselas*.

their children, but the very thought of that is now immoral. Marriages are better left to love, and love will unerringly single out the one perfect mate in the whole world and make his or her identity known in a soul-shaking flash of perception. Such is the romantic credo, with its article of love at first sight.

That there is such a thing as interest or desire at first sight no one can doubt who has spent two minutes on any city street. The pivoting of male heads at every rump that minces by is one of the great comic gestures of the urban scene. But those who believe in love at first sight would be the first to insist that love and desire are not identical.

Those who do not believe in love at first sight would say that love often has its beginning in desire, but grows into affection through association. Even maternal love, they might point out, has to grow. The great majority of infanticides occur very soon after the child's birth, before the mother has become, as we say, "attached" to it.

A very little arithmetic serves to dissipate the idea of "soul-mates". There are, roughly, one thousand million men and one thousand million women living on the earth. Assuming that the searching lovers have looked into the faces of ten thousand of the opposite sex, they have still seen only one hundred-thousandth of the available material, an effort that in anything really important would be regarded as trifling.

But even that gives far too bright a picture. The ordinary young man or woman on arriving at the marriageable age probably does not "know", in the sense of being able to speak to, two hundred people. Half of these, we will assume, are of the same sex, though the actual proportion is probably much higher. Of the hundred that might, biologically, be possible mates, eighty at least will be ruled out by social and æsthetic considerations. The young are extremely sensitive to differences in age, for example. To a boy of twenty a woman of thirty is an aged hag, a girl of fifteen a silly child. A young woman of twenty has a slightly greater tolerance for men older than she is, but even less for boys younger. The young are avid for distinction, and considerations of prestige weigh more heavily in the matter of a partner then than later. Any deviation from the group norm of prettiness or handsomeness in a partner is embarrassing, any peculiarity of pronunciation or dress humiliating, the slightest blemish disgusting. Twenty out of the known hundred is probably far too high; ten would be nearer it. But of the acceptable ten not all are available. Some are not yet ready for marriage or are emotionally concerned elsewhere. It would be a fortunate youth who knew five acceptable and available girls. And a further, quite severe, limitation is imposed by the fact that he must be acceptable to them. Then it must be just the right time for both of them. One would think, all these things taken into account, that no one would ever get married, and under the soul-mate theory no one ever would. But, actually, most people do, and most marriages prove more or less tolerable. It is apparent that, whatever theories they profess, most people marry just about the first person acceptable, available, and willing, and manage to get on somehow.

A further argument against love at first sight is furnished by the large number of those who have married a second time and found the second marriage happier than the first. One survey found that ninety per cent of those questioned about their second marriage regarded it as happier than the first.[1] Some of this may have been spite against the first partner. People would be loath to confess a second failure in marriage, which would begin to look as if *they* were hard to get on with. Second marriages, too, would be made at a more mature age, with the advantages of less hope, more experience, and—most likely—more money. And the comparison would not be fair until the second union had lasted as long as the first. But, on the whole, the report was probably accurate.

Two other illusions of courting are that jealousy is a sign of love and that absence makes the heart grow fonder.

Young men and women in love often misinterpret a show of jealousy in the object of their affection as proof that their passion

---

[1] See Arthur Garfield Hays: "They Tried It Once", in *Why Are You Single?* p. 235.

is reciprocated. But, like many other conclusions reached by young men and women in love, this can be a dangerous error. Jealousy is more likely to be a sign of self-love, a measure of which, of course, is mixed up with any love affair. The true nature of jealousy may perhaps be suggested by comparing the grief felt at the loss of a loved one by death with the resentment and injured pride at the loss to a rival.

The disastrous rate of divorce among the young couples separated during World War II ought to disprove the adage that absence makes the heart grow fonder. Temporary absence may heighten desire, but true affection, which is founded upon a community of interests, is bound to grow less as the separation continues. Statistics are unavailable, but it is a common experience in large families that interest in one's brothers and sisters declines as space and time interpose.

Of the two proverbs relating to love, that "Opposites attract" and "Similitude is the mother of love", the former is more often heard, though the latter seems more consonant with the facts.

Although Dr Horace Gray, of the Stanford University School of Medicine, found, in an analysis of two hundred and seventy-one married couples, that introverts seem, on the whole, attracted to extroverts, a number of other studies have shown that in social matters likeness attracts or, at least, unlikeness repels. Sir Francis Galton, in his investigation of the temperaments of English scientists seventy years ago, found that in choosing a husband or wife "harmony strongly prevails over contrast", and his conclusion was confirmed by Lord Raglan, who said: "We are really attracted by and marry people like ourselves".

Professors Burgess and Wallin, in a study of one thousand engaged couples, discovered that similarity in background and interests was the rule. Dr E. Lowell Kelly, in an earlier examination of thirty-three hundred engaged couples, found striking similarity in each couple, not only in social background, but in a whole series of personality traits.

One of the most curious reports in this field was that made by Marvin Koller, who, in 1948, investigated the distance from their homes which various males in Columbus, Ohio, ventured in search of a mate. The median was thirteen blocks. The bolder blades, twenty-four to twenty-seven, went farther; but the younger men, splendidly impatient, went less. Men over thirty-five averaged less than seven blocks. Whether they were decrepit, desperate, or cynical, or whether Columbus is so rich in attractive, marriageable women that it made no difference, the report did not say.

Similar eagerness or apathy was found by other investigators in Duluth. Analysing three hundred marriage licences issued in that city, Messrs Marches and Turbeville discovered that 5.67 per cent of the couples lived at the same address,[1] 20 per cent lived within five blocks of each other, and 42 per cent lived within twenty blocks.

This doesn't seem to indicate a very thorough search for the perfect mate or any far-reaching desire to find one's opposite; but at least it shows that men do better than mice—which rarely go more than thirty *feet* for their mates.[2]

One type of opposites that seems to attract is religious opposites. Even among Roman Catholics, where such marriages are most strongly opposed, almost half are now mixed.[3] Those who are about to make such unions are usually warned by their spiritual guides that they are risking unhappiness, and they are certainly risking a higher probability of divorce than if they married one of their own faith. Although religious differences

[1] Hmm!

[2] For Dr Gray's study, see the *Journal of Social Psychology*, May 1949, pp. 189–200. For Galton, see his *English Men of Science* (London: Macmillan and Company; 1874), p. 27. Lord Raglan was so quoted in the *London Daily Telegraph* (reporting his speech before the British Association), September 8, 1934. For Burgess and Wallin, see an article by Dr James E. Bender in the *New York Times Magazine*, December 8, 1946. Dr Kelly's findings were reported to the Midwestern Psychological Association, at their Chicago meeting in 1940. Koller's reports appeared in the *American Sociological Review*, October 1948, pp. 613–16, and June 1951, pp. 366–70. Joseph R. Marches and Gus Turbeville published the results of their study in the *American Journal of Sociology*, May 1953, pp. 592–6. The mice were studied by Professor John T. Emlen, of the University of Wisconsin. See *Science Digest*, March 1949, p. 37.

[3] See the *American Ecclesiastical Review*, July 1948, for an estimate, by Clement S. Mihanovitch, that in 1946 it was 40 per cent.

have, no doubt, embittered many a marriage, and certainly have exacerbated marriages already embittered for other reasons, they rank very low as a cause for divorce. The Reverend John L. Thomas, of St Louis University, in a study of seven thousand marriages, found religion listed as a cause of family discord in only 2.9 per cent of the cases, only one tenth as often as drink and one eighth as often as adultery.[1]

The unhappiness resulting from religiously mixed marriages seems to accrue, to a large extent, to the pastors themselves, for the chief religious consequence of them seems to be an increase in irreligion. The question was investigated by Professor Murray H. Leiffer, of the Garrett Biblical Institute, who found, in a study of seven hundred and forty-three "mixed" marriages, that the commonest adjustment was for one or both of the partners to stop taking an interest in church. Those sects that maintain special schools for the children of their adherents have noticed that a depressingly large proportion of the children of mixed marriages go to the public schools. "It is abundantly clear" to Professor Leiffer "that interfaith marriages have unfortunate results for organised religion".[2]

One of the pitfalls of love, wholly unsuspected by the amorous youth seeking the ideal maiden, is that impersonating the ideal maiden has long been a preoccupation of not-so-ideal maidens. The deception, however, is often to the young man's advantage; for the ideal maiden is never thought of as clever, the not-so-ideal impersonator must be clever, and a clever wife is desirable. Any man is better off if by accident he gets an intelligent wife; but if he does get one, it will only be by accident, for the male ego, especially in its highly sensitive courting days, demands a submissive inferiority from the female. "A woman," Jane Austen tartly observed, "if she have the misfortune of knowing anything, should conceal it as well as she can."

[1] See an AP dispatch from St. Louis in the *Chicago Sunday Tribune*, February 1, 1953, pt. 1, p. 25.
[2] The *Christian Century*, January 19, 1949, pp. 78–80; January 26, 1949, pp. 106–8.

No formula for box-office success in a social-comedy movie is more certain than to have a cocky heroine enter some field generally regarded as a masculine preserve, achieve some initial, superficial success, and then become so entangled in difficulties that she has to be extricated by the hero, who, smirking forgiveness and tipping the audience the wink, offers her his brain for salvation and his shoulder for submission and tears.

Women are still, for the most part, dependent on men for their livelihood, and most of them take care not to appear more intelligent than their escorts think they ought to be. According to a study of coeds, reported by Professor Mirra Komarovsky in the *American Journal of Sociology*,[1] many college girls deliberately play dumb to please their dates. Forty per cent of the girls she interviewed admitted that they lied about their grades, making them out to be *lower* than they were. They gave up arguments when they saw that they might win, lost card games on purpose, begged for explanations of what they already knew, knowingly mis-spelled words in their letters, and generally "jigg'd, lisp'd, and ambled" in the seductive manner that so annoyed Prince Hamlet.

Of course, there is deception on both sides. In the male it is called chivalry, which is further disguised by being regarded as mere consideration for others. But chivalry is distinguished from kindness, shown to be more courting than courtesy, by the fact that it is not practised outside of one's own marriage group. No Southerner, for example, however chivalrous, would offer his seat on a public conveyance to a Negro woman.[2]

It has been suggested[3] that modern chivalry may have even more sinister intentions, being instilled into boys by mothers in whose sexuality there is a large measure of hostility, as a means

---

[1] November 1946. The findings are restated in Mirra Komarovsky: *Women in the Modern World* (Boston: Little, Brown and Company; 1953), pp. 77–82.

[2] John Dollard (*Caste and Class in a Southern Town*, New York: Harper & Brothers; 1949, pp. 288–9) observed that much more antagonism is tolerated in the South from Negro women than from Negro men. But, then, the women are less to be feared.

[3] By my learned colleague, Professor Lambert Ennis.

of incapacitating them later in the war of the sexes: "They drill
boys into feeling that to offend a woman is to commit a mortal
sin, and these boys are helpless in mature life when their own
interest requires them to hold their own against an aggressive
woman."

In return for his chivalry the man receives "inspiration".
That woman is man's inspiration is one of the most deeply
entrenched of amorous illusions. It is widely believed, or at least
asserted, that men who achieve greatness do so because there is a
trusting and loving woman behind them, one who had faith in
them when their own confidence wavered. This is the central
message of the biographical movies and of those thumbnail
sketches of the famous which incite the mediocre to be conventional. In many of these narratives the woman is allowed
works as well as faith: there is often more than a hint that the
idea upon which the great one's greatness rests was originally
hers, but that she let him have it and contented herself with
reflecting his glory.

The suggestion naturally appeals to many women because it
makes them seem to be the power behind the throne and conceals
the drabness and emptiness of their actual role. Mrs Dale Carnegie states the myth in its classic form when she says (in her
How to Help Your Husband Get Ahead, N.Y., 1953) that it is a
wife's duty to keep her husband in a continual state of productive
enthusiasm, to "build him up" by complimenting him on his
necktie and otherwise convincing him that he is a success. She
must egg him on and never, never—even in jest—allow him to
doubt his own superlative greatness. She herself, she confesses,
has been of assistance to her own distinguished spouse by whis-
pering people's names to him when he had forgotten them and
by suggesting (she having read his book) topics of conversation
that would be flattering to the person spoken to. As a deplorable
example of one who was *not* inspired by his wife, she mentions
Samuel Taylor Coleridge. But one wonders if in so doing she
has not violated one of her own canons; for the contrast between
Coleridge's writings and those of her own husband—which her

example forces on the reader's attention—could hardly reinforce Mr Carnegie's self-esteem.[1]

It is true that many women do sustain their men's good opinions of themselves, and that many men do seek balm for the hurts sustained by their vanity in "the healing pool" of a woman's compassion. But the encouragement of self-pity is not inspiration, and men do less rather than more because of it.

Women are more often goads than inspirations. Many a man who has achieved middling success in business, or that "solid" professional success which consists largely of a good income, owes much of it to the proddings of an ambitious wife. The wretch is kept in a continual state of guilt regarding his obligations to his family, an "inspiration" which has maintained a great many life-insurance agents in comfort, but which has also led to more embezzlement and defalcation than all the blondes and race-horses that ever failed to pay off.

But nine out of ten men who have done anything really significant have probably done it more in spite of than because of a woman. More wives are jealous of their husbands' work than of their mistresses—if only because many men have work and few have mistresses.[2] The wives don't see it that way, of course. They just feel "neglected", and reproach their husbands because they don't live "the way other people do", "don't go out any more", and because he's "always at the office".

Naturally, if a man is engaged in some exhausting project, a slave, whether male or female, can be helpful. His wife (it has to be a wife; a mistress won't) can see that he is well fed and protect him from harassments and interruptions. She can shush the

---

[1] "Poor, dear Sara", it must be admitted, was not the chief source of Cole-ridge's inspiration. But he was a tough proposition. As for his ego, when his spirits were up he needed no help; when they were down, the eleven thousand virgins of Cologne could not have comforted him. Sara did, how-ever, perform one wifely function: she bore him four children and reared three of them, with precious little help from him, to be among the most brilliant figures of their generation.

[2] Husbands are probably even more jealous of their wives' work outside the home and, usually, insanely jealous of their success. He is an extraordinary man who is not humiliated by any non-domestic accomplishment of his wife's.

children or, better still, see to it that there are no children. She can answer the telephone, decline all social invitations, stall off creditors, earn some additional money, do without anything for herself which would take any of his time or thought—and when the goal is finally reached and he is famous and rich and she is faded, plain, and uninteresting, she may make her final contribution by not contesting the divorce he is almost certain to seek.

But nagging comes easier and probably accomplishes more. "I ought to get married," Chekhov wrote in his notebook. "Perhaps a cross wife would cut down my visitors by half." More than that, she would have seen to it that he wasted less time in smoking and daydreaming. Nothing like a shrill tongue and a sullen brow to keep a man cowering productively in the lee of his desk!

And, conversely, nothing like a really loving wife for wasting time. There is an old poem that examines the various kinds of wives and their effects. He that marries a scold, it says, will find his wit sharpened. He that marries a sulk will find his gall stimulated. And so on, a benefit from each misfortune. But he that marries a loving wife—that has the cushion of her compassion to fall on, the joy of her beauty to divert him, and the gratification of her whims to occupy him—he may live and die a happy man, but he'll never amount to a damn:

> But he that's matched with a turtle dove
> That hath no spleen about her
> Shall waste so much life
> In love of his wife,
> He had better be without her.[1]

[1] Anonymous Elizabethan or Jacobean. Quoted by Aldous Huxley: *Texts and Pretexts* (New York: The Macmillan Company; 1933), pp. 191–2.

CHAPTER TEN

Family Matters

T HE POPULARITY of June as the month for weddings is
sometimes explained on the grounds that summer is the
most pleasant time for a honeymoon. But this sounds like
an effete rationalization. May was probably the first month that
allowed much walking out and houghmagandy, and June the
earliest reckoning. Then March was considered the best month
for childbearing, because the mother would be fully recovered
by harvest time and able to work. There was a Scotch proverb:

> *He's a fool that marries at Yule;*
> *When the corn's to shear*
> *The bairn's to bear.*

Once wed, in whatever month, the couple will find themselves
face to face with a formidable array of fallacies and superstitions,
for there is nothing in the world so hedged about with doubts and
delusions as the relations of the sexes.[1]

In regard to the sexual act itself, the lover whose ardours are so
feeble as to permit him to seek advice will find himself confused
by contrarieties, for folk-wisdom extols and abhors continence.

---

[1] The author has dealt with pre-natal influencees, conception without
coition, "inbreeding", "telegony", false pregnancies, fears of sterility, elimi-
nation of the "unfit", means of foretelling the sex of an unborn child,
children crying in the womb, and so on, in an earlier volume, *The Natural
History of Nonsense* (New York: Alfred A. Knopf; 1946).

The vague term "debauchery", much in use among our grand-fathers, covered a multitude of sinnings and included among its wages duels, paternity suits, venereal infections, and a dread but mysterious consequence known as a "weakening of the germ plasm". All this, of course, took place in relation to the male; debauchery in the female was unthinkable.

Buffon was greatly exercised about this "weakening", and opposed the castration of farm animals on the ground that it threw too heavy a burden upon the uncastrated, whose energies, as a result, were unequal to those of the female, so that the progeny were "tinctured with feminine qualities". Or else the females, disappointed, "languished", conducted their "sluggish amours" halfheartedly, and so produced only "insipid beings".

There has long been much concern about the debilitating effect of too much love. "These gymnicks inordinately taken", Walter Shandy informed his brother, are likely to "dry up the radical moisture", impair the strength, and weaken the mind. And he was only passing on to the impressionable captain what he had read in Aristotle and what is repeated daily in Y.M.C.A.'s and poolrooms. "It is a common belief," says Simone de Beauvoir, "that a man loses his muscular strength [in coition] and his clear-headedness, and that his phosphorus is used up and his sensitivity dulled."[1]

Physicians, however, are inclined to believe that the languor usually felt is due to a temporary nervous and physical exhaustion, not to a vital loss.

Some who do not insist that sexual intercourse is directly harmful yet maintain that continence is beneficial and prolongs life. Sir Thomas Browne insisted that there was a material diminution with each act, that "the propagation of one is the

[1] Simone de Beauvoir: *The Second Sex* (New York: Alfred A. Knopf; 1953), p. 161. Even worse horrors are whispered. In 1939, when Chicago was visited by the seventeen-year locust, the author encountered an awe-struck greensman on a Chicago golf course who was of the opinion that the insects' shed skins—hollow, chitinous shells then to be found on every tree—were all that was left of the males after they had performed their reproductive function.

minoration of another", and hence that "an impotency or total privation prolongeth life".

But some of the great debauchees of history have lived to a respectable age. August of Saxony-Poland, respectfully surnamed "the Strong", died at sixty-three, Catherine the Great at sixty-seven, and Casanova at seventy-three.[1] And life-insurance statisticians assure us that the married live longer than the single. Singleness, to be sure, does not guarantee celibacy, but it certainly warrants the assumption of a higher rate of continence. The most energetic rake rarely equals the normal activity of an ordinary married milque-toast.

Those who, on the other side of the argument, insist that continence is injurious are usually driven, today, to claiming that the injury is psychic. But even that is dubious. Complete abstinence might be injurious to mental health if the continent person chose to worry about it; but there is no evidence that it has any deleterious psychical effects. Priests and nuns, because of their regular lives, are probably more healthy than the average.

One sometimes hears that sexual intercourse is good for kidney ailments in women. It used to be a common joke in saloons. George Ade records that when a he-man ordered gin in the old-time saloon, he invariably excused himself on the grounds that he was taking it for his wife's kidneys. Vance Randolph says the remark is common in the Ozarks when a man takes a drink of whisky, and others have reported it from various parts of the country. The meaning (which seems to have escaped Ade, who was a modest and naïve bachelor) is: "Alcohol is an aphrodisiac, and my drinking some of it will set in motion a series of events which will ultimately benefit my wife's kidneys." Urologists, though, say that it isn't, it won't, and it doesn't.

Those who recommend continence as the best form of birth control sometimes allege that contraceptives cause sterility and

---

[1] Mere men may be comforted by Casanova's admission that his remarkable powers declined in the middle thirties and were completely gone by the late forties.

even cancer, and insist that, even if they don't, they "destroy all respect for marriage".

That the use of contraceptives induces sterility or cancer must be regarded as "not proved". Of course, if a woman uses harsh chemicals or an ill-fitting pessary, she may harm herself; though to say that bad contraceptives may do harm is not to say that contraceptives do harm. And, if the discussion is going to be put on the basis of physical consequences, surely the amount of physical harm done to women by overbreeding must outweigh many, many times whatever damage even bad contraceptives have done.

Statistics simply do not bear out the more general aspersion, that contraceptives destroy respect for marriage. "Respect for" is a vague term, but it is hard to see how anyone can show a more healthy respect for marriage than by getting married, and marriage and the practice of contraception seem statistically related: the United States must be almost the largest producer and consumer of contraceptives in the world, yet it has the highest marriage rate in the world; Ireland, which prohibits the importation, manufacture, sale, distribution, or even discussion of, contraceptives, has now almost the lowest marriage rate in the world.[1]

Although no figures could possibly be procured, it is hard not to correlate the marked increase in marriage in America and the marked increase in early marriages (both of which indicate the highest possible respect for the institution) with the spread of contraception. "It seems reasonable to believe," state two of the soberest authorities on population trends, "that young people, knowing that marriage does not necessarily involve continence, parenthood or abortion, are more ready to marry than they would be were they reasonably certain they would have children born at rather regular and frequent intervals if they do not practise continence or abortion."[2]

---

[1] See Table I, p. 71, in *Why Are You Single?* The statistics were compiled by Dr. Louis I. Dublin.

[2] Warren S. Thompson and P. K. Whelpton, quoted in *Science News Letter*, June 24, 1933, p. 388.

A common belief in regard to the sexual life of women is that desire ceases with the menopause. Continuation of sexual interest past this period used to be regarded as "contrary to the laws of nature". "Mutiny in a matron's bones", Hamlet called it. It was felt that Providence had provided a period devoid of desire in which women especially (Providence, for some reason, had not arranged quite the same period for men) could "in the calmness of reason look forward without regret to the end of mortal existence".[1] The nonagenarian Sarah, eavesdropping on angels, burst out laughing at the very thought of having pleasure of that nature when it had ceased to be with her "after the manner of women".

There is hardly a gynaecologist today, however, who does not admit that desire after the menopause is widespread and normal. Dr Kinsey and his associates found that a woman's sexual vigour outlasts a man's and that when the fear of pregnancy has vanished, desire often increases.

Gratification, of course, is another matter. Æsthetic considerations and the comparative scarcity of attractive men compel most unattached older women to resign themselves to clubwork. But the force of the old longing is dramatically and pathetically illustrated by the ravages made among them from time to time by unscrupulous swindlers who use their masculine charms as bait. An interesting case history—for the benefit of those who do not frequent night clubs—is supplied by the antics of the aged Marchioness d'Urfe with the amused and slightly embarrassed Casanova.

Pregnancy is as full of fallacies as of fears. Life is dull for a pregnant woman, and until quite recently was even duller. Eating was one of the few pleasures permitted, and its excesses were often justified by the assertion that a pregnant mother had to "eat for two".

So she does, but that doesn't mean that she has to take a second helping every time. All that the foetus is or hopes to be he owes

[1] Nicholas Francis Cooke: *Satan in Society* (Chicago: C. F. Vent Company; 1889), p. 163.

E

to his mother, but, so far as mere bulk goes, that isn't very much when spread over eight hundred and forty meals. Most gynaecologists now try to stop their patients from eating too much; excess weight is just that much more to be carried around, and adds to the mother's exhaustion.

A contrary idea, which is gaining in popularity, is that if the mother restricts her diet the child will be smaller and she will have an easier time of it at delivery. But investigations do not always bear this out. Some obstetricians claim to have reduced the weight of babies by dieting their mothers, but it was noticed that despite the meagre diet forced upon Germany and Austria in World War I the weight of newborn infants in those countries did not decrease. And investigations in England, Guttmacher says, have shown that though income and calories in the diet are directly related, the average birth weight is almost identical in the three income classes.

That dieting the mother will reduce the infant's size seems to be posited on the assumption that there is a camaraderie between mother and foetus, that it's share and share alike; if the mother pushes away the tempting pie, the foetus will restrain itself too. But, alas, such are not the ways of Nature. The foetus is a parasite. It will take whatever it wants, whenever it can, in complete indifference to the self-sacrificing character, or even to the physical well-being, of its host.[1]

Among the lowly there is sometimes a sinister contrary belief: that the health of the expectant mother and that of the child vary inversely. In Quebec a healthy woman who has lost several children is often thought to have taken over their health. One woman, in poor health, was quite pleased at the death of two of her children at birth, because it meant that her health would improve and "it couldn't hurt them just to be born and die".[2]

Even more bewildering than the taking in of food is the giving it up again. Many women assume that nausea and vomiting are

[1] ". . . the mammalian embryo . . . is quite definitely parasitic upon the mother in whose womb it develops."—Geoffrey Lapage: *Parisitic Animals* (London: Cambridge University Press; 1951), p. 15.

[2] The *Journal of American Folk-Lore*, vol. 32 (1921), p. 127.

as inevitable in pregnancy as swelling. Joanna Southcott, the prophetess, who believed herself, at the age of sixty-three, to be pregnant with Christ at His Second Coming, insisted, as proof of the gravity of her gravidity, that she was extraordinarily squeamish. And many women insist that morning sickness is a sign of a healthy baby.

But it is not an invariable sign, because one third to one half of all pregnant women go to term without it and bear as large a proportion of healthy children as their wretched retching sisters.

This has raised the question of whether morning sickness is "natural", a question that must be infuriating to those afflicted with it. None the less, it is a mysterious performance, and no one knows for sure just why or what it is.

There are, as is to be expected, many explanations. Some say that it is a sign that the child will be born with a thick head of hair—that the hair is tickling the mother inwardly. Very few physicians hold with this. They are inclined to attribute it to "the toxæmias of pregnancy, as yet unisolated". That sounds more impressive, but it's simply a stately way of saying that some women throw up when they're pregnant because something makes them throw up when they're pregnant. Others, middle-of-the-roaders, think that hormonal changes may induce qualms that the mother's fears exaggerate into nausea. Some psychiatrists have advanced the theory that morning sickness is a symbolic (and in severe cases often a successful) rejection of the child. Their theory is supported by the fact that the affliction is not universal, that it has not been observed in any other mammal, and that it seems to occur more among the well-to-do than among the poor. It is opposed by the facts that it is sometimes observed in women who, certainly at the conscious level, desire passionately to have a child, and that some women have suffered from morning sickness before they knew that they were pregnant.[1]

A peculiar circumstance that supports those who claim that morning sickness is psychic in origin is the fact that many men

[1] For much of the information in this section, the author is indebted to Dr Albert S. Tenney, of Orange, New Jersey.

vomit when their wives are pregnant, and a few even go so far as to have pains when their wives are in labour. Some attribute this phenomenon to fear, some to sympathy, and some, more cynical, to the alcohol with which the husband may have been consoling himself.

Among many primitive peoples the father goes to bed and groans during the delivery and often stays in bed after the mother gets up to do the necessary work. Marco Polo observed this custom in Chinese Turkestan, and his account of it no doubt helped to earn him the reputation of being a liar—though his doubters could have found a similar custom almost on their own doorstep, in Albania and in Corsica.

There have been many attempts to cast light on this widespread and curious custom of *couvade*. Anthropologists have suggested that the father is pretending to be the wife, so that the evil spirits will attack him instead of her; but this smacks suspiciously of modern, Western chivalry. Other anthropologists, with more likelihood, have suggested that the father must take special care of himself lest he suffer some injury which sympathetic magic would transfer to the child. Or it may be that by seeming to share in the child's delivery he demonstrates his paternity.

The contemporary American father is expected to pace the floor and be generally distraught at the time of his wife's delivery. It doesn't require any great histrionic effort, because he has good reasons for being uneasy. She may bear triplets or quadruplets and ruin him (the Dionnes and the Diligentis have raised the ante to at least six if it is to pay off). He may have to go to work and be wild at not getting his sleep. Or he may feel it necessary to make a show in order to assert his virility and demonstrate that the child is his.

Many men feel guilty. They love their wives, and now, through an act of theirs, their wives are in danger! The same feeling often weighs upon them all through the period of gestation, not merely at its conclusion. William Steig's drawing of pregnancy as a vast sphere almost filling an entire room and overwhelming a terrified little man in a corner reflects the normal male's feelings in the presence of a gravid woman. Sex, that hidden thing, is so monstrously in the open. Taboos, terrors, and reproaches charge the air, and guilt cries out to mountains of responsibility to fall upon it in atonement.

There is a vast oversolicitude for the woman. She is suddenly felt to be extraordinarily fragile, and there is great concern lest she be jostled. Long before L. Ron Hubbard added Dianetics to the world's supply of innocent merriment, the common man believed that if the mother sneezed, the baby was buffeted about, or if the mother bumped into a table, the baby had its head staved in.[1]

The alarm is exaggerated, however. Pregnancy is a natural condition, and Nature, foreseeing that men might be careless and even rude, suspended the fœtus in the amniotic fluid like a tadpole on a string inside a water-filled balloon—where it can be heard splashing around. Any pressure on the mother's abdomen merely jolts the child and it floats away. Women who have attempted to induce abortions by throwing themselves downstairs have been astonished to learn how indifferent to their discomfort a healthy embryo can be. Guttmacher had a patient who jumped off a sixteen-foot cliff to rid herself of an unwanted child, broke both legs, and had a normal delivery at term. Alexandre Dumas' account of the woman who produced monsters to order for circuses by binding her stomach during pregnancy would be received today with lifted eyebrows.

Women themselves have many groundless fears of this kind during their pregnancies. Some think they must not sleep on their backs, some think they must not sleep on their stomachs; but it makes no difference to the fœtus, who is upside down anyway. Many women fear that if they lift their hands above their heads they may strangle the fœtus in the umbilical cord or overturn it so that there will have to be a breech delivery. But in both fears they are either ignorant or forgetful of the anatomical facts.

---

[1] Mr Hubbard is quoted in *Look* (December 5, 1950, p. 83) as giving these experiences, among others, as typical causes of "engrams".

There is a rooted belief that "the fœtus grows only while the mother is sleeping"—as though they took turn and turn about. And many women are convinced that it is a nocturnal animal, "with studied malice choosing the night" to move about. But Guttmacher says it is not so: women lying in bed have less to divert their attention, and hence are more conscious of the child's movements.

Doctors and laymen alike are so impressed by the discomforts attendant upon deliveries in the early hours of the morning that they have come to think that most babies deliberately select this time for their entrance upon this great stage of fools. Statistics, however, particularly those based on the studies of Maximilian Meyer, who analysed more than one hundred and thirty thousand births occurring over a period of twenty-two years, show that births are evenly distributed throughout the twenty-four hours.

There is a good deal of uneasiness in the popular mind about Cæsareans, and one often hears "Once a Cæsarean, always a Cæsarean", and is told that no woman can have more than three Cæsareans. Neither assertion is true.

Dr Guttmacher, Associate in Obstetrics at Johns Hopkins, says there is nothing in the belief that one Cæsarean necessitates that all future deliveries be Cæsareans: "It is wholly unnecessary to repeat the section, unless of course the cause for the original operation is still present."[1] And while it is customary to sterilize a patient at her third Cæsarean, it is not obligatory, and a number of ardent women who like babies or operations unusually well have, at their own request, undergone the experience more often. Four is not uncommon, and there have been five, six, eight, and—it is said—ten.[2]

[1] See Kate Holliday: "Why Not a Caesarean?" *Woman's Home Companion*, February 1950.
[2] Dr Guttmacher records four women who have had four Cæsareans each and one who had five. Dr Eleanor Fordon Hamilton, herself a pediatrician, has had five children by Cæsarean section (*Chicago Sun*, August 24, 1947, p. 19); Mrs Margaret Thommes has had eight (*Chicago Sun-Times*, September 23, 1952, p. 22); and it is said that a Dublin woman holds the record with ten.

Many women think that each operation leaves a separate scar, a sort of procreational service stripe. But this is not so. The scar of the previous operation is always removed.[1]

It is instructive to remember how fixed certain errors were in the past, and by what unimpeachable authorities they were upheld. Think of the millions of children who for thousands of years were tightly swaddled lest they injure their limbs by moving them around. Every physician and midwife in the civilized world and most medicine men among savages prescribed this custom. Any other procedure would have been heresy. Yet modern science condemns it as harmful in the extreme, and it is a tribute to the sheer toughness of life that whole generations were not crippled by it. In some cultures, of course, such as those of the Chinese and the Flathead Indians, countless generations *were* crippled and distorted by following the best practices of the day as recommended by the most solemn savants.

An almost equally venerable custom, only now disappearing, is that of binding or swathing the mother's abdomen after childbirth, though enlightened doctors have seen its dangers for centuries. In all but Cæsarean cases, most obstetricians now dispense with it. Dr H. J. Stander, Professor of Obstetrics at Cornell, says that he is convinced that the binder "has no influence upon the involution of the uterus, nor upon the restoration of the figure". Indeed, he adds, it may be harmful in the latter respect "by inhibiting the movements of the abdominal wall".

The medieval justification for the binder was the assumption that the departure of the fœtus and the placenta left a lot of space in which the other organs might wobble dangerously about. The womb, in particular, was thought to be a wandering organ and hysteria (Greek *hystera*, womb) thought to be caused by its tickling as it moved about.[2]

---

[1] Alan Frank Guttmacher: *Into This Universe* (New York: The Viking Press; 1937), p. 264.

[2] Men, not having wombs, couldn't get hysterical. When men had tantrums and wept and tore their hair and beat their heads against the ground, they were displaying strength of character. One of Freud's earliest heresies was saying that men got hysterical, too.

Lactation has its illusions, no less than parturition. One of the commonest of these is that the size of the breasts indicates a woman's power to furnish milk. The assumed endowment of the Balinese women, for example, is sometimes accounted for in folk-anthropology on the grounds of natural selection. The lack of condensed milk and other blessings of civilization among these simple people, we are told, necessitates their having an ample natural supply on hand or on chest.

But there are a number of illusions involved. One is that the Balinese women have breasts differing in any way from those of other women, and another is that there is a correlation between the size of the breasts and the amount of milk they produce. "The size of the breasts," says an eminent authority, "seems to bear no relationship to this peculiar gift. The only index is the test of performance." Flat-chested women are often more lacti-fluous than their protuberant sisters.

Many well-meaning people urge a nursing mother to drink beer, under the impression that it has special virtue as a galacta-gogue. But any other potable liquid will do as well.

If a nursing mother takes in enough beer, she can get herself, and in consequence her child, drunk, as some of the alcohol passes into her milk.[1] In moderation this seems to do no great harm, and some thoughtful mothers charge themselves with a stiff highball before nursing on the evenings when they are going out. This dulls their own maternal pangs at the thought of the separation and puts the infant into a profound slumber, making it more convenient for the sitter.

---

[1] After World War I, Nauru Island in the Pacific was mandated to Australia. The natives drank a great deal of strong home brew made from fermented palm leaves and were tipsy much of the time. Prohibition was put into effect, and while, no doubt, this was good for their souls, it proved disastrous for their bodies. Infant mortality rose to fifty per cent within six months. An investigating committee found that their diet was low in vitamin B_1 and that the infants got enough for subsistence only when their mothers were full of the vitamin-rich hooch. The toddy was allowed again. The mothers got drunk again. And infant mortality fell at once to seven per cent. See J. B. S. Haldane: *Science and Human Life* (New York: Harper & Brothers; 1933), pp. 227–8. Haldane refers his readers to "An account of the Nauru affair given by Bray in the *Proceedings of the Royal Society of Medicine* for 1930".

Whether it does harm for a nursing mother to smoke is fiercely debated. The Anti-Tobacco League feels that it is very bad, though the majority of doctors are inclined to view it lightly. Waggish pediatricians have been known to oppose it on the grounds that the ashes drop in the baby's eye.

Now that the family, as our fathers knew it, has ceased to be, it has become the object of a great deal of romantic glorification, and we are told a great many things about it that don't accord with the facts. We hear of the "simplicity" of family life in former days, and exasperated bachelors, annoyed at the amount of attention and concern that children now get,[1] frequently insist that our ancestors managed to rear dozens of children with less fuss and bother than we expend on one or two.

It is hard to know quite what is meant by the "simplicity" that allegedly characterized family life in the past. No one who is familiar with Aubrey's *Brief Lives*, the *Paston Letters*, Burton's *Anatomy of Melancholy*, the Elizabethan dramatists, or the writings of the Brontës, Flaubert, or Dostoievsky can believe that it was emotionally simpler. And physically it was, in many ways, much more complex. Two hundred years ago most men were farmers, carpenters, hunters, soldiers, botanists, farriers, schoolteachers, and veterinarians all in one. They had to be. Their women were cooks, gynaecologists, pediatricians, herbalists, weavers, dressmakers, tailors, laundresses, and—in such operations as making their own soap—chemists. They were oppressed by superstitious fears and saddened by the ceaseless ravages of death. They were early disfigured by malnutrition and disease, and they died prematurely of sickness, overbreeding, and overwork.

As for rearing their children "with less fuss and bother", the grimmest fact of all in their lives was that they *didn't* raise very many of them. Until very recently—well within the past century—most human beings died in infancy. A committee of the House of Commons investigating the subject in 1765 found

---

[1] The next great liberator of mankind will be he who frees suburban parents from the P.T.A. and the Cub Scouts.

that only seven out of every hundred children under a year old in the care of the parishes survived. Benjamin Franklin was told at the Paris institution for *Enfants-Trouvés* that nine tenths of their charges died soon after admission. Of the twelve thousand seven hundred and eighty-six children admitted to foundling hospitals in Dublin between 1792 and 1797, twelve thousand five hundred and sixty-one died on the premises.

Nor was this solely the lot of the poor. Queen Anne bore nineteen children, none of whom survived. Mrs Thrale, with every advantage that wealth and intelligence could give, kept three out of her twelve children. Dr Johnson comforted Boswell on the loss of an infant son with the reminder, which seems harsh to modern ears, that in losing only one out of four he was keeping " more than his share".[1]

So taken for granted, through most of the nineteenth century, was the death of children that beginners in the *McGuffey Readers* were urged to be kind to their little brothers and sisters because "they will soon be gone". And books of consolation for bereaved parents were as much in demand then as books of advice for harassed parents are now.[2]

For the unhappy parents never seemed to get used to it. These myriad deaths did not come undreaded or pass unlamented. The tears were as hot for the tenth child as for the first. Letters and diaries are filled with endless forebodings, heartsick apprehensions, and pitiful lamentations. Little ones sickened and wasted away or were cut off with cruel suddenness by fevers. It was the *flowers* that the grim reaper was always thought of as mowing down with his icy breath, and the efforts to save the babies were as pathetic as they were futile. We who are accustomed to formulas and bottle-feeding can form no idea of what

[1] For the Dublin statistics, see W. E. H. Lecky: *History of Rationalism* (New York: D. Appleton & Company; 1903), vol. 2, p. 234 n. For Franklin, see the Hill-Powell edition of Boswell's *Life of Johnson* (Oxford: The Clarendon Press; 1934), vol. 2, p. 398, n. 4; and for Mrs Thrale, see the same, vol. 3, p. 109. For Queen Anne, see the *Dictionary of National Biography*.
[2] Such as William Logan: *Words of Comfort for Parents Bereaved of Little Children* (London; 1868), 560 pp.

it meant only sixty or seventy years ago to a mother when she found she could no longer give milk. The well-to-do found a wet nurse. But it was a risky business; many children died of diseases contracted from wet nurses. And it was often a cruel business; for the wet nurse's own children often died for lack of the milk she had to sell to others.[1]

Then—as far as "fuss and bother" are concerned—the large families that our ancestors are thought to have taken so lightly destroyed the women. Sometimes one wife would produce the dozen children recorded on the gravestones, but it often took two or three; and so there were desolate orphans, distraught widowers, and exasperated stepmothers to add to the general stress.

One of the favourite themes of moral alarmists is that "the family is disintegrating". Certainly it is changing. Modern living conditions do not, as a rule, permit the old to live on with their children and grandchildren. This unquestionably means more loneliness and emptiness for the old, but it also means less humiliation for them and less irritation for the others.

The great agency charged with "breaking up" the family is divorce. And certainly more homes are broken up by divorce than used to be, though that many of them would have been worth living in had the divorce not taken place is doubtful. Obviously those most nearly concerned and presumably best informed did not think so.

The picture is not quite so dark, however, as viewers-with-alarm sometimes picture it. The old-fashioned family was nowhere near so stable as they imagine. It was, in fact, not so stable as the modern family. Prostitution flourished under the double standard. Men kept mistresses more openly. Desertion

---

[1] Samuel Johnson was put out to wetnurse when he was a few weeks old and returned shortly blind in one eye and disfigured for life. The woman had scrofula.

"Of the two women known to have wetnursed little Archie [Douglas], both lost their own children in the process, a fact which no one seems to have taken any notice of whatever. It was the natural order of things."— Lillian de la Torre: *The Heir of Douglas* (New York: Alfred A. Knopf; 1952), p. 138.

and bigamy seem to have been widespread. But all of these factors fade to insignificance when compared with the death of one or both parents. Death, not divorce, is the great disrupter of families. Even yet, more children under eighteen are orphaned annually in the United States than are affected by divorce. Since death is classified as "an act of God", it is never thought of by the moralists as *the* great force that breaks up families. But it is. And science, which is often blamed for the change in attitudes and customs that has led to the increase in divorce, is rarely credited with being *the* great preserver of the family by having increased life expectancy—so that more parents live until their children are grown.

For the fact is that *fewer* families are broken up today than were sixty years ago. The increase in divorce has been more than offset by the decline in the number of families broken up by death. Although a changed institution, the family is a more stable institution today than at any time for which statistics are available,[1] and the increased stability is owing almost entirely to science: to lowered mortality, to a better understanding of psychological difficulties, to the eradication of venereal disease, to an increase in education, and to improved birth control.

[1] See Louis I. Dublin, in collaboration with Mortimer Spiegelman: *The Facts of Life: from Birth to Death* (New York: The Macmillan Company; 1951), pp. 77–8. Dr Dublin is responsible only for the figures; the deductions are not necessarily his. For further facts on the instability of the old-fashioned family, see an article by Dr Ray H. Abrams in the "family stability" issue of the *Annals of the American Association of Political and Social Science*, November 1950.

CHAPTER ELEVEN

The Monstrous Regiment of Women

THE real virtue of the old-fashioned family, though most men would no longer dare say so openly, was the subservience of its women. But *that* is past! According to many prophets, the shoe is now on the other foot, and we are faced with the menace of women's domination. From all sides we hear of the coming "matriarchy". Clubwomen exult while clubmen scrounge deeper into their leather chairs and double the number of their doormen.

Do such fears (or hopes) have any basis in fact? Are they merely the nightmares of misogynists or the fantasies of feminists? Could they be an inverted erotic dream, more a symptom of the present than an indication of the future?

Certainly the tensions between men and women seem to have increased and come very close to open war. Some irritation is, of course, inescapable and even pleasurable; but many things in the modern world have combined to raise the normal tensions between the sexes to an unprecedented height.

The evidence is all about us. Popular fiction, written largely for women, is characterized by a marked animosity towards men. The heroines of the best-sellers are usually female Don Juans seeking love vicariously for their readers, not for happiness or security, but for the chance it offers of "getting back at" the

arrogant male. Opposed to this, the male writers of contemporary
fiction, almost unanimously, see women as cold and selfish, fear-
fully destructive through the power that love gives them over the
generous and noble sex. Where an ideal woman is portrayed, her
complete and unreal self-effacement and subordination are even
more revealing.

Among the subliterate one finds the same sentiments expressed
in radio and television jokes about the tyrannies of marriage, in
the acceptance of henpeckedness as the normal state of the
married man, and the conviction, reiterated to tedium, that
women are childish, illogical, verbose, and silly. There is hardly
a newspaper in America that does not carry some daily feature
that reflects this antagonism. In point is a widely syndicated
cartoon whose humour consists entirely of the stupidities and in-
eptitudes of a shirking, illiterate, and irresponsible stenographer.

Such creatures exist, of course, and are fair game for satire.
But can anyone conceive of the obverse being syndicated? What
paper would think of buying a cartoon whose humour consisted
of the ignorance and stupidity of a boss being continually met and
tactfully corrected by an intelligent stenographer? Yet that
situation also exists. Statistics are hardly worth compiling, but it
would be interesting to know how many comic strips end with a
woman shattering a vase over a man's head, driving him out of
the house, or, in the more modern strips, luring him into some
fatal trap or attempting to shoot him or stab him when his back
is turned.

It might be argued that the direction of the violence is merely
a matter of chivalry, but there is too much of it and it is too
warmly greeted for it to be dismissed wholly as a polite convention.

It seems, rather, a manifestation of deep insecurity in contemporary men. The passive subjection of women has been one
of the mainstays of masculine assurance, and the effect of their
revolt has been traumatic. There is no one against whom we
turn with greater fury than one who has formerly ministered to
our vanity and now dares to assert independence. Men hate an
"uppity" woman. Ours has been a Jane Crow society for several

thousand years, and the master group always fears its slaves more than any foreign enemy; at the least stirring of the helots, the ruling caste is subject to terrible imaginings.

But does anything in the present situation suggest that complete reversal of male and female roles in our society which is anticipated by those who think we are headed for a matriarchy? Is it likely, for instance, that women will become the chief breadwinners while men perform domestic chores? Will women become the executives, men the stenographers and clerks? Will men be reduced to charming ornaments among the rich and drudges among the poor? Will they be denied equality under the law, prohibited from voting or managing their own property, kept illiterate, excluded from the professions, and restricted to severe monogamy, while their wives flaunt their gigolos and patronize male prostitutes? Will they, in brief, be put in the position that women were in up until fifty years ago, when "patriarchy" flourished?

It doesn't seem likely.

In the first place, it may be doubted that a true matriarchy has ever existed. There have been, and are, matrilinear societies—societies, that is, in which descent and family connection are traced through the mother rather than, as with us, through the father. And in most primitive cultures women have had, and do have, more power and dignity, more personal freedom, and more say in public and domestic affairs than has been accorded them, until recently, in Christendom or Islam.

A matrilinear society, however, is not the same thing as those mythical societies in which, from tales of the Amazons on down through the ages, women were imagined to be completely dominant. There are many accounts of such groups, but none of them has been verified, and they probably owe more to fantasy than to observation.[1] Women are not the only ones who indulge in fancies of being ravished without responsibility.

---

[1] "The theory of gynaecocracy is in truth a dream of visionaries and pedants."—Sir James Frazer: *Adonis, Attis, Osiris* (New York: The Macmillan Company; 1932), vol. 2, p. 211.

But no amount of erotic dreaming, however disguised as science, can change certain facts. Women are slighter than men, lighter and less muscular—not so much as it pleased our grandfathers to assume, but still definitely so. Then they must bear the economic and physical handicaps of pregnancy, childbirth, nursing, menstruation, and the menopause. No one of these incapacitates all women all of the time, but the combination of them certainly prevents women, as a group, from excelling or even equalling men in war and work.

Curiously enough, they seem, despite this, to be *biologically* stronger than men, and the fear of their dominance may find support in the recent discovery of that fact. They live longer. They seem emotionally more stable. They are less subject to many diseases. And so on. But that doesn't change the fact of their comparative physical weakness and the disadvantage at which it puts them.

It is true that women are now competing with men in industry, but that can lead to their subjection as easily as to their dominance. Industry, which now requires more manipulative skill and patience than brute strength, has found out that women can perform most of the tasks formerly performed by men, and has developed new techniques and machines to take advantage of that fact. In consequence there are now more than eighteen million women in the American labour force. They are there to stay and, from all indications, to increase. But while this represents, from one point of view, a form of emancipation,[1] it may actually represent the opposite. More than eight and a half million of these women are women without men—single, widowed, or divorced;[2] so that there is the possibility that, like the social insects, we are creating a great mass of unsexed workers.

One of the central facts of life today is the excess of women.

[1] Dr F. Zweig (*Women's Life and Labour*, London: Victor Gollancz; 1952) found that the overwhelming majority of English women in factories preferred the factory work to housework.

[2] See *Women as Workers*, issued by the Women's Bureau of the Department of Labour, July 1952. This report (p. 23) estimates that women-without-men constitute 45 per cent of all women in the labour force.

Twenty years ago there were more marriageable men than marriageable women in the United States; but the conditions prevailing in less fortunate countries have in this, as in so many other things, finally caught up with us, and we now have many more women than men, and will apparently have even more. Just what has brought about the change is not clearly understood. Most of the emigrants were men, and that would account for the old surplus of men. In part the change may be due to hygienic practices of modern society which give the natural biological superiority of women a chance to assert itself.

Whatever the causes, the facts remain. According to Amram Scheinfeld, who bases his figures on estimates of the Census Bureau, there was, in 1930, an excess of more than one million men in the United States. By 1950 there was an excess of more than one million four hundred thousand women, and the changing ratio was accelerating. To be sure, many of these women are beyond the ordinary marriageable age—though that doesn't prevent them from adding to the competition—but there are enough of them within the marriageable age to doom about one out of every thirteen girls to spinsterhood.[1]

The prophet Isaiah, in a mood unusually gloomy even for him, foretold a frightful time when "seven women shall take hold of one man", offering to support themselves if only they might bear his name "to take away their reproach". We have not yet come to any such alarming pass, but this change in the ratio of men and women is one of the most significant and far-reaching facts that women must now face. It is one of the chief underlying causes of divorce (divorce is a sort of staggered polygamy, and reflects the highly moral, or cowed, nature of contemporary men; the modern philanderer no longer keeps the extra woman as a mistress—she must be a wife even if it requires him to

---

[1] See Amram Scheinfeld: *Women and Men* (New York: Harcourt, Brace & Company; 1944), p. 193; *Statistical Bulletin* of the Metropolitan Life Insurance Company, May 1942; *Time*, December 1, 1952, p. 11; and *Science News Letter*, March 6, 1954, p. 147, where the Metropolitan Life Insurance Company is quoted as predicting more than eight million widows in the United States by 1960.

divorce the wife he already has) and, to some extent, of the increase in promiscuity among women. There just aren't enough men to go around.

What the lasting effects of all this will be, no one knows; but it is against all reason to assume that it will increase the dominance of women over men.

The surplus women are finding employment in offices and factories, and so competing with men, but they have made practically no impact on the professions and the executive classes. Much is made of the few who reach even the second or third rank of distinction; but the fact is that after three generations of nominal equality in most things and a full generation of political equality, the woman who has entered the professions or reached a minor executive position is still news. Women have taken over public-school teaching, but ninety-nine per cent of the principals and superintendents are men. Except in women's colleges and women's divisions of co-educational colleges, where is a woman dean or a woman college president to be found? Only six per cent of those listed in *Who's Who* are women, and many of them seem to have paid for their eminence with celibacy or childlessness. Forty per cent of them are unmarried, and almost half of those who are married have no children.[1]

It is in the sphere of *mores*, however, rather than in the economic sphere, that the combination of the excess of women and their new freedom has produced the greatest changes; and their independence in personal matters is the real basis of such bogeys as the fear of an impending matriarchy. When an inferior status in another is taken for granted, any attempt on that person's part to assert equality will be regarded as an act of aggression. The white chauvinist sincerely believes that he is being shoved off the sidewalk if a Negro dares to share it, but the chauvinist's

[1] *Science News Letter*, February 4, 1950, p. 77, reporting the findings of Dr Clyde V. Kiser and Miss Nathalie L. Schacter, of the Milbank Memorial Fund. Does anyone imagine, to press the argument further, that the creation of the WAC and the WAVE means that women are now headed for the top brass in the Army and Navy? Or does it mean new sources for labour battalions?

appraisal of the situation is not likely to be accepted by those who are free of his hates and fears.

Although no modern woman with any intelligence need be as humiliatingly dependent on the lordly male as her grandmother had to be, it is doubtful that her new freedom gives her any great edge on him. For, as women are at a physical disadvantage in competing with men in industry, they are at a psychological disadvantage in sexual freedom. Their indulgence in it, like their entrance into industry, *now that they outnumber men*, contains as much danger of their subjection as hope of their mastery.

The sexual desires, or needs, of women are more pervasive than those of men. A woman attains complete satisfaction—in so far as anyone can—in the involved and prolonged business of bearing and raising children. To be successful, she must have not only a satisfactory lover, but a satisfactory husband and a satisfactory father for her children. She must, in other words, have a satisfactory *marriage*. A satisfactory *affair* is not enough.[1]

There seems to be little doubt that women are seeking sexual pleasure for itself (as men do) with more directness and freedom than heretofore. But those who do so are taking greater risks than their masculine equivalents. Not merely physical risks— those are less for a woman now than they have ever been, though still greater than the physical risks a man runs—but psychological and social risks as well.

For beyond the pleasure of the moment, the woman wants marriage. And the female adventurer has a tough row to hoe. She has plenty of bait, but no hooks. The world she wants to enter is fiercely competitive. Few holds are barred. The demimonde wouldn't last a week if it adopted the ethics of café society. And the long-run effect of such competition can only be to extend the evil. Men have always been wary of marriage, and they will surely be less inclined than ever to accept its burdens

[1] " . . . Dr Kinsey . . . further states that his findings indicate that the average woman marries to establish a home and a long-term relationship with her husband and to have children, rather than to find sexual gratification."—Anne G. Freedgood: "Dr Kinsey's Second Sex", *Harper's*, September 1953, p. 27.

and restrictions when they can obtain what they assume to be its delights more cheaply and pleasantly elsewhere. And on the whole it is likely to be the more desirable men who will behave that way. The clinging vines—those who seek a mother or a housekeeper rather than a mistress or a companion—will, of course, continue to want marriage.

Because of the ruthless competition for men, every American woman has become a lady of fashion and is on the firing line at least twelve hours a day. Every magazine ad, every radio and television commercial, and every shop window reminds her that her chief business is to allure men. Perfume is a good example. Forty years ago advertisements for perfumes stressed the innocent freshness they conferred. Today they are offered as mantraps: "Frenzy", "Surrender", "Menace", "My Sin", "Intoxication", and "Tabu". Nothing but postal regulations, apparently, has prevented some manufacturer from going the whole hog with "Orgasm". Soaps, face creams, and even jewellery are advertised as if they were aphrodisiacs, and spinsterhood is openly threatened to those who scorn their aid.

Nor is the threat idle. The danger is real, and every young woman knows it and governs herself accordingly. The shopgirl who skimps on food and lives in a hovel in order to dress as much like a movie star as she can (and the resemblance is often amazing, considering the difference in means) is no fool.[1] It would be no comfort to be better fed, but to remain single. She is like a soldier in action who jettisons his rations but hangs on to his ammunition and keeps his rifle clean.

Some bold social physicians, such as the late Professor Ralph Linton of Yale, have advocated polygamy as a possible solution. They argue that it will not only take up the slack of surplus women, but will extend the range of choice and re-introduce a little wholesome natural selection. But this argument is based on the assumption that a woman would rather have a part interest in

[1] Zweig (*Women's Life and Labour*, p. 124) suggests that fashion is a battle in which the working girl seeks to obviate class differences in clothes while the woman of wealth and leisure seeks to make them as conspicuous as possible.

a virile man than full ownership of a twerp, and it collapses because of the further assumption that people will be reasonable about such matters. Furthermore, it ignores some of the facts of polygamy, which, after having been tried out for several thousand years by several hundred million people, has been pronounced, by most who have given us any intimate account of it, to be unsatisfactory for everyone except the reigning favourite of the moment.[1] Most women would probably prefer divorce and remarriage, promiscuity in the single state, or adultery.

It is true that many things support the illusion of an impending woman's world. The industrial revolution took the man out of the home and left the woman its unchallenged mistress. His skills are now exercised elsewhere, and the authority and confidence that come from their exercise—things that formerly earned him the respect of his wife and children—are now left at the factory or office. He comes home a visitor whom exhaustion has often made peevish and whom familiarity has made, if not contemptible, at least unimpressive. Then, in most cases, he comes home to some cramped space where privacy, peace, and dignity are impossible. The wife, increasingly likely to be exhausted from *her* factory work, is irritable or demands sympathy. There is an explosion, followed by endless recriminations. Save at the most degraded levels, custom no longer permits the man to assert a physical dominance, and, save at the highest levels, he is probably unable to assert an intellectual dominance or even an equality. One of the salient features of American middle- and upper-class life is the superior education and cultural attainments of the women.

---

[1] For testimonials to its unpleasantness, see Rebecca Hourwich Reyher: *Zulu Woman* (New York: Columbia University Press; 1948) and Anna Leonowens: *Siamese Harem Life* (New York: E. P. Dutton & Co.; 1953). It is pictured as a more tolerable state—indeed, sometimes as a pleasant state—in Kimball Young's account of Mormon polygamy, *Isn't One Wife Enough?* (New York: Henry Holt & Company; 1954), but Professor Young, in his interesting and valuable book, makes it plain that Mormon polygamy was unusual. It was enjoined upon the faithful as a religious ideal, and it carried over, in practice, many of the values and attitudes of the monogamy that the early Mormons had grown up in. It was, really, plural monogamy, and it was not without its woes and difficulties.

So the man laughs it off, or sulks and snarls, and gets out of the house or apartment at the first opportunity. Somewhere, the chances are, he will encounter one of the surplus women who will baby him and flatter his vanity. There are far more surplus women, however, than surplus living quarters and, especially if there is the added pull of children, he will probably return to his wife, guilty perhaps at first, but in time merely sullen. Where there are no children, divorce is already more common than continued marriage.

Below the surface a vicious spiral strikes down to the roots. Women, resentful of their husbands, dominate their sons, producing mama's boys. Or fathers, resenting their wives, seek too determinedly to rule and make their sons dependent or rebellious. In both instances, the number of men who would make desirable husbands is lessened. Then many men losing their psychic security have lost their potency, and they hate and fear the aggressive, demanding woman.

A mess, yes; a matriarchy, no.

CHAPTER TWELVE

Youth and Age

Infancy and childhood seem girt about with fallacies, from the first indignant wawl with which we protest against being so unceremoniously dragged into the world up to the pimples and poetry of adolescence.

That cry with which we exhale the first air we ever breathe is the subject of doubt and controversy. It used to be generally believed that if a baby did not cry at once it should be spanked or plunged into cold water so that, having something to cry about, it would inhale in order to lament. And certainly many babies *have* begun to breathe after being so treated; but it is now doubted that the spanking or the shock had any bearing on the situation. The essential stimulus of our first breath, as of our last, seems to be a concentration of carbon dioxide in the lungs.[1]

Wiseacres sometimes regard the possession of fingernails as conclusive proof that a baby was born at term. Where it is a first child, born prematurely, this has led to some unwarranted assumptions about the pre-marital conduct of the parents. But premature babies have fingernails, perfectly formed.

Perhaps the knowing ones feel that if the nails were formed earlier they would be long enough at term to scratch the mother, a thing that Providence would not allow. But let them meditate upon the gestation and delivery of the porcupine.

Other illusions are stated with equal assurance. Thus one often hears it said that babies have an "instinctive" fear of noise.

---

[1] See "Initiation of Respiration at Birth", by Professor Yandell Henderson of Yale, in *Nature*, August 25, 1928, p. 283.

However, William A. Hunt, who made a special investigation of this, did not find it to be true. Using ultra-slow-motion cameras, Professor Hunt took pictures of the responses of sixty babies to sudden loud noises, and found that even a revolver shot at fairly close range elicited more interest than concern. Thirty-three of the babies didn't cry at all when the revolver went off, and seven others who had been crying stopped when they heard the sound. All of the babies, though, stretched or wiggled their toes.[1]

Many a first father on seeing the odd-shaped head of his first child has gloomily commenced to compute the probable cost of maintaining an imbecile, only to be cheered up, on his next visit, by observing that the baby's head has assumed a more normal shape. It is often believed that the improvement was the result of manipulations by the guilt-stricken obstetrician who had crept by night into the maternity ward and done what he could to remedy his earlier botchery.

Fears and fancies, though, are alike unfounded. The head of a newborn infant is malleable and, especially in first deliveries when the membranes have ruptured early and the mother's pelvis is small, is often squeezed into the shape of an egg. But after three or four days it automatically assumes its proper shape. Babies delivered by Cæsarean section before labour has begun, and breech babies, freed from any such pressure on their heads, are always born with normal heads.

Parents sometimes fear that the distortion might have a bad effect on the brain; but the brain is a semi-liquid mass and within limits seems none the worse for being pushed around. The Flat-head Indians distorted all their skulls, but—aside from the limitations implied in their continuance of the practice— seemed, so far as we know, intellectually none the worse for doing so.

One does not have to be an over-anxious parent to fear that a baby will kill itself by holding its breath in its paroxysms of rage.

[1] Professor Hunt reported his findings to the American Association for the Advancement of Science in December 1936. See *Science News Letter*, January 9, 1937.

Certainly the distorted, often cyanotic, faces of these infuriated brats, and the dreadful silence that mounts in tension until it and the parents' anxiety are relieved by a scream of anger, are enough to shake the stoutest calm. And one does read stories in the papers of babies who have killed themselves by deliberately holding their breath.[1]

Most pediatricians doubt, however, that a normal child could kill itself in this manner. Breathing is largely a reflex action set in motion by the concentration of carbon dioxide in the lungs, and even if the child could control it, it is hard to believe that it could know, at the age at which breathholding is common, that this particular act would constitute a threat against the parents. Where children have died of asphyxiation in a tantrum, it is thought that there must have been something wrong with them, such as, perhaps, a diseased thymus.

Mothers have enough genuine worries, but few seem content with them; they must make up some extra ones. Among the fallacious fears with which they torment themselves none is more common, pediatricians say, than that the second year of a child's life is particularly dangerous. Years ago there may have been some slight basis in fact for the belief: during its first year the child would be constantly under its mother's surveillance, but in the second year, as yet too young to fend for itself, it would be superseded by the next, inevitable, arrival and left to the slender mercies of its not so very much older brothers and sisters. This would account for accidents and external dangers, but it's probably reaching too far to try to find a rational basis. The belief is that the child itself is in some way more delicate, more vulnerable to disease, in its second year.

The most dreadful consequences may ensue, in mothers' imaginations, from the most innocent acts. If a child tries to walk too early, it will become bowlegged. If it is tickled, it will

[1] Two such cases were reported in the Chicago papers within two months of each other, one in East St Louis and the other in Louisburg, N.C. See the *Chicago Sun-Times*, September 20, 1949, p. 3, and the *Chicago Daily News*, November 10, 1949, p. 1. See also an article on the subject by Dr Theodore R. Van Dellen, the *Chicago Tribune*, January 16, 1954.

stutter. If it bites its nails, it will have stubby fingers. If it sucks its thumb, it will be hideous. If it crosses its eyes for fun, the disfigurement will become permanent. And so on through a ghastly catalogue of alarms and excursions into fantasy, mostly needless.

Bowlegs are due to a deficiency of calcium in the bones, and hence are primarily a problem of nutrition. Perhaps the belief that they are the result of trying to walk too early is the last remnant of the age-old conviction that children should be tightly swathed or swaddled to prevent them from injuring themselves by moving their limbs. Modern authorities think that if a child wants to walk it is not likely to be too early for it to try. Forcing it to walk by holding it up and shoving its legs about is, of course, a different matter.

If tickling babies causes them to stutter when they grow up, then many more boys than girls must have been tickled when they were babies, for many more boys than girls stutter.

Biting the nails and gnawing the cuticle may make fingers look stubby, but when the habit is stopped the nails will grow out, none the worse, and can be manicured to give the fingers whatever tapering shape they were capable of assuming in the first place. A lung abscess, by the way, will sometimes club the fingers; and the sight of some unhappy person so afflicted may be viewed (like the Venus de Milo) as a frightful consequence of biting the nails.

Orthodontists, who have showed that one out of every six cases of malocclusion may be wholly or in part attributed to thumb-sucking, feel that the practice should be sternly discouraged. Some advise smearing the child's thumb with myrrh or some other bitter substance. Some urge that the hands be bound, to be released only at mealtimes, under adult supervision. Dr Edward S. Mack of San Francisco recommends[1] that all thumb-suckers over three and a half years old have a set of inward-curving tines cemented to the back of their upper front

[1] In the July 1951 *Journal of the American Dental Association*. A picture of the device, the most horrendous prophylactic since the chastity belt, may be seen in *Time*, July 9, 1951, p. 34.

teeth. He grants that it is a vicious-looking device and that the wearing of it would be humiliating as well as uncomfortable, but he thinks that it would bring the child to maturity with straight teeth. After two or three absent-minded attempts to suck it, the thumb might have to be amputated; but that's a problem for the digitologist and no concern of the orthodontist.

Child psychologists, however, point out that a baby is born with a sucking reflex—some fœtuses suck their thumbs! The child, they say, has to suck something, and if that something is not available, it must make do with whatever it has on hand. Thumb-sucking, they aver, is "as normal as breathing" and attempts to stop it may well lead to maloccluded personalities.

Torn between these conflicting authorities, faced with having to choose between a buck-toothed snerd or a neurotic nitwit, many a frustrate mother has given up and started to suck her own thumb.

Modern babies probably suck their thumbs a great deal. Hygiene, caoutchouc, and the brassière restrict their opportunities for natural gratification. The thumb does not appear to be fully satisfactory, however, for millions of them never seem to get completely weaned; years later they celebrate Mother's Day and smoke cigarettes.

If they take up the smoking too early, they will give their mothers still further cause for concern, for it is widely believed—or at least told to boys—that smoking stunts growth. There's no evidence that it does, and some that it doesn't. Mickey Norman, of Paterson, New Jersey, who commenced to smoke cigars at the age of fourteen months and consumed an estimated thirteen thousand stogies before his nineteenth birthday, grew to be six feet tall.[1] In so doing he has cut out for himself, it would now seem, a considerably better than average chance of developing cancer of the lips, tongue, and lung; but at least he isn't the runt the neighbours predicted he would be. It may be that boys who are undersized in the first place are more inclined to take up smoking in order to be "big".

[1] The *Chicago Daily News*, March 10, 1950, p. 1.

Mothers sometimes warn their children that it is dangerous to look cross-eyed in fun, as the condition may become permanent.[1] But the fear—despite even Montaigne's support of it[2]—is groundless. Crossing the eyes is a complicated muscular performance, and there is no more chance of its being suddenly fixed than there is of a ballet dancer's being frozen, like a bird dog, in the midst of a strenuous cavort. The mugging offspring may actually be benefiting themselves—wholly apart from preparing for a brilliant career as a comic in television—by exercising their powers of convergence and fusion.

Some children are cross-eyed at birth, or become so soon after. In others the condition does not develop until some time between the second and the fifth years. The mothers of some of these latter may well think at first that the child is merely fooling and hence to blame for its own disfigurement; especially if a maternal warning had been given in the early stages and seemingly disregarded, as nearsighted and deaf children are frequently accused of wilful neglect of the lessons they cannot comprehend.

There is a general opinion that strabismus can be outgrown, and friends often misadvise the parents of a cross-eyed child to wait until the child has had a chance to use his eyes in school before doing anything about it. Ophthalmologists disagree, however; they feel that it simply allows that much more time for the eye muscles to become set in an abnormal position.[3]

A once-widespread notion about children and their eyes was that piercing the ear lobes improves the sight. Alfonso XIII of Spain had his ear lobes pierced when he was a child for this purpose—though it certainly does not seem to have helped his political foresight. One would have thought the idea was

---

[1] "`. . .` like they say how you might cross your eyes and then you can't uncross." Lena Grove, in William Faulkner's *Light in August*.

[2] "Mothers have reason to rebuke their children when they counterfeit having but one eye, squinting, lameness, or any other personal defects; for, besides that their bodies being then so tender, may be subject to take an ill bent, fortune, I know not how, sometimes seems to delight in taking us at our word."—"Not to Counterfeit the Sick Man," *The Essays of Montaigne* (Modern Library edition), p. 260.

[3] See "Eyes and Eye Doctors", *Hygeia*, December 1949.

completely extinct, but Miss Gracie Barrie, a comedienne, was
quoted by Nate Gross, in his "Town Tattler" section of the
Pictorial Review, in 1948, as saying that her doctor recommended that she pierce her ears in order to improve her sight.[1]
Of course Miss Barrie may have only been plying her trade. Or
it may have been just publicity—for Miss Barrie, that is, hardly
for the doctor. H. Allen Smith reported that he found the subject
still being discussed as a vital issue in the letters column of *The
Times* when he was in London in 1950. A Spanish-born correspondent had written in to say that it is all a matter of when it is
done. It must be done in childhood to be effective. She added, in
confirmation, that she had recently visited her native village in
Spain, where it was customary to pierce the ears of all baby girls,
and had found very few old women wearing glasses.

Certain diseases are still regarded as "children's diseases", and
it is widely felt that "they might as well have them and get it
over with". Our stouthearted parents used sometimes to put a
healthy child in bed with a sick one because "it would get it anyway", and patients are easier to handle in job lots.

Many parents hold to the old theory, though few today would
definitely court infection. They argue, for instance, that mumps
is more severe in an adult and that, therefore, it is better to have
it while you are young.

It is best, of course, not to have it at all, and the same goes for
measles and the lot. "Children's" diseases (they can all be contracted by adults) are now regarded as serious afflictions, grave in
themselves and often the cause of even more grave after-effects.
Whooping cough, which was formerly often regarded as merely
an inconvenience to the sufferer and an annoyance to others, is
now known to cause more deaths than infantile paralysis,
diphtheria, scarlet fever, and measles all put together. And where
it is not fatal it may cause permanent damage to the brain (so
warns the Illinois Public Health Department) because of lack of
oxygen in the brain during the paroxysms of coughing. "Many
studies," the Illinois Public Health Department warned in 1950,

[1] The *Chicago Herald-American*, December 12, 1948.

"have revealed undesirable personality changes directly traceable to a severe attack of whooping cough."[1]

Even more callous is the dismissal of certain pains as "growing pains". Growing is not a painful process, and the aches which our fathers pooh-poohed and which many parents still dismiss with a hearty quip may be rheumatic and indicative of a condition that will have serious consequences later. The child's only recourse is to get himself transferred to a properly run orphanage or to wait until he can pooh-pooh his parents' arthritis as mere "ageing pains".

Most modern parents, however, are more fearful than callous, and are in continual anxieties, many of which are unjustified. There is a frightening belief, for example, which is entirely false, that a child who has sustained a head injury must not be allowed to go to sleep. It is, apparently, one of the many associations of sleep and death. A child who goes to sleep after a head injury has probably sustained a concussion, and a physician should be called; but, once the injury has been sustained, there is nothing wrong in the sleeping.[2]

Rusty nails still inspire terror, and rightly so, because a rusty nail, which must have lain out and probably been buried, is more likely to be contaminated with the germs of tetanus than a clean nail, and, if it is stepped on, may carry the anaerobic germs deep into the tissues where they can thrive. But the rust itself, iron oxide, is perfectly harmless. None the less, there is a custom, still practised in country places, of greasing a nail or a needle that has been stepped on so that it won't rust, it being assumed, apparently,

[1] The *Manchester Guardian*, August 24, 1950, p. 14, says that at St. Albans "a conspicuous number of children are still marched round and round the gasworks by anxious parents as a cure for whooping cough". The *Guardian* and the Gas Board are of the opinion that this strange practice, known elsewhere in England, "derives, presumably, from a mistaken interpretation of the doctor's advice about a change of air". The *Guardian* lists other popular cures, many of which are plainly based on sympathetic magic. A fish is put in the child's mouth and then thrown into a river, where it "gives" the whooping cough to the other fish. Or a piece of the child's hair is mixed with meat and the meat fed to a dog. This may be a semantic confusion between two meanings of "give".

[2] In many parts of Germany it used to be believed that immediately after the death of someone in a house, all who were sleeping there must be awakened; otherwise their sleep would pass over into death.

that the rusting of the nail induces suppuration in the wound by sympathy.

A minor belief that comes as an anticlimax after all these weighty worries, and one which must be a modern fallacy, is that overshoes "draw" moisture from the feet. Actually, all they do is to prevent the evaporation of the normal exudation, but parents —already sere and desiccated—have forgotten how exudant young glands are. Etiquette and our own drying-up enable us to ignore the humiliating fact that we who regard ourselves as self-contained are but sponges through which there seeps a stream of food and water, and in and out of which suck and puff little gasps of nitrogen, oxygen, carbon dioxide, and assorted mephitic vapours. Were our sight keener, we would perceive that every man ambles about in a cloud of steam issuing from his own pores.

Multiple births have always fascinated—and sometimes frightened—people, and there is a great lore about them that is only just beginning to be replaced by scientific facts.

Although the Dionnes and the Diligentis hold the official record in a tie, stories of even more remarkable fecundity are a part of the folk tales of every land. Marcin Kromer, in his history of Poland (1568), says that the Countess of Cracow, on January 20, 1269, bore thirty-six children at one delivery. Anne Hutchinson, for daring to disagree with the Puritan clergy, brought forth "thirty monstrous births at once", the Reverend Samuel Clarke asserts, a monster for each of her "monstrous heresies". But the all-time record has been held for centuries by the Dutch countess Margaret of Henneberg, whose story became an indispensable part of any collection of salacious marvels. The story was that the Countess, who apparently believed in birth control, scornfully refused alms to a poor widow who appeared at her door with a babe on each arm. On the Friday before Palm Sunday, 1276, the Countess was delivered of three hundred and sixty-five children, "in bigness all like newbred mice". One hundred and eighty-two were sons and one hundred and eighty-two were daughters and the odd one was a hermaphrodite. The children were baptized en masse in two basins by the Suffragan

Bishop of Utrecht, who, in quite understandable despair, named all the males John and all the females Elizabeth. What he named the hermaphrodite is, unfortunately, not recorded. Immediately after the baptism, the children and their wicked mother died. All accounts of the episode conclude by silencing doubt with the assurance that the two basins are yet to be seen in the church at Loosduinen.[1]

Even twins have never been accepted as a matter of course. Some legendary heroes have been twins—Castor and Pollux, Romulus and Remus, Jacob and Esau—but, for the most part, twins have been regarded as unlucky and many primitive people kill at least one of them.[2] They are sometimes regarded as definite proof of the mother's immorality.

Professor Horatio Hackett Newman, who made one of the most complete studies of multiple human births known, says that it is commonly believed that twins are not as bright as other people. Certainly, with the exception of the Piccards, who had to go up into the stratosphere and down into the Cimmerian depths of the ocean before they were noticed, no pair of twins has ever attained great renown. None the less, Professor Newman (who is himself a twin) is convinced by extensive tests that he and his assistants have carried out on a large number of twins that twins are the mental equals of single-born individuals.

The popular belief may have its basis in the fact that twins, being always talked about and regarded with curiosity, are set apart a little, and hence are often shy. Then many parents dress twins exactly alike without realizing that this emphasis on their likeness to each other also emphasizes their unlikeness to other children. Twins are thrown together more closely than other siblings, so closely, with so many identical possessions and experiences, that they do not *need* to talk as much as other children, and

---

[1] The story has been in print in English ever since James Howell's *Familiar Letters* (4 vols., 1645–55). The best modern account of Countess Margaret and her "biggsweld wombe" is to be found, with references, in Professor Hyder Rollins (ed.): *Pepysian Garland* (New York: The Macmillan Company; 1922), p. 121 ff.

[2] J. M. Robertson: *A Short History of Morals* (London: Watts & Co.; 1920), p. 62.

often develop speech late. And all of these things could seem to be dullness.

Parenthetically, there are several illusions about the intelligence of children. The common belief that "summer children are brighter" than children born in the other seasons may, originally, have had some magic association with the sun. A few planned-parenthood enthusiasts have tried to find a rational justification for the belief by suggesting that the more intelligent parents would have arranged to have their children in the milder season. But tests have failed to establish the fact, and so any explanation is unnecessary.[1]

That children learn more easily than adults has been axiomatic for millennia. "Sely childe," says Chaucer, "will alday sone lere." But it is doubtful. Children so delight in learning new things, are so energetic in their eagerness, so swift, pliant, and merry in their pursuit of knowledge, and so innocent in their happy display of it, that the assumption that they learn more easily than adults seems obvious. Yet the late Professor Edward L. Thorndike demonstrated, on the basis of a great deal of experiment and observation, that childhood is not the best age for learning. The mind is less acquisitive after sixty-five, but any age below forty-five, he believed, is better than the ages from ten to fourteen.[2]

Learning takes time, and children have more time than adults. Unless an immediate need for the knowledge can be shown, the learner must be induced by promises or impelled by threats, and not only are adults less amenable to either, but there is no one greatly interested in promising or threatening them. But show an adult the need for learning, or establish rewards that do appeal to him—such as more money, a favoured position, or even admiration—and he will learn faster than the child.

[1] Dr. J. A. Fraser Roberts, of Bristol, gave intelligence tests to two hundred and forty-four pairs of children at Bath, each pair born to the same parents but one in the winter and one in the summer. The summer children had a slight superiority, but so slight as to be negligible. See his report in the *British Medical Journal*, March 4, 1944.

[2] Edward L. Thorndike: *Adult Interests* (New York: The Macmillan Company; 1935).

F

Returning to twins for a moment, there is a curious belief that one out of every pair of twins is sterile, an error that may be a false carry-over from the situation among cattle. When a cow produces a male and female twin, as a cow does once in a while, the female, called a freemartin, is always sterile. But this is owing to the fact that in cows even dizygotic twins are enclosed in one amnion, where the hormones of the male fœtus sterilize the female. But in human beings dizygotic twins—and twins of different sex must be dizygotic—are enclosed in separate sacs, a circumstance now attributed to their separate inception, though formerly ascribed to Providence as "an admirable provision to inspire men from the germ with the laws and rules of chastity".[1]

Strangely enough, such are the ways of error, though the delusion about human beings is common, the fact about cattle is not generally known. It is safe to assume that most readers of Aldous Huxley's *Brave New World* were puzzled by his use of "freemartin" to designate the more complaisant of his pneumatic young ladies.

Among the bogeys in the dark realm of sex which must distress many an expectant mother, especially if she reads the tabloids, is the fear of giving birth to a hermaphrodite; but despite the whisperings about the local "morphodite" which one hears in every village, true hermaphroditism—the possession of fully developed organs of both sexes by one individual—is almost unknown.[2] The anatomical difficulties practically preclude the possibility.

Stories of hermaphroditism find their support in certain ambiguous people in whom the vestigial organs of the opposite sex, which we all carry, have had an unusual development. Bearded ladies are a feature of every circus, and men with fully

[1] The sentiment is taken from the *Observations sur la practique des accouchements naturels* by Cosme Viardel (1671). The wording is that of Dr George T. Elliot, Jr, translating from Viardel, p. 165 of the *New York Medical Journal*, vol. 3 (1866).

[2] See Hugh Hampton Young: *Genital Abnormalities, Hermaphroditism and Related Adrenal Diseases* (Baltimore: William Wood & Company; 1937) and his "Some Hermaphrodites I Have Met", the *New England Journal of Medicine*, 209: 1933, pp. 370–5, for a description of fourteen cases which Dr Young had seen at the Brady Urological Institute, Johns Hopkins Hospital.

developed breasts exist and have been photographed. The Chevalier d'Eon, a celebrated figure in eighteenth-century London and Paris, was, apparently, one of these, and did everything in his-or-her power to increase the confusion of the public, dressing as a man one day and as a woman the next.[1]

A tragic case of this nature was that of Elvira de Céspedes. The Holy Inquisition prescribed two hundred lashes and ten years' imprisonment to help her make up her gonads.[2] Today surgery and endocrinology have helped hundreds of such unfortunates, but the most they can do is to increase the preponderance of whatever seems to be the dominant sex. Even then, however, there are psychological difficulties so great that some doctors believe it more advisable to strengthen what the patient believes him-or-herself to be rather than what he-or-she actually is. The case of a boy in Troy, Ohio, shows the dangers latent in such a situation. Brought up as a girl until he was eighteen, and believing himself to be a girl, he was, at that age, by means of an operation, "changed" to his true sex. But he could not adjust himself to his life as a male, and after ten unhappy years murdered his father (for some taunt) and later committed suicide.[3]

Most common instances are those individuals, not hermaphrodites at all, in whom the true sex has been concealed by some anatomical peculiarity. Typical of these was that Marie Germane, examined by Paré and Montaigne, whose male organs had apparently been retained in the body cavity until an unusual exertion late in adolescence suddenly liberated them. Paré said she had leaped a ditch while "earnestly pursuing hogges". Montaigne said she was playing leapfrog. Both agreed, whatever she was doing, that she "went up a maid and came down a man". It took the authority of a cardinal to get her change of sex officially recognized, and she was regarded as one of the wonders of the age.

[1] There is an account of the Chevalier in the *Dictionary of National Biography*.
[2] See H. C. Lea: *History of the Inquistion in Spain* (New York: The Macmillan Company; 1906-7, vol. 4, pp. 187 ff.
[3] See Associated Press dispatches for December 3, 1948.

Then, to confuse the issue further (the more confusing to the common man as it is one of the very few things he is *not* confused about), there are those who, physically normal, desire to be accepted as members of the other sex. Some men have even been willing to be castrated in order to be more womanish, and others have been eager to follow their inscrotumable example.[1] But most of the impulse of this sort seems to be—as one would expect in a society in which men enjoy a favoured position—in the opposite direction. Many women want to be men, and it is not so surprising that some should pose as men as that they should succeed as completely as some of them have. One of the most famous was Hannah Snell, who in 1745 (before the day of pre-induction examinations) enlisted in the British Army. She deserted, entered the Navy, and served as a sailor for several years. She was wounded at the siege of Pondicherry and, even though her true sex had become known, was awarded a pension and became an out-pensioner of Chelsea Hospital. During her military career she was several times on the verge of marrying young women smitten with her soldierly charms. Many of these women have married other women and lived for years as "husbands" with, so far as is known, happiness all round.[2]

One often sees a story in the newspapers about some little boy who has been reared as a girl. In extreme cases he has been dressed in frilly dresses and given a doll to play with, but usually he has merely been allowed to grow long curls and the news story centres around the cutting off of the curls. The father is said to have put his foot down, the boy is shown in some pose of manly satisfaction, and the mother is often shown as crying because she has "lost her baby".

The reasons given for keeping the boy a girl are "We wanted a girl" or "I just couldn't bear to see him grow up", and both are doubtless sincere, at least at the conscious level. A psychoanalyst

---

[1] Two such appeared before Judge Morris Ploscowe, in New York, in February 1953. He remanded both youths for further investigation.

[2] For a collection of some remarkable instances of women masquerading as men, see Chapter Two, "James Allen: The Man Who Was Not," in Dingwall: *Some Human Oddities*.

would view the matter more seriously, seeing in it the deter-
mination of a neurotic mother to emasculate her son. But there
may also be in it a residuum of the very old belief that strength
lies in the hair, a belief that found expression in a number of
proverbs, particularly among the Germans, to the effect that
cutting a boy's hair before he was seven would impair his
health.

Among many peoples—the Chinese and the Irish among
them—boys were often dressed as girls to deceive malignant
spirits that might harm anything so valuable as a boy, but would
not be interested in anything so worthless as a girl.[1]

There are nowhere near so many illusions about the aged as
about the young. Fear abates with hope. The outcome of the
years is grimly certain; only the Great Delusions remain, and
even they are held with increasing faintness as *the* Fact of Life
approaches.

A handful of fallacies about the old may, however, be mar-
shalled. One hears that they need less sleep than younger folk,
that they need less food because "their stomachs shrink".
Shrivelled gums mumble rumours of third sets of teeth, and dim
eyes gleam hopefully at stories of renewed sight. Fantastic tales
of longevity camouflage the imminence of the grave, and mankind has agreed to crown the whole pathetic fabric of imposture
with the reputation for wisdom.

The elderly, as every young slugabed knows, have a detestable
habit of getting up early and a still more detestable habit of
boasting about it during the waking snatches of their dozing
days. Few observations are more often on their lips than that
they don't need as much sleep as they did when they were
young.

What they really need are more topics of conversation. These
would keep them awake longer in the evening, and that, in turn,
would let them sleep later in the morning. Dr Roger F. Lapham,
of the Cornell University Medical School, states emphatically

---

[1] See "Male child disguised as a girl", *Standard Dictionary of Folklore*
vol. 2, p. 67.

that old people need *more* rest than young people, and he adds that they usually get it, in fragments if not in one solid stretch.[1]

Most old people have less inclination—and fewer opportunities—to stuff themselves than they had when they were younger. The number of taste buds may diminish, and with the loss of teeth eating often becomes—though no healthy young person would ever believe it possible—more effort than it's worth. Few of the old are so fortunate as to have anyone who cares whether they eat or not, and the common belief that "old folks' stomachs shrink" is a convenient dismissal of an unpleasant problem. Except for the senile degeneration of its tissues, however, the stomach does not shrink with age; the old need as much food as they ever did after the growing, exceptionally active, years of youth.

No hope is too preposterous to generate its own supporting evidence. That life will renew itself within us, and that youth will spring like a phœnix from our ashes is too pleasing a wish to be abandoned without making some effort to preserve it. Most place the transformation beyond challenge by locating it in another world; but many are determined to find evidence of it here on earth, and among the hopeful signs that they hug to their bosoms none is more common than the story that some aged person, happier than others, but a harbinger perhaps of better things for all, has grown a complete third set of teeth.

Reports of those who have done so are a staple of news: Mr Richard Thompson, of Florida, aged ninety, throws away his false teeth because a new set of natural ones renders them at first uncomfortable and at last unnecessary; Mr Fred Weekly, of Chicago, aged ninety-three, holds a mirror before his open mouth to silence the incredulous; Mr Frank Basey, of Denver, aged eighty-five, obliges the cameraman by holding a teething ring in his mouth and adds further to the human interest by attributing his third set of teeth to chewing tobacco for seventy-three years.

[1] Roger F. Lapham: *It's In Your Power* (New York: Essential Books; 1946).

He is of the opinion that chewing tobacco is "good gum fertilizer".[1]

It may be. Some dental scientists aver that third sets of teeth have actually grown in human jaws,[2] but most are inclined to believe that such claims are based on nothing more than the belated appearance of supernumerary or impacted molars, teeth that have been dormant in the jaws since youth.

Many old people, finding that they can read as well or even, sometimes, better without their glasses, joyfully believe that they have "renewed" sight. Alas, it is only the continuing of the process that caused them to use spectacles in the first place. The lens of the eye gets harder with age and its hardening increases its index of refraction. This makes it a better magnifying glass, but it is no better as an eye; whatever advantage may be gained for close sight is paid for by the greater dimness in the distant vision.

There is an old gag about a fortune-teller who made a mother happy by assuring her that her infant son would be a famous man if he lived long enough. When the mother eagerly asked: "What will he be famous for?" the fortune-teller said: "For having lived so long."

The desire for fame and attention is strong. Most old people have no other distinction than their age, and it is not surprising that quite a few of them attempt to be interesting by adding extra years or decades. The more imaginative throw in a recollection of some historical event or gather reflected glory by connecting themselves with some famous figure of the past. George Washington's coloured mammy kept dying, in the papers, throughout the second half of the nineteenth century, and Barnum kept resurrecting her. Zaro Agha, the old Turkish fraud who visited America in the early 1930's, was able, after a little prompting

[1] *Time*, August 29, 1949, p. 78; the *Chicago Sun-Times*, March 31, 1953, p. 14; the *Chicago Sun-Times*, April 23, 1950, p. 12.
[2] See Leo Kenner: *Folklore of the Teeth* (New York: The Macmillan Company; 1928). Dr Kenner, relying on Drs Montigel and Kerstig, thinks it remotely possible. Dr Floris van Minden, writing on the subject in his column in the *Chicago Sun-Times*, February 8, 1947, p. 15, is definitely of the opinion that "There is no third set—but false ones".

from his press agent, to remember Napoleon distinctly. And anyone who listened to the tales of the G.A.R. veterans as their ranks thinned with age was amazed at the number of Union soldiers who had happened to be at Gettysburg the day Lincoln delivered his famous address.

Most famous of all pseudosupercentenarians was Thomas Parr, who professed to be one hundred and fifty-three at the time of his death and claimed to have threshed wheat when he was one hundred and thirty. When he was one hundred and five, according to the *Dictionary of National Biography*, "his vigour was so far in excess of his discretion that he was constrained to do penance in the church of Alderbury for having begotten a bastard child". He was brought up to London in 1635 as a curiosity by the Earl of Arundel, and there overate himself and died. He was buried in the south transept of Westminster Abbey, not far, fittingly enough for one so imaginative, from the Poets' Corner, with an inscription that attests many, though not all, of his alleged accomplishments.

Dr Maurice Ernest, an English physician who has devoted forty years to an investigation of the subject, is inclined to doubt most claims of longevity exceeding, or even reaching to, one hundred. It is his opinion, which he documents, that "there is no proof to show that any member of any animal species has ever reached 114".[1] The authentic record, he thinks, is held by Pierre Joubert, of Quebec, who lived one hundred and thirteen years and one hundred days—with the Honourable Katherine Plunkett, of Ballymascanlan in Ireland, the runner-up with one hundred and eleven years, three hundred and twenty-seven days. Pierre Joubert had another distinction: he was one of the very few people who have lived to extreme old age who thought he was younger than he really was. Most of them overestimate their age.

Many stories of astonishing longevity may be the result of honest ignorance. Dr Ernest tells of a tombstone in Suffolk which

[1] See the *New York Times*, November 7, 1946; *Science Digest*, August 1947, pp. 1–4.

listed the deceased's age as 207—but it turned out that this was an illiterate stonecutter's idea of how to write twenty-seven. The tablet over Macklin, the eighteenth-century actor, in St Paul's Church, Covent Garden, states that he was one hundred and seven at the time of his death; but when the coffin was exhumed in 1858 the coffin plate revealed that he was only ninety-seven.[1]

That wisdom increases with age is one of mankind's oldest and most pathetic fallacies. Experience breeds caution, it is true; greed sharpens cunning; and a growing sense of one's weakness teaches thrift and prudence. But these are base elements of wisdom at their best. The great thoughts of the world, the exciting aspirations, the imaginative visions, and the generous impulses belong to youth. With the increasing average age of our population, popular magazines carry more and more articles recounting the great accomplishments of some men in their old age, but these are only the exceptions, and almost all the same men did better in their youth. Furthermore, most of the distinguished work done by great men in their advanced years owes its distinction to the technical proficiency and the erudition that only a long life can produce. If every human being who ever lived had died at the age of forty, the stock of the world's wisdom would be little diminished. Surveying the work of five hundred philosophers, Dr Harvey C. Lehman, of Ohio University, found that their most important work was produced when they were in their thirties.[2] Most of the world's great poetry was written and most of its paintings painted by young men. Even mathematicians had their great thoughts in their youth, and while many distinguished musicians have fortunately continued composing late into life, their later works have rarely equalled their earlier.[3]

[1] They were not numerically minded in the past. Exactness in dealing with figures is a recent accomplishment of a minute fraction of humanity. The English Parliament of 1371, as a fair sample, levied a tax based on the assumption that there were 50,000 parishes in England. There were 8,600.

[2] See his *Age and Achievement* (Princeton, N.J.: Princeton University Press; 1953).

[3] See Catherine Morris Cox: *The Early Mental Traits of Three Hundred Geniuses* (Stanford, Calif.: Stanford University Press; 1926).

CHAPTER THIRTEEN

Autointoxication

IN THE past forty years more than one million people have been killed by automobiles in the United States. This is almost twice as many as have been killed in all the wars in which we have ever engaged. Some fifteen to twenty million others have been injured, more than a million of them permanently disabled. This is twenty-six times as many as have been wounded in all the wars in which we have ever engaged.[1] Property damage resulting from automobile accidents adds up to more than three thousand million dollars a year. Father Dominic Devas urges motorists, "that unfortunate class", to have the medal of St Christopher "honourably and firmly affixed to their cars", and certainly it is time to invoke some sanctification, conjuration, charm, or spell, for the situation is obviously beyond rational control.

Every sixteen minutes someone in the United States dies in a motor accident. For the sheer horror of it, we have to go back to the medieval plagues. The dead lie along the highways in windrows. The shrieks and moans of the mangled almost drown out the curses of those who have struck them. He that would now be a friend to man and live by the side of the road must build a hospital, not a house. And he should have an understudy, for the

[1] *Science News Letter*, August 1, 1953, p. 80; November 14, 1953, p. 330; March 20, 1954, p. 192. We lead in numbers because we have the most cars, but other lands have even higher rates: "France has over four times as many fatal traffic accidents per 100,000 drivers as the U.S. . . . one in eleven French drivers, in his lifetime, kills someone. . . ." (*Time*, September 3, 1951, p. 37.) (These figures had better be suppressed, lest they be taken as a challenge.)

number of those killed every year while befriending the injured is large.

Things are getting worse, too, and if the manufacturers make good—as they surely will—on their promises of more power and more speed, they are going to get much worse.

Probably the most astounding element in the whole situation is the public indifference to it. Everyone knows what is happening. There are few people who have not at some time or another seen an accident. There is hardly a family in the country that has not sustained a casualty. There are special greeting cards for those who have been run down by cars. Insurance policies are computed on the assumption that every car will have at least two collisions. And yet—a ten-year-old child could formulate rules that would put an end to it!

Obviously there is more here than meets the eye. Such a state of affairs would not continue unless it gratified something deep in our psyche, and as the slaughter goes on, with ever accelerating ferocity, we must face the central fact: we like it. However much we may lament and protest, we are plainly having a wonderful time. To be sure, our pleasure is concealed, as so many of our vices are, by being disguised as moral indignation and false solicitude, but the enjoyment shines innocently through.

Psychiatrists and safety directors now assume that any man who is the victim of a series of avoidable disasters has in some way courted his misfortune. If a man falls down a manhole once, it is an accident; if he falls down a manhole twice, it is a coincidence; but if he falls down a manhole twenty times, it is a pleasure. Of course the pleasure may not be in the falling, but in what he unconsciously hopes to get out of it. He may want sympathy. He may want an excuse to quit his job. He may hope to sue the city. He may want to triumph over an opinionated neighbour who has insisted that no man has ever fallen down a manhole twenty times. He may be seeking a precipitous return to the womb, in full Freudian paronomasia. Or he may just enjoy the publicity. But, however obscure the motive or painful the fall, he likes it.

And there can be little doubt that we like our automobile accidents. There wouldn't be so many of them if we didn't.

That we like to see and hear about them, to the last clinical detail, can hardly be denied. The prevailing temper of the crowds that collect so eagerly at the scene of an accident is invariably pleasurable excitement. The newsreels and the popular magazines batten on the horrible. Their gloatings are, of course, like the unctuous exultations of the announcers as they give the statistics of mortality on holiday week-ends, always presented as contributions to safety; but he is a simpleton indeed who believes that the endless pictures of injured women with dresses disarrayed and broken limbs exposed are intended as aids to traffic control. The only things they affect are the circulations of the readers and the magazines. The publication of "And Sudden Death" by the *Reader's Digest*—one of the most successful "strokes" of modern journalism—is the supreme example. Touted as a grim warning, it was actually one of the most uninhibited debauches of pure sadism that our age has ever enjoyed, and there is not the slightest evidence that it prevented so much as a hangnail.

That most accidents are directly caused by at least one of the parties involved in them has gradually come to be the opinion of men who have devoted years to the problem. It is interesting—and sad—to read the bulletins and analyses issued during the past thirty years by the insurance companies, the highway departments, and the traffic institutes. Up until about 1937 their reports had a distinct note of hope: a few more educational campaigns, better road-engineering, stiffer law-enforcement, shatterproof glass, new headlights, and so on, and the situation would be under control. But safety campaigns educated, the engineers broadened the roads into runways and banked them into speedways and elaborated the intersections into Chinese puzzles, the manufacturers put shatterproof glass and sealed-beam headlights into every car—and the deaths went up and up and hope went down and down.

On the introduction of traffic lights, it was thought that they were the answer; but repeated studies have shown that they *add* to the hazards. The city of Wilmington, Delaware, in a study of sixteen hundred intersections over a fifteen-year period, found that the ratio of death at light-controlled crossings was more than eight times that at unmarked crossings. Of course, the lights were presumably installed at the more dangerous and crowded intersections, but that is not the entire explanation. Traffic lights tempt the reckless and disarm the prudent; the best they can do, as Wilmington's chief engineer expressed it, is to *proclaim* danger; they don't eliminate it.[1]

Many—particularly those who hope to profit by their construction—still insist that bigger, better, broader roads, with special illumination and over- and under-passes and steam pipes to melt the ice, are the solution. Statistics don't bear them out, however. Seventy-five per cent of fatal smashups occur on straight roads. The safety record of the new superduper turnpikes is appalling.

Then there is the cost. The very mention of this is un-American, but arithmetic has never yet yielded to ballyhoo, and facts are facts, however annoying. The latest estimate of our full national "needs" in the way of new and improved roads is a modest sixty thousand million dollars,[2] and accepting this sum at its full face value we come to some remarkable conclusions. Assuming that the roads built with this much money will be adequate for the next thirty years, that if they are not built the present number of traffic fatalities will continue, and that if they are built every single one will be prevented, it works out at about one hundred thousand dollars for every life saved. But as this considerably exceeds the per-capita wealth of the country, we must either regard those killed in traffic as a privileged group and deny ourselves necessities in order to save them or accept them as expendable in the interest of breaking the tedium of Sunday afternoons.

The latter seems advisable as well as economical, for though, no doubt, traffic accidents have destroyed hundreds of thousands

---

[1] See the *Reader's Digest*, October 1949, p. 12.
[2] See "Our Roads Are Going to Pot", *Harper's*, September 1950, p. 35.

of innocent victims, they have, at the same time, aided natural selection, a salutary process that is being progressively restricted in almost every other department of life. For the experts seem, finally, to have decided that the problem is primarily a psychological one. They seem discouraged, even a little exasperated: "Drivers usually have no one but themselves to blame for accidents"; most accidents result from "stupidity and bad manners"; "Highway safety is a problem which . . . must be solved by each individual for himself"; and "Automobile accidents are the result of individual carelessness".

But is "carelessness" quite the word? Is a man "careless" when he scoots out of line to pass twenty other cars on a hill, when he cuts in savagely, races through a red light, or smashes the gates at a railroad crossing to smear himself broadside against a passing train?[1] Why are there relatively far fewer accidents involving taxis, buses, and other commercial vehicles than private vehicles? Is it that commercial drivers care more or, perhaps, less? Could it be that men who drive for wages (aside from chauffeurs) do not identify themselves so completely with the car they are driving, do not find their pride so deeply connected with its performance?

The fact must be faced that the automobile seems to be particularly conducive to the sort of behaviour which causes accidents. There are, first of all, certain physical factors. The exhaustion that comes from driving a car and inhaling its fumes is insidious, resembling mild drunkenness rather than ordinary tiredness. Then the continual shock of driving frays the nerves and strains the temper. But more dangerous are the psychological factors. The immense power, obedient to the slightest pressure of the foot, encourages a feeling of aggressive potency, particularly in the weak, the frustrated, the defeated, those who are suffering from feelings of inferiority, those whom the insecurity and competition

---

[1] In about 27 per cent of car-train accidents, it is the car that hits the train. "Ninety-six per cent of the motorists involved in serious grade-crossing accidents are thoroughly familiar with the crossings at which the accidents occur, according to a Baltimore and Ohio Railroad study."—*Science Digest*, November 1950, p. 82.

of the modern world are multiplying by geometric progression.[1]
Lolling on foam cushions, soothed by syrupy music, sweeping
along with a hypnotic hum, the surface of the earth smoothed
down to a gentle undulation, the very air warmed to please—
how easy to deem oneself a god! And how terrible the godlike
wrath visited on the impious wretch who would dare to disturb
one's dreams or question one's divinity! Pan, the beast god, he
who inspired panic, slept on summer afternoons, and the Greeks
felt that the heavy sultriness was charged with menace, for he
was violent in the most dreadful extreme if accidentally awakened.

Into every driver's mind as he hurtles towards an oncoming
car at a comfortable seventy miles an hour, there must at some
time have flashed the thought: "Suppose this guy coming at me
is crazy!" It's a playful little homemade thriller, a gruesome
whimsy to relieve the moment's boredom, but the real joke, the
hidden topper, is the considerable statistical chance that he *is*.
Nothing in most types of mental disturbance incapacitates a man
or woman from learning to drive a car, and now that almost
everyone drives, there is bound to be a vast number of the feeble-
minded, of psychopaths, neurotics, epileptics, mild paretics, and
other disturbed people on the highways. Of ten thousand problem
drivers referred to Detroit's traffic clinic, one hundred were
found to be committably insane, eight hundred and fifty were
feeble-minded, and one thousand were former inmates of mental
hospitals, lacking the emotional stability to drive safely.[2] The
violent crashes with which so many stolen joyrides end are perhaps not wholly accidental. Dr Walter Bromberg has suggested
that they may have a psychological meaning. "The speed of the

[1] Carol Lane, Women's Travel Director for the Shell Oil Company,
lectures on driving before women's clubs. She says that nine out of ten
women tell her that the thing they like most about driving is the "sense of
independence" it gives them.—*Parade*, January 21, 1951, p. 7. The author
has been assured by members of the Chicago and Evanston police forces,
and by officials of various traffic schools and safety organizations, that
resentful people, people who feel they are discriminated against, are bad
drivers—because, apparently, the car releases their aggressions.

[2] From the report of Dr Alan Cantry, psychiatrist of Detroit's traffic
clinic, before the annual convention of the National Safety Council, in
1953.—*Time*, November 2, 1953, p. 104.

machine," he believes, "is absorbed into the psyche of the driver and tends to express his aggression as well as to serve his pleasure." And as "an act of aggression without an object . . . is a frustrating experience, . . . the terminal smashup, often caused in part by alcoholism, is frequently an unconsciously determined act which is aimed at removing the frustration of objectless speed".[1]

The real danger, however, the fact that dwarfs all other considerations, is that about half the population seems mildly paranoiac when driving a car. It is amazing what delusions of grandeur and persecution seize otherwise sane-seeming men and women once they get behind a steering-wheel. Any attempt to pass them is an affront, to be resisted to the death. Any hesitation in letting *them* pass is studied insolence, to be repelled with violence. The slightest delay of others at a green light is a malicious prank; the least impatience of others at *their* delay is a violation of the Constitution. And so they go, chafing and raging, until, worn out with a hundred tantrums, they arrive home limp and exhausted, discharge the dregs of their bile upon their cowering families, and crawl to bed to gather strength for the next morning's ordeal.

These are but the milquetoasts, and in their milder moments. More manly fellows assert themselves, show the other driver "where to get off at", "put him in his place", which, often enough, is the hospital or the grave. Sometimes, for good measure, they put themselves and their families there with him. The more socially conscious and more energetic may undertake to educate those whom they regard as poor drivers by shouting at them, crowding them over, dazzling them by the glare of their headlights, and, sometimes, heading directly at them with a burst of speed and swerving aside at the last moment. Or at least, one assumes, intending to swerve aside at the last moment; the police cannot always be sure just what a corpse's intentions were.

Most "causes" of accidents are only contributory factors. They are merely the conditions under which if you behave in a

---

[1] Walter Bromberg: *Crime and the Mind* (Philadelphia: J. B. Lippincott Company; 1948), p. 126.

certain way you are likely to have an accident. (The experts compute that "on the average a person violates a safe practice three hundred times" before he is injured in consequence.) But the behaviour is the thing, and much of the behaviour seems to be motivated by what De Quincey called "the glory of motion". Motorists collide at intersections, not out of carelessness so much as out of resentment at the other fellow's daring to cross their path. Drivers get out of their lanes and race to death at the summits of hills because they are furiously determined not to endure the "persecution" of the cars dawdling in front of them. Autoists[1] speed as much to save face as time, and frequently and literally lose both.

The safety campaigns and the work of the engineers are highly commendable, but the most that they can do is to create circumstances under which safety is possible if the public wants it. But there is little indication that any large segment of the public wants it—wants it, that is, enough to pay the necessary price. Probably eighty per cent of these killings and maimings could be stopped at once if cars were properly inspected, traffic laws enforced, and drivers' licences issued only to those who have demonstrated their ability to drive, their familiarity with the laws, their financial soundness, and their emotional stability.

That, of course, is like saying that there wouldn't be any trouble if people weren't troublesome. It is a counsel of perfection, irrelevant in its reasonableness. For the automobile is basically *un*reasonable—is bound up, that is, and intertwined with, much that is unreasonable in ourselves and in the world that we, and the car, have fashioned in the past fifty years.

All the follies and fallacies of gadgetolatry have flowered in the automobile. Never has any people played such a trick on themselves as we have with the horseless carriage. Within fifty years this djinni has become our master. Two generations ago it was a rich man's toy. It is now the poor man's necessity, and

[1] Not to be confused (as *Time* would say) with *autists*, psychotics who are "absorbed in phantasy to the exclusion of interest in external reality " (Merriam-Webster), though the inclination to confuse them is almost irresistible.

drains from him more than anything else he owns, directly in cost and maintenance, indirectly in taxes.

Nothing in our history has received such an immense subsidy. A legislator may vote against housing, national security, the Bill of Rights, or public health, and hope to keep his job, but if he opposed any measure that favoured automobiles he would be out. The American citizen will sleep in tenements, trailers, basements, or tar-paper shacks. He will eat adulterated food, wear shoddy clothes, and ache for lack of medical care—beefing, to be sure, as is his inalienable right, but putting up with it. But let anything or anyone threaten the jiggling ecstasy of joyriding and he will rise up in maniacal wrath.

Even where he derives no benefit, the citizen seems content if public funds are only spent on the automobile. What is it, apparently, to the people of Chicago that their garbage is uncollected and their teachers underpaid, their books and movies censored by a minority, their police in cahoots with the crooks? Have they not the solace of contemplating the Outer Drive, that great sweeping boulevard with its mechanical partitions, its lanes within lanes, its arabesque underpasses, and its army of attendants? True, it is used, congested as it is, by probably no more than twenty per cent of the population, while a mile to the west the remaining eighty per cent cling to the greasy straps of the antiquated, unsanitary, dilapidated, dangerous—and expensive!—Elevated, as it screeches its tortuous way among decaying warehouses and hovels. And its use cuts the public park in two and makes going from one part of it to another extremely hazardous, unless one walks a mile or two to a crosswalk. But no one seems to object. The automobile is a god, and nothing spent in its service is begrudged.

It is a jealous god, though, and demands heavy sacrifices. It begot the assembly line, which begot the boom that begot the bust. It begot the bomber, which begot the bogey that is begetting Armageddon. It has surrounded our moribund cities with ever widening, ever dying circles of suburbs. It has littered the countryside with billboards and ramshackle vegetable stands whose vegetables are often the staler for having been hauled out from the city in the first place. It has girdled every town and village with neon-lit sties of dreary mirth. It has brought the driveteria, where ptomaines are palliated by carbon monoxide. It has reduced the home to a dormitory over a garage and the age of innocence to something under ten.

Great as these evils are in the aggregate, they are, like all true evils, necessary evils. For the chief joker now in the automobile problem is that we *can't* get rid of it. We are literally bound captive to its wheels and led in triumph down the Gadarene turnpike. There is not a major industry in the country—rubber, textiles, glass, iron and steel, and oil, with all their subsidiaries— that is not now dependent upon the automobile industry. One out of every seven United States workers builds cars or contributes to their building. Their manufacture, sale, and servicing totals twenty-five thousand million dollars a year, one fifth of all retail trade. The collapse, or even the faltering, of the automobile industry would reduce every one of us to beggary.

Not that there is much likelihood of beggary coming *that* way; we love our cars too passionately. The amount of riding we do almost defies comprehension. The Automobile Manufacturers' Association estimated that in 1952 the people of the United States travelled five hundred thousand million passenger miles in their cars! How much of this was conducive to the riders' well-being is anybody's guess, but whoever puts it higher than ten per cent is confusing human beings with migratory geese.

It is awe-inspiring to contemplate merely the time required in this extraordinary performance. Assuming that these miles were driven at an average speed of thirty miles an hour—that is, that each one took two minutes of someone's time—it means that approximately two million years of human life was spent in this rhapsody on rubber.

It will be claimed, of course, that it saved time, that distances had to be traversed and that going in the car was the most efficient means of traversing them. But this claim is fallacious. Those who seek to defend the automobile would do better to stress its convenience and comfort. For convenient and comfortable it certainly is, particularly for trips, and we are much given to tripping. You can pile your stuff into it (usually three times more than you need, it being easier to pile it in than to make a selection) at a local address at one place and proceed directly to a local address in another place without having to lug or heave from one vehicle to another. Granted that there are no collisions with the law or other motorists, no flat tyres, empty gas tanks, vapour-lock, or frozen radiators, you can arrive at the second address calm and unruffled, which is more than can be said for any other form of travel. Furthermore, the automobile is an excellent shopping bag. And it is the finest umbrella ever devised, a fact of great importance to men in a country where the umbrella is regarded as slightly effeminate.

But a time-saver the automobile is not. For long distances trains and planes are quicker. For middle distances—the usual run, say, from the suburbs to the shopping centres—proper public conveyances, which would exist and could function if it were not for the private cars, would be quicker. For anything under two miles, in any city of one hundred thousand people or over, a bicycle can beat a car right now. And for anything under a mile, it's quicker to walk.

Most automobiles are used in and around cities, and in the larger cities they have about nullified themselves as time-savers. There are just too many of them for them to do anything but creep behind each other. The state of New York has thirteen thousand miles of paved roads, yet its cars and trucks if placed bumper to bumper (as they *are* placed much of the time) would extend for fourteen thousand miles.[1] Fort Collins, Colorado, whose expansion has probably been typical of the smaller town, had an average of five hundred vehicles a day on its main street when it paved that street forty years ago. Today it has approximately nine thousand. An advertisement of the Portland Cement

---

[1] *Time*, August 4, 1952, p. 21. That extra thousand miles is puzzling until one reflects that it is probably taken care of by the comparatively less space filled by those cars that are being towed away from smashups, on their hind wheels only, by tow trucks.

Association, from which these figures are taken, fails to state what the extra eight thousand five hundred cars are doing. But it doesn't need to. Any American knows what they are doing: they are cruising slowly around the block waiting for one of the original five hundred to vacate a parking space. And the advertisement, which says proudly that the concrete, after all these years, is as even as ever, is discreetly silent concerning the temper of the inhabitants.

More than tempers is lost in traffic. The average vehicle speed in congested streets is about three miles per hour. The Boston Fire Department has found that its motorized equipment can't get to fires as fast as its horse-drawn equipment could fifty years ago. This is confirmed in London, where it has been discovered that horse-drawn traffic moved twice as fast as motor-propelled.[1] If you are injured in Chicago's Loop, you could be taken to the nearest hospital in a wheelbarrow faster than in an ambulance.

All of which contributes to the deterioration of the cities. The biggest single capital investment our society has is in city properties, and this investment is threatened with catastrophic depreciation as the cities become increasingly congested. City merchants are discovering to their dismay that the horseless carriage trade is becoming more and more reluctant to come beyond the suburbs.

The whole cost of living is affected by it, in a hundred hidden ways. An example is furnished by soft drinks. One would not at first connect the increased cost of soft drinks with traffic congestion, but they are not unrelated. Because of traffic congestion, the Coca Cola company, for example, has found that it must purchase more trucks to make the same number of daily sales calls in New York City. These, in turn, cause their bottling plants to jam up at check-in time, with the driver-salesmen (each selling less per day because he can't get to as many customers) getting overtime for sitting around in his cab waiting to settle the

[1] *Time*, March 23, 1953, p. 36. The study was made by the Royal Automobile Club.

day's business.[1] And for a glimpse into the future, businessmen can turn with alarm to Rio de Janeiro's super traffic jam of November 1949, which tied up ten thousand cars and made two hundred thousand office workers three to five hours late to work—which cost an immense city, that is, a full day's productivity.[2] Megalopolis seems, finally, to be grinding to a choking standstill, destroyed by the automobile that built it. It looks as though we will have to get rid of either the cities or the cars; but as the car is necessary for working in the city, and working in the city is necessary to be able to afford the car, it is difficult to know where to begin.

The present bubble of illusion is parking-meters. So far few have profited by them except their manufacturers and those politicians who may have received something from the manufacturers. The theory is that they will pay for themselves in a few years and that the cities that have installed them will reap a rich harvest. But it is plain from the already-dilapidated state of many of them that the cities will have to invest large sums in their repair before the harvest can be garnered; and that even when it is garnered, it will be less than anticipated by the amount needed to keep them operating. For they, like all mechanical devices, must have their attendants, and they will need particular attention because they are subject to particular abuse from resentful motorists, who, at the least imperfection in their performance, shake, kick, and whack them with a violence greatly in excess of any good it might do.

In so far as meters have achieved anything, they have forced the penurious and the penniless to park a little farther afield—or, rather, the feeble-minded or those exasperated unfortunates who find they have no change; for it takes very little actuarial acumen to perceive that it costs more than one cent to drive to the unmetered side streets.

Parking is as much a part of operating an automobile as starting and steering. The time, money, and emotional energy

[1] See *Fortune*, January 1951, p. 79.
[2] See *Life*, November 14, 1949, pp. 21-7.

expended on it have to be deducted from the "economy" and "convenience" of using a car; and in the minds of some there isn't much economy or convenience left. Dr Johnson never showed greater wisdom than when he cut short Boswell's excited description of a self-propelled vehicle that he had seen by saying: "Sir, the man now has his choice; hereafter he may go alone or he may take his machine with him."

But not even Johnson, brilliant as his prophetic vision was, could have foreseen the full burden of taking the machine with you. You are lucky, in any large American city, if you can find a parking spot in less than ten minutes' cruising, and luckier still if it happens to be within five minutes' walk of where you want to go. There are usually municipal parking lots, but they are farther out. There are garages and parking lots right in the shopping centres, but they are regularly so congested that if you get in at all you are fortunate to have your car taken off your hands in five minutes and more fortunate if you have to wait only ten to get it back. However you arrange it, parking will take the best part of half an hour.

It will take money, too. If you cruise until you find a spot at the kerb, you can charge up a gallon of gas and pro-rate the occasional ticket. If you use the municipal lots, there are a medium charge for parking and added bus or taxi fares. If you park right downtown, you pay plenty. And somewhere, if you are a strict accountant, you must add the value of your time and the cost of repairing the fenders, a cost which, on the new cars, where each fender is half of a side, bids fair in the aggregate to equal the national debt.

There are always hidden costs to be considered and these hidden costs are exceedingly important in any estimate of the real cost of the Great American Delusion. For the catch in the car as a time-saver is the time it takes to earn the money it takes to save the time it saves.

You can go from Evanston to the Loop, for instance, in ten minutes less by car than by the Elevated, and it is easy to regard that as ten minutes saved. But an average car requires more gaso-

line—about a dime's worth—than could be bought with the El
fare. Parking will more than consume the ten minutes saved;
and earning the money to pay for the parking and the extra cost
of the gas will take a man earning four thousand a year approximately half an hour. So that the time lost by using the car is half
an hour.

That, however, is reckoning only the operating costs of one
journey. Actually, it may require many times that amount of
time, for an automobile is a far more expensive thing than the
ordinary owner will let himself know. Depreciation is hard to
compute, but if we accept the OPA's estimate of ten per cent
every six months, and choose twenty-four hundred dollars as an
initial valuation, we have forty dollars a month right there. State
and municipal taxes and insurance will add at least another fifteen
dollars, and garage rent, whether paid directly or concealed in
higher house rent or building costs, sticks on another twenty
dollars. That's seventy-five dollars a month, without taking the
car out of the garage.

More and more people, especially those who live in cities, are
dispensing with garages altogether, letting their cars stand bumper
to bumper in the streets day and night. But when one considers
the deterioration of property values in such streets (not to mention the deterioration of the cars themselves), this hardly constitutes a saving. Indeed, most of those who live on such streets,
creeping between bumpers and fenders in momentary expectation
of being maimed, would gladly pay twice the cost of a garage, if
they had it, to live elsewhere.

There are other costs. The expense of the maintenance of
roads from day to day—traffic police, the changing of lanes, the
upkeep of signs—is immense. The mere paint used to mark
streets and highways for traffic costs about three million dollars
a year.[1] The city of Chicago spends close to one hundred thousand dollars a year replacing street lights and traffic signals that
are knocked down. It is true that there would have to be some
of this with any traffic, but forty million private cars make a

[1] *Science News Letter,* November 8, 1952, p. 303.

difference in degrees so great as to be a difference in kind. We have poured over thirty billion dollars into roads since the car appeared, and everyone knows that these roads are ruined and inadequate and must be completely rebuilt. As has been said, experts think this can be done for sixty thousand millions more, but their estimates are based on our present rate of travel; whereas everyone knows that the more roads the more travel, and that any estimate short of the entire population in motion at every moment will be inadequate.

All of this has to be paid for, and the individual citizen, whether he owns a car or not, has to work a considerable amount of his lifetime to pay for it. The obvious expenses of a car make it the fourth item in the average family budget, just below rent, food, and clothing. The concealed expenses probably move it up to third place. Even among cultivated, well-to-do people, the car takes more of the family income than all other pleasures—books, music, sports, movies, theatre, and television—put together.

Professor Oliver E. Baker, of Maryland University, computed that it costs as much to maintain a car as to rear a child, and he believed that there is a definite negative correlation between the two activities: "As the sales curve of automobiles goes up, the curve of births goes down." But the professor has overlooked something. It really costs twice as much to rear a child, for as soon as the child is old enough, it will demand a car of its own!

Sir Charles Galton Darwin believes that the future belongs to the race or nation that can longest resist "the bribe of the motor car". They, he thinks, will have the families, the population, and, therefore, the power.[1] But there is little doubt that, having gained the power, they will use it to produce cars in which to ride blissfully to extinction.

The loss of life and the suffering caused by automobile accidents involve values that eclipse any computation of time saved or lost. Yet there is a loss of time which must be added to the

[1] Charles Galton Darwin: *The Next Million Years* (London: Rupert Hart-Davis; 1952), p. 148.

total reckoning. Every accident involves a loss of time. An hour is spent at the spot and in conference with the police, the other party, and the insurance companies. Then there are several trips to the garage, consuming at least a couple of hours; and, as most policies are fifty-dollar deductible, there must be anywhere from ten to thirty-five hours of work to meet the expenses. Where the accident results in physical injury, these things are multiplied many times over; and when it causes death, they are increased to awe-inspiring figures. If the average age of the thirty-eight thousand killed by automobiles each year be fixed at thirty, and if each of the hundred thousand injured be assigned only a week's loss of time, we shall have to add over one million years of human life to the grand debit.

Altogether, it's quite a bill! Making the most favourable interpretations and deductions, it adds up to the fact that the American wage earner devotes from one tenth to one fifth of his time to his car, its purchase, maintenance, and use.

That it saves him an equivalent amount of time can hardly be maintained. He must, therefore, regard it as a luxury or a burden or perhaps both. Not that his so regarding it will enable him to get rid of it if he can't afford it or doesn't want it. He has to have a car to hold his job; very few people live within walking distance of their work any more, and public transportation is wholly inadequate. Invention has been the mother of necessity.

But he has food for thought. If he chooses to regard his automobile as a luxury, he should, if he is rational, weigh it against the other pleasures that an equal amount of the national wealth could purchase: better housing, better health, increased security, more books, games, music, or anything else he can think of. If he regards it as a burden, he should pay some attention to the various means—better city-planning, rehabilitation of slum areas, proper public transportation, control of national resources, etc.— which have been proposed to relieve him of it.[1]

He will, of course, do neither. For when it comes to his car,

---

[1] He may even come to doubt that what is good for General Motors is, of necessity, good for the country.

he has no intention of being rational. The cynic may grin at the official classification as "pleasure" vehicles of the twisted and splintered wrecks one sees dripping blood and gasoline at major intersections; but the fact remains that the automobile *is*, fundamentally, a pleasure vehicle. And the common man would no more submit his car to a mercenary accounting than he would enter his mother in a beauty contest. It is his romance, upholstered and on springs. It is his magic carpet, complete with radio and heater. It is his solace: he may be henpecked at home and browbeaten at work, but in the sweet intervals of coming and going he is a god at whose slightest bidding a hundred horses spring forward. He has achieved divinity with a down payment.

It is his caste mark. It is his entry in the social register, spread open for all to read. And it is his love song. F. Scott Fitzgerald said that the most passionate desire of his youth was to loll at the wheel of a Stutz Bearcat with a half-sneer on his face. Changing the model to suit the times, it is the yearning of all young men. While the car may limit the size of the family, it is certainly instrumental in getting one started. There is no more irresistible mating call than the imperious horn at the kerb. Fogies and fossils start up in wrath at its raucous summons. But rose-lipped maidens hear it and obey—while less fortunate young men dedicate themselves anew to their dream of owning a jalopy.

Nor does the glory fade with the years. The American is in love with his car (and the Turks, Tongas, and Tibetans would be if they could afford one). The phallic symbolism of most of the ornaments on the hoods is pitifully naïve. It is the common man's trylon and his perisphere, his pride and his delight. The man who leaves his car in the street all night may be moved as much by affection as by parsimony. He can get up in the night and look at it. He can polish it on Sunday. He is its slave, but as a lover is a slave. For at bottom this symbiosis of the American and his car, a social phenomenon to be ranked with the Tulip Mania or the Dancing Mania, is a love affair.

CHAPTER FOURTEEN

The Evil that Men Do

I T IS hard to know how those who insist that "crime does not pay" expect to be understood. Do they mean that the swag is small for the effort involved, that fear and shame prevent its enjoyment, or that the certainty of being apprehended makes the risk foolish?

In ways they don't intend, of course, crime does pay. It obviously pays the makers of toy pistols, the publishers of crime comics and murder thrillers, and the producers of crime movies and radio shows. The exploitation of crime for amusement is a big business. Then half our politicians wouldn't be where they are except for opposing crime, and the other half wouldn't be where they are except for supporting it.

To what extent the individual criminal profits from his activities is difficult to determine. The moral cliché, that crime does not pay, is often used to emphasize that the delinquent would have done better, from a purely mercenary viewpoint, to engage in some legitimate effort. And, indeed, in many holdups, especially those which terminate in murder, the amount obtained is fantastically small when one reflects on the risk taken and the suffering, often extending through whole families and generations, inflicted. But in many other instances, it must be confessed, criminals, even of this low order, do very well. We must always bear in mind that the few who are caught and convicted are the failures. We don't know much about the successes. Whoever robbed the mint in Denver or the Brinks Express Company in

Boston did better for themselves, financially, than they could have hoped to do in an ordinary industrious lifetime. The Kefauver investigations made it plain that criminals in the aggregate take hundreds of millions of dollars from the national wealth, and that most of them enjoy their gains in undisturbed tranquillity. The individual income-tax returns of the Capone gunmen in Chicago "reveal illicit profits in recent years totalling millions of dollars".[1]

And even these, of course, are pikers. Much of what is called big business—misrepresentation in advertising, lobbying, the securing of preferential treatment in purchasing, taxes and tariffs and rebates, the giving of executive bonuses and huge pensions, the paying or receiving of exorbitant commission fees, the control of union fees for the benefit of the officers, and so on, and so on—is simply what on a smaller scale is called intimidation, bribery, and theft. The usurer differs from the cozener, often, only in the fact that the usurer makes the laws. Even justice is, as Shaw said, sometimes no more than the wholesale department of what in retail is called crime.

It is in this half-world between legitimacy and illegitimacy, where the lawyer replaces the bodyguard, that many large personal fortunes are being made today. Crime is there euphemized as "shrewdness", "slickness", and "knowing one's way around", but it still pays.

Above those who profit within the pale of legality, in an ascending scale of reward, tower the real Titans of crime—the heroes of mankind, the conquerors, the enslavers, the destroyers, and the dictators. The Punic Wars, one of the really great crimes of history, paid Rome handsomely. Spain lived for centuries on the spoliation of the Moors and the ruin of Mexico and Peru. The stately homes of England were mortared more with blood and tears than with sweat, and the extermination of the American Indian and repeatedly breaking faith with him has been one of our most profitable undertakings.

[1] See Virgil Peterson: "Crime Does Pay", the *Atlantic Monthly*, February 1953, p. 40.

Crime seems to pay as much in glory and ego-satisfaction as in
wealth. The bigger criminals, as Senator Kefauver has showed
us, may shape the destinies of states and secure immunity for
themselves by selecting the law-enforcement officers. Some of
the more grateful or more innocent appointees even call them
up to thank them or send them bread-and-butter notes. Sheriffs,
mayors, and governors seem pleased, at times, to be invited to
their parties. The ordinary citizen cannot hope for any such
distinction for himself, but he revels in the newspaper accounts
of their luxury, lusts over their molls in the rotogravure, respectfully observes a moment's silence when solemn voices interrupt
his radio programmes to announce "Al Capone is dead",[1] and,
in a final gesture, dips his handkerchief in their blood to secure a
prized memento to hand down to his posterity.[2]

There surely can be no one so innocent any more as to believe
that crime does not pay because it is certain to be punished.
Hereafter it may be, but a reckoning on this earth is statistically
remote. The Chicago Crime Commission estimates that
"approximately ninety-seven per cent of the burglaries and
ninety-one per cent of the robberies committed in Chicago in
1951 did not even result in an indictment for the offence committed".[3] And an indictment is a long way from a conviction,
and a conviction sometimes a long way from serving a sentence.
The Wickersham and Seabury investigations twenty years ago
agreed that a criminal had about a ninety-nine-per-cent chance
of escaping punishment. As a matter of fact, our whole prison

[1] Chicago programmes were interrupted with special announcements of
this momentous event.
[2] Those who jostled to dip their handkerchiefs in John Dillinger's blood
may have been more pious than morbid or may have been merely seeking
a valuable home remedy. An executed criminal is thought to exude a
special manna. It was formerly believed that a child could be cured of
scrofula by being lashed with the rope with which a murderer had been
hung, and the sale of the rope was one of the hangman's perquisites. There
is, or was, in Sicily, a cult of veneration of the souls of departed malefactors,
with its own church, the *Chiesa delle Anime de' Corpi Decollati*, at Palermo.
The decollated, if propitiated, served as a special protection against holdups!
See E. Sidney Hartland, F.S.A.: "The Cult of Executed Criminals at
Palermo", the *Journal of American Folk-Lore*, vol. 21 (1910), pp. 168–79.
[3] Peterson: "Crime Does Pay", p. 39.

system is geared to the expectation that there will not be more than one conviction for every twenty felonies committed.

The more mercenary the crime, apparently, the less the chance of arrest and conviction. Those who kill for jealousy or personal hatred are easily caught. They are amateurs and, often, completely satisfied with their act (for there are many ways in which crime can pay), make little effort to escape. Holdup men, whose killings are usually incidental to the business of robbery, are harder to apprehend, and once they get away from the scene of the crime, as they usually manage to do, are taken only occasionally, and then by accident. But the professional "killers", hired murderers who kill cold-bloodedly for pay, the ones whose fate is most germane to the validity of the assurance that crime does not pay, are almost never apprehended. Their motive is obvious. Their act is often public, and the police usually have a pretty good idea of who instigated it, paid for it, and profited by it. But nothing can be done. Or, at least, it is to be hoped that nothing can be done; for certainly nothing *is* done. There have been approximately seven hundred such killings in Chicago in the past twenty-five years, and less than ten convictions.[1]

The public is the more perplexed by this state of affairs because of its growing faith in the lie-detector, a credulity that in its absolute form must be ranked among modern fallacies. It seems to the man in the street that all the police have to do is to round up all suspects, subject them to this unerring device, free the innocent, and punish the guilty.

It is a very old approach to the problem of the criminal. All ages have had their lie-detectors. The Greeks hung pebbles from branches and listened to them as they were blown against the sides of a caldron. The Romans were convinced that truth was to be found in the arrangements of chicken guts. The Saxons felt that if a man's word was doubted, the thing for him to do was to pick up a red-hot poker. The Inquisition was of the opinion that nothing produced dispassionate veracity so surely as tearing a

---

[1] Chicago's record in this respect is *better* than that of twenty other American cities.

limb from its socket, crushing the bones of the foot, or driving splinters under the nails. The Russians seem to think there is some antipathy between truthfulness and wakefulness and, apparently, do not expect even reasonable accuracy until the person being questioned has been at least forty hours without sleep.

In America, with our faith in machines, we rely on the "lie-detector".

The very name is misleading. The thing is simply a recording device. It has not—and does not profess to have—any knowledge of truth or error whatsoever. What it does is to record changes in heartbeat and respiration, and sometimes whether the subject is sweating profusely. Its use as a test of veracity is based on the assumption that when a man tells a lie he is disturbed, and that his disturbance will show in his respiration and pulse.

In most cases it probably will. The polygraph, as the machine is properly called, is not used unless the suspect professes to be innocent and willing to co-operate. He is bound to the stake, often parrying for his life and usually on edge. Into a series of innocuous questions is introduced something relevant to the crime. The subject has known from the beginning that some such thing was coming, that the examiner was playing with him as a cat with a mouse, and here, suddenly, it is. If he is totally innocent of the matter, he may not perceive the import of the question at all; it may seem just another irrelevancy. But if he is guilty, the chances are that there will be the tension, the gasp, the sweating, and the pounding heart that the machine measures and records.

But there are some serious limitations, as all who have worked with the device and written about it have made plain. Some people don't mind lying at all. Some diseases make pulse and respiration subject to erratic changes. A stupid subject might fail to see the implication of some pertinent questions, while a highly imaginative subject might see implications where none existed. Then, fear is not the only emotion that heightens respiration and pulse; anger does the same thing, and many subjects get angry.

And, lastly, even where the record indicates guilt, it may not be *the* guilt the examiners are particularly concerned with; a man may have other things hidden in his life which he fears will be revealed in the course of the questioning.

All in all, the experts believe that under the best of circumstances there may be as much as twenty-five per cent of error in the polygraph's findings, and that is certainly enough (as the best of the experts themselves insist) to exclude its findings from being accepted as evidence in court.

This does not mean, however, that it does not have a value. It is a very useful instrument in criminal investigation. Even though the courts will not accept its record as evidence without the accused's written consent, the answers given often furnish the police with clues that lead to evidence that can be submitted in court. The very belief that the machine can infallibly detect lies has led many a guilty man to confess before he was put in its seat. Most criminals are comparatively uneducated men, but such words as "pneumograph" and "sphygmomanometer" would strike terror into even learned hearts.

There is another value to it, too, as Professor Fred Inbau has pointed out: if the police believe it works, they are less likely to employ such archaic instruments of interrogation as the night stick or a rubber hose.[1]

A curious usefulness of the lie-detector is in *dis*proving confessions. Every notorious murder is sure to elicit a number of false confessions, confessions supported by the detailed re-enactment of the claimed crime. Every state in the Union is put to expense and trouble to prevent some of its citizens from committing suicide in this manner.

Confessions, however obtained, have to be checked and rechecked. The history of penology is full of people who have

---

[1] See Richard B. Morris: *Fair Trial* (New York: Alfred A. Knopf; 1952), pp. 432–3, for a comment on the lie-detector's limitations. And see Jules H., Masserman and Mary Grier Jacques: "Do Lie-Detectors Lie?" the *Nation*, April 19, 1952, pp. 368–9. Above all, see Fred E. Inbau: *Lie Detection and Criminal Investigation* (Baltimore: The Williams and Wilkins Company; 1953).

G

confessed to crimes they never committed. The Boorn brothers, a famous example, confessed to killing their brother-in-law Colvin, supplied the police with full details, and were sentenced to be hanged. Their sentence was commuted to life imprisonment, and after some years Colvin turned up hale and hearty. As also did Topsy, the niece of Louise Butler, who had been sentenced to death after furnishing the most minute and gruesome account of killing the said Topsy. John Johnson confessed to the brutal murder of little Annie Lemberger in Madison, Wisconsin, in 1911, was barely saved from lynching, and had served ten years of a life sentence before it was definitely established that he could have had no part in the crime.[1] A Chicago mother took poison after confessing that she poisoned her two-year-old son—surely the dreadful seal of remorseful veracity. Yet the inquest showed that the child had died of natural causes.[2] Five confessants strove for the dishonour of having slain the "Black Dahlia" in Los Angeles in 1947, each belittling the others' confessions and insisting that his own was the only reliable one. The police decided that they were all nuts, an attitude that so infuriated one of them that he wrote an indignant letter to *Life* protesting against the flippant disregard of his claim.[3]

Not a month passes but someone, somewhere, confesses to some crime that he or she could not possibly have committed. So common, in fact, are such confessions that such states as have laws indemnifying the wrongfully convicted usually make an exception of those who have contributed to their own conviction.

One of the most frequently voiced opinions in popular criminology is that crime is caused by "secularized" education and that the one sure cure for it is "a religious upbringing". The late Fulton Oursler said that "secularized education in our public schools" must be held accountable for "much" of the "more than eighty per cent increase" in our prison population in the last ten

[1] For these and many other instances, the incredulous are referred to Edwin Borchard: *Convicting the Innocent* (New Haven, Conn.: Yale University Press, 1932).
[2] The *Chicago Sun*, January 4, 1945, p. 13.
[3] *Life*, March 24, 1947, p. 18.

years. The Division of Christian Education of the Protestant Council of the City of New York is of the opinion that children not receiving religious education "are a menace to society, to themselves, to our country and our country's future". The National Reform Association says that we must restore religion to the schools "or perish through secularism and crime". Mr J. Edgar Hoover has stated frequently that attendance at Sunday school is the solution for juvenile delinquence. Father Robert I. Gannon, president of Fordham University, gave the old assertion a new and grim touch when he said that for every [public-school] classroom that was built, it was necessary to build two cells for the insane and one gallows.[1]

These are bitter words and would make a man wonder if a public-school commencement is any more than a witches' Sabbath, were it not that statistics fail to support them. For the facts —established in a dozen surveys, many of them reported in religious journals—are that most criminals have *had* a religious upbringing. The vast majority of convicts claim a sectarian affiliation. The percentage of the "religious" in prisons is far in excess of their percentage in the general population. Despite Mr Hoover, most delinquents have "been inside a church", and many are constant attendants. Seventy-two per cent of the more than six thousand boys apprehended for criminal activities in Detroit in 1950 attended church, forty-five per cent of them regularly. Nor is this solely an American phenomenon; studies have shown much the same situation in England, Holland, and Australia. And Westermarck quotes Mohammedan authorities to show that it pertains in Islam too.[2]

[1] Fulton Oursler, speaking over the radio, Sunday, June 9, 1946; the statements of the Protestant Council and the National Reform Association are quoted, with references given, in V. T. Thayer: *Religion in Public Education* (New York: The Viking Press; 1947), pp. 77, 80; Father Gannon was quoted to this effect in the *Brooklyn Tablet*, December 14, 1940.

[2] For statistics on the religious affiliations of criminals and delinquents, see a statement by Father George B. Ford, *PM*, February 29, 1944; William Adriaan Bonger: *Race and Crime* (New York: Columbia University Press; 1943); J. B. S. Haldane: *What Is Life?* (New York: Boni & Gaer; 1947), pp. 107, 109; Donald Powell Wilson: *My Six Convicts* (New York: Rinehart & Company; 1951), p. 254; Thayer: *Religion in Public Education*, p. 110;

This, emphatically, does not mean that a religious upbringing leads to crime—though if the statistical tables were reversed, much would probably be made of it. It may even be argued that they are to the churches' credit, since they indicate how largely they work among the poor, from whom most criminals are recruited.

If it were true that a religious upbringing prevents crime, there ought to be little crime at those times and in those places where the entire education is religious. The Middle Ages, for example, ought to have been practically free from crime, and the jails in Spain and Italy ought to be almost empty. But—if we may trust the homilists, and that's about all we have to go on—the Middle Ages were times of dreadful violence and debauchery; and the jails of those lands that support a sectarian education seem to be just as crowded as those of less fortunate countries.

Those who approach the problem of crime scientifically do not agree that there is any one solution. Crime, they say, is the product of complex forces. Most delinquents, they find, "hail from relatively localised urban and rural areas, with well-defined conditions of social deterioration". Criminals have usually grown up in poverty-stricken squalor, amid illiterate, quarrelling, and often criminal, siblings. They are below the average in education and physical health, with—as a class—a high incidence of mental

---

Father Leo Kalmer: *Crime and Religion* (Chicago: Franciscan Herald Press; 1936); Father McCaffrey: "The Church and Crime", *Commonweal,* December 14, 1932; Edward Westermarck: *The Origin and Development of Moral Ideas* (London: Macmillan & Company; second edition, 1917), vol. 2, p. 735. Jesse James had a religious upbringing, and was, indeed, a devout man all his life. He did not swear, smoke, or carry on with women. He always read the Bible before undertaking one of his professional enterprises, and definitely expected to go to Heaven when the time came.

Incidentally—on the question of whether or not crime pays—the James brothers have certainly paid handsomely. Some 450 novels have been written about them. Hundreds of short stories have recounted their glories, and even an entire publication, *The James Brothers' Weekly,* was devoted to them. Six major movies have been made about them, and countless serials. Frank Tousey alone "made more money printing stories about Jesse James than Frank and Jesse made in all their lives as bandits". See Jesse James in the *Dictionary of American Biography;* and Homer Croy: *Jesse James Was My Neighbour* (New York: Duell, Sloan & Pearce; 1949), pp. 243, 245.

deficiency. The hovels in which they live are crowded with unwanted children, and they spend their leisure in the streets, among bad companions, with "vicious, commercialized recreations". And, in addition, as all slum children do not become criminals, and all criminals are not drawn from the slum classes, there are personal factors. Many delinquents have suffered from delayed growth spurts that produced psychological tensions that sought relief in anti-social behaviour. Psychiatric examinations of delinquent boys have revealed that many of them have severe internal conflicts springing from poor interpersonal relationships. They were, more than others, stubborn, egocentric, impulsive, emotionally insecure, and "touchy". Many criminals (like many great men) are below average height.[1]

If these things are so, then, plainly, no one thing, however laudable, will cure crime. The worst forms of poverty will have to be eradicated. Slums will have to be cleared away, education extended, supervised recreation provided, families limited, and health—mental as well as physical—improved. Even that won't get rid of all crime, but it will get rid of a lot of it.

But such conclusions, though inescapable to the student and the logician, do not bother the common man. His concern with crime is more likely to be limited to such specific problems as whether or not one may hit a man wearing glasses, whether a citizen can make an arrest, whether a shoplifter must leave the store before he can be seized, whether a butcher can serve on a jury, whether a Mason has ever been hanged, whether there must be a body before there can be a conviction for murder, and whether a condemned man, if not killed on the first attempt at hanging or electrocution, is or is not entitled to go free. These are the questions that enliven bars, divert lunchrooms, estrange friends, hone wits, and, like the brook, go on forever.

---

[1] The statements in this paragraph are founded on Sheldon Glueck: *Crime and Correction* (Cambridge, Mass.: Addison-Wesley Press; 1952); Sheldon and Eleanor Glueck: *Unravelling Juvenile Delinquency* (New York: Commonwealth Fund: 1951); and Nathan Peyser: "Character Building for Crime Prevention", Chapter 6 in Sheldon and Eleanor Glueck (eds.): *Preventing Crime* (New York: McGraw-Hill Book Company; 1936).

Many a myope has been challenged in many a tavern to take off his glasses and waive the special immunity they are thought to confer; and many a timid schoolboy has blessed the specs that saved him from the local bully who knew that "you go to the reformatory for roughhousing a guy with glasses".

Of course if one who must wear glasses can be persuaded to take them off, or if they are knocked off, he is even more helpless than he was, and an even easier prey. But it is doubtful that any such consideration enters the mind of the attacker. There is simply a folk belief that "it's a prison offence to hit a guy with glasses".

Actually, the law makes no such distinction. It is true that if a man is hit in the eye when he is wearing spectacles he may be more seriously injured than if he had not been wearing them, and hence the hitter liable for a more serious offence, but the law confers no privilege to hit men without glasses.

The larcenous impulse latent in every shopper's heart leads to a great deal of speculation as to the exact point at which one becomes a shoplifter. And it is generally agreed to be the front door; only after one has crossed the lintel with unpaid-for goods can one, in popular opinion, be charged with shoplifting.

Donald Powell Wilson, in his semi-fictional best-seller *My Six Convicts*, gives the myth an almost classic expression in his anecdote of the lighthearted and light-fingered safecracker who, granted a day of freedom as a reward for opening a jammed safe, planted stolen merchandise in the pockets of a detective who was sent along to keep an eye on him. "Connie", as the prisoner was called, then waggishly reported the detective to a floorwalker and capped the whole hilarious scene by extracting a mass of purloined articles from his own pockets and stacking them on a counter. "It's no misdemeanour, y'know, to collect merchandise in a store," he informed the "mystified" floorwalker. "You can't arrest nobody till they get out on the street with it. After all, they might be intendin' to pay for it."[1]

---

[1] Wilson: *My Six Convicts*, p. 131. Writing in the *New Republic*, May 28, 1951, p. 4, Joseph Fulling Fishman states that the official records of Fort Leavenworth contain no mention of the temporary release of an expert safecracker to open a safe.

Setting aside the high degree of improbability of the entire anecdote, the problem is not so simple as Connie is made to express it, either for the shop or for the lifter. A store would not stay long in business that seized everyone who carried an article to the window or even to the door to have a better look at it. But it wouldn't stay solvent if it confined its pursuit of thieves wholly to the adjacent sidewalks. Each arrest has to be a matter of individual judgment and individual risk. Some courts have held that a store is justified in making a brief detention on the basis of a reasonable suspicion. Others have held that stores are liable even where an honest mistake was based on a strong presumption.[1]

There is a subsidiary myth that if a woman is falsely charged with shoplifting, she can have her choice of the finest mink coat the terrified store has in stock. But this, too, is dreaming. Arrests are never made unless the suspect has concealed the article in question and seems to be departing with it; and under those circumstances, no matter what motive could be established, it would be difficult to collect the value of a mink ear muff.[2]

It is true that any citizen can make an arrest, but it's a ticklish business. Usually, he is so empowered for any crime committed in his presence, but only for a felony committed elsewhere. *The New Yorker* had a satisfying anecdote of a citizen who saw a traffic cop violate a traffic ordinance and forthwith arrested him and compelled him to write himself a ticket. But either the cop was overawed at the magnificence of the act or that particular state had an unusual statute, for the violation of a traffic ordinance does not ordinarily (despite the attitude of some traffic cops) constitute a misdemeanour or felony.[3]

In discussions of the duties and limitations of citizenship one sometimes hears—more often in England than in America—

[1] William L. Prosser: *Handbook of the Law of Torts* (St Paul, Minn.: West Publishing Company; 1941), pp. 148–50.

[2] Mr. L. E. Edwards, superintendent of Special Service at Marshall Field and Company, told the author that he had heard this story for twenty years and that there was nothing to it.

[3] Anyone with an itch to arrest his fellow citizens without first getting himself deputized would do well to read Prosser: *Handbook of the Law of Torts*, especially pp. 161–2.

that butchers are ineligible for jury duty because their calling has so inured them to death that they would be indifferent to the death penalty. Dryden, Swift, Leigh Hunt, Lamb, and Hazlitt are among the authors who have helped perpetuate this opinion, an opinion, it hardly need be said, with no basis in law or psychology. Some go so far as to explain the excusing of physicians and surgeons on the same ground, but here—though the exemption is a fact—the reason is obvious: they have to be available in case of sickness or accident.

That no Mason has ever been hanged is a tenet of American folklore. "They are notoriously immune to hanging," says Mencken. The expression of the belief is almost always tinged with reproach and admiration. It is felt, apparently, that a great many of them *ought* to have been hanged—but they must be accorded, however grudgingly, the respect which we as a nation reserve for those who successfully beat the rap.

And, indeed, a hanged Mason *is* a rarity. Richard Savage was a Mason, and he was condemned to be hanged in 1727 for the murder of James Sinclair, but he was pardoned and lived on for many years. Benedict Arnold may have been a Mason, yet he took his neck whole to Westminster Abbey! Almost every lead ends up in disappointment: if the suspect is executed, it turns out that he wasn't a Mason after all. However, a recent discovery has settled the matter. The most famous American ever hanged was a Mason. Old John Brown was made a Mason in Hudson Lodge No. 68, at Hudson, Ohio, on May 11, 1824, perhaps through the influence of his uncle, Gideon Mills, who was the first Worshipful Master of the lodge.[1]

That there can be no conviction for murder without a body's being produced as unquestionable evidence that someone has been murdered is widely held, even by murderers. Thus a Mr Clark, of California, after burning the body of a Mr Schick, also of that state, in an oildrum behind his house, complacently told the police: "You can't convict me without a body."

---

[1] Ernest C. Miller: *John Brown, Pennsylvania Citizen* (Warren, Pa.: Penn State Press; 1952), p. 10 and notes 41–2.

But his assurance proved unjustified. Many men (including Mr Clark) have been so convicted. Courts are not always as inextricably entangled in technicalities as laymen think. Thus, in the case of *Commonwealth* [of Pennsylvania] v. *Lettrich* the defendant was convicted of the murder of her sister's eight-day-old illegitimate child, though the baby's corpse was never produced. The court reasoned, not illogically, that as it had been established that the child had last been seen with its aunt, and as it could not of itself go anywhere, and as it was missing, there was a strong inference that her statement that she had put it in the furnace was correct.

Those who contemplate committing the perfect crime and are relying on a complete disposition of the body as an element in its perfection are advised to read Mr Haydn Hilling's "The Case of Decasto Earl Mayer" in the *Washington Law Review* for May 1947 before they proceed. It may exercise a salutary restraint upon a dangerous confidence. Mayer, with the assistance of his mother, Mary Ellen Smith, murdered James Bassett in order to procure his automobile. There were no witnesses to the act other than the principals, and the body was never found. Mayer was apprehended after some very astute detective work, and there is little doubt that he would have been officially hanged had he not anticipated the law by tending to the business unofficially himself. The trial court, in a special memorandum, stated that "the *corpus delicti* in a homicide case can be established by circumstantial evidence".

The common belief to the contrary may be due to a confusion of the *corpus* of the essential *corpus delicti* with *corpse*. But the *corpus delicti* is the body of the crime, not the body of the victim, and its "establishment" simply means that it must be shown that a crime has been committed. Thus the spontaneous combustion of a newly insured house, amid a pervasive aroma of kerosene, is, at least to the average insurance-adjuster, the *corpus delicti* of arson.

Of course, it is easier to establish that a man has been murdered if his body, bearing marks of violence that could not have been self-inflicted, can be produced. But it is not essential. A strict interpretation of the rule, as Judge Storey observed, "would amount to a universal condonation of all murders committed on the high seas"; and as the conditions of modern life make it easier and easier to dispose of a body, the rule will probably be more and more relaxed and inferences more frequently relied on.

The electrocution of Willie Francis on May 9, 1947 for the murder of a druggist at St Martinsville, Louisiana, ought to have given at least a temporary check to the belief that a condemned man cannot be sent twice to the chair, gallows, or gas chamber for the same offence. Francis had been placed in the chair on May 3, 1946, but something had prevented his being killed. Some said that the current failed. Francis's lawyer, J. Skelly Wright, averred that the officials were too drunk to know what they were doing. In any event, the condemned man was taken back to his cell and his execution delayed by appeals to the Louisiana courts, the State Pardon Board, and, eventually, the Supreme Court of the United States. Whatever pleas were advanced, the popular feeling in Francis's favour was based on the belief that in going once to the chair he had paid his penalty; [1] but as the sentence read that a current of electricity was to be passed through his body "until he was dead", it is hard to see how the various boards and courts could have ruled otherwise than they did.

The most famous case of this kind was that of Captain Kidd, who was hung at Wapping, on May 23, 1701, between the high- and low-water marks, as custom dictated for a pirate. The rope broke at the hanging, but it was re-tied and he was re-hung. Kidd, by the way, was far from being the colourful villain that legend has made of him. He was connected, in his operations, with some of the most respectable people in England. His trial was, by modern standards, unjust; and he was convicted not of

---

[1] A minority of the Supreme Court held that a second journey to the chair for Francis would put him in double jeopardy and constitute cruel and unusual punishment.

piracy, which he stoutly denied to the end, but on a trumped-up murder charge.[1]

In former days, before the hangman's knot and the autopsy ruled out any possibility of resuscitation, it was believed that if a hanged man could be revived he would be entitled to live, and several attempts were made to rescue a man in this manner. A John Smith, of Malton, who was hung at Tyburn on December 24, 1705, was cut down and revived after hanging for fifteen minutes. His was actually one of those melodramatic cases where a reprieve arrived after the noose had been adjusted and the prisoner swung off the ladder. He became a distinguished cadger of drinks and raconteur and was known as "Half-hanged Smith".[2]

Of such attempts the most notorious was that arranged for the Reverend Dr Dodd, an eighteenth-century forger whose condemnation, because he was a clergyman and because he underwent a highly publicized repentance, had aroused immense feelings of pity and horror. A room and a physician were ready close at hand, and at the expiration of the legal minimum of suspension his body was to be claimed and efforts made to revive him. But the experiment was frustrated by the very popularity that led to its inception; the crowd at the hanging was so dense that the body could not be got through it in time.

[1] See Morris: *Fair Trial*, pp. 33–68: "The Politicians and the Pirate."
[2] See T. H. White: *The Scandalmonger* (New York: G. P. Putnam's Sons; 1952), p. 74.

CHAPTER FIFTEEN

Ishmael

ALTHOUGH few criminologists today would undertake to identify the criminal "type", the common citizen has no hesitation. After every exciting crime, scores of eager informants call the police to report "suspicious" persons who had been "acting queer" near the scene of the crime.

What emerges—apart from a great deal of extra work for the police—is an interesting illustration of what seems "suspicious" to the common man, the appearances and actions that are vulgarly thought to mark a criminal. Professor Hans von Hentig has collected hundreds of these identifications and finds that there is a great conformity among them. They project a sort of "devil" image, and the devil is, in brief, the nonconformist, the outsider, the unsuccessful. The morose, the sad, the tired, the unshaved, the unkempt, and the sickly are suspect in the eyes of the conventional citizen: pale men, bearded men, "swarthy" men, men whose eyes have "a wild gleam", and men who don't give their wives expensive funerals. [1]

Conversely, those who pass unsuspected are the tall, the handsome, the smiling, the seemingly well-to-do, the clean-shaved, and the neatly pressed. It is not easy to secure a conviction on a criminal charge when the defendant, if male, is tall and blond or,

---

[1] Hans von Hentig: "The Suspect: A Study in the Psychopathology of Social Standards," the *Journal of Criminal Law and Criminology*, vol. 39, no. 1, May–June 1948, pp. 19–33.

if female, is demure and wistful. A grandmother, if she conforms to the stereotype, is unassailable. And despite the fact that crooks seem especially fond of winter resorts, a tan is popularly regarded as a badge of innocence. That Secretary Fall was a member of the Cabinet did not seem to disturb the American public half so much as that his skin was bronzed from the great outdoors, that he wore a wide-brimmed felt hat and bore himself as one inured to the saddle.

Newspaper readers never seem to cease being amazed to learn that evildoers, when not doing evil, are much like other people. The dread Dillinger was shot down as he emerged from the local movie, redolent of popcorn. The "Terrible Touhys" avoided arrest by fading into a stodgy, respectable neighbourhood—where they were held in high esteem. When John Hamilton the lethal gangster was finally seized, he was feeding the baby in its high chair. "Ma" Barker, the devoted mother of the notorious Barker brothers, who was shot by the FBI in 1935, was the sweetest old lady who ever cased a joint. When Mrs Mae Smith and her daughter were arrested in 1940, near Chicago, and charged with being accomplices in an abortion ring, with abduction, and, possibly, with complicity in the wholesale murder of infants, it was found that they had kept a joint diary. Was this a document of unparalleled horror, filled with ghastly meditations and gruesome plans? It was not. It was domestic, sentimental, tender, a repository of exemplary thoughts. Interspersed with recipes for apple hodgepodge and blueberry crisp were notations of Shirley Temple's birthday and the anniversary of the death of Rin-Tin-Tin.[1] "Golf-Bag Sam" Hunt, one of Chicago's more resourceful hoodlums, had a brilliant inspiration when he substituted a golf bag for the more conventional gun case. What could have disarmed suspicion more effectively than this indication of suburban leisure, of solid, healthful conformity? Even his victims were deceived.

Because the criminal is, plainly, in popular fancy, an outlander, it is not astonishing to hear it asserted, as it often is, that

[1] See the *Chicago Tribune*, May 2-8, 1940.

immigrants are more criminal than the native-born and that the majority of the "criminal classes" is drawn from the "foreign-born elements", especially those inclined to be swarthy.

But repeated studies have showed this to be false. In 1931 the Wickersham Commission reported that "in proportion to their respective numbers the foreign-born commit considerably fewer crimes than the native-born (of the same age and sex)". In 1937 the arrest rate per 100,000 adult population was 514.2 for the native whites and 212.1 for foreign whites,[1] and these figures have been substantiated by further investigations conducted by the FBI.

The most dangerous criminals of all wear an even more disarming disguise. In so far as the ordinary man permits his fancy to dwell upon the dark possibility of his being done in, he will probably expect the attack to come from some thug, fiend, jealous rival, or vengeful competitor. Statistics indicate, however, that if it is to be, it is most likely to come from a loved one. Someone near and dear will pull the trigger, swing the axe, or pour the arsenic into the soup. "Family conflicts," says Dr Frederic Wertham, speaking from a long experience as a psychiatric expert in murder trials, "cause more murders than revenge, gangster killings and insanity put together." From the researches of the Metropolitan Life Insurance Company comes corroboration: domestic quarrels, particularly over money, lead to three times more homicides than gangster killings. Nor does this mean fiendish plots to gain Uncle Lucullus's millions; the sum in dispute seems to average about twenty-five cents. It is, as they say, the principle of the thing. Most of the causes of domestic killings seem trivial to those not immediately concerned —a late dinner, resentment at a rebuke, annoyance because someone else was served first.[2]

No figure is more firmly fixed in the Pantheon of Popular

[1] From Samuel Tennenbaum: "Some Truth About Immigration," the *American Mercury*, May 1947, p. 484.

[2] Frederic Wertham: *Dark Legend* (New York: Duell, Sloan & Pearce; 1941), p. 39. For a summary of the Metropolitan's report, see *Science News Letter*, March 11, 1939, p. 152.

Horror than the "mad killer". Any particularly attrocious murder is sure to be ascribed to a "fiend", and the word carries a suggestion not only of hellish cruelty, but of hellish subtlety as well. One of the chief characteristics of the insane murderer, in the common conception, is his diabolical cleverness. "You should have seen how wisely I proceeded—with what caution—with what foresight—with what dissimulation I went to work," Poe's madman exulted, gloating over the success of his homicidal cunning.

Nothing could be further from the fact. For though it is felt that the insane are frightfully clever in perpetrating and concealing their monstrous killings,[1] they are neither one nor the other. Dr Louis H. Cohen, Professor of Legal Psychiatry at Yale, and Dr Thomas E. Coffin, Professor of Psychology at Hofstra College, insist that *lack* of subtlety is the distinguishing mark of the demented killer. Indeed, they suggest that the question of sanity or insanity might well be settled by the crime: if there is method or advantage in it, there is also, they believe, a measure of sanity.

In "The Pattern of Murder in Insanity" the professors conclude, after examining many cases, that murders committed by the insane are characterized by their senselessness: "No one 'in his right mind' would go about committing a murder in such a senseless fashion." The insane murderer "consults none of the usual conveniences of crime". His motives are neither mercenary nor self-advancing. He never kills for gain; "it apparently requires some sanity to murder for profit". He rarely shows any forethought or cunning or judgment in his choice of time and place—nor often, to the sane mind, in his choice of victim. He doesn't bother to find a suitable weapon, and makes little or no effort to "get away" with the crime. It takes no sleuth to find him because he makes no attempt at concealment. He rarely resists arrest, but usually gives himself up to the police at once and assists them in every way that he can.[2]

[1] As in *The Lodger*.
[2] The article by Drs Cohen and Coffin will be found in the *Journal of Criminal Law and Criminology*, vol. 37, no. 4, Nov.–Dec. 1946, pp. 261–87. Exhibitionism is becoming more frequent from an automobile: "One of

This last fact negates another popular delusion, namely that murderers frequently evade their just punishment by pretending to be insane; for the first element in the pretence would have to be a disregard for their own safety. The popular idea seems to be that the sanity or insanity of the accused is determined wholly by intelligence tests or by eccentricities in his behaviour, and that these can be faked. But if the tests are administered by a competent psychologist, this would be almost impossible. Unless the suspect had actually worked with the tests, he would not know which indicated one age level and which another; and the moment the examiner thought he was malingering, he would give him a mixture of texts from various age levels and probably catch him answering some from the higher levels while deliberately missing some from the lower.

To begin with, the criminal who intended to "fake" insanity would have to perform his crime in a different manner from that which sanity would suggest. He would have to do it openly, with no regard for his own safety. He would have to plan it in such a way that no ordinary motive could be perceived. And he would have to make no effort to escape. Then he would have to have an unusual knowledge of, and skill in mimicking, psychotic behaviour, and very few people have either. Indeed, there are not many things about which popular ideas are more grossly inaccurate than how the insane look and act. The few who try to simulate insane conduct generally overact their part. Cohen and Coffin believe that a man would have to be close to psychotic to put on anything like a convincing performance.[1]

Furthermore, if a criminal were possessed of the knowledge and skill to act out insanity successfully, he would be more likely to lose than to gain. For if a man is declared insane after commit-

---

the evidences of the neurotic character of this type of offence is that no effort is made by the perpetrator to obscure the licence plate and thus avoid detection."—Manfred S. Guttmacher and Henry Weihofen: *Psychiatry and the Law* (New York: W. W. Norton & Company; 1952), p. 114.

[1] Guttmacher and Weihofen: *Psychiatry and the Law*, p. 280.

ting a murder, he isn't just turned loose. He is committed to a hospital for the criminal insane, an institution likely, in many ways, to be far grimmer than a penitentiary and far harder to get out of. Even if, after successfully deceiving the psychiatrists into thinking him insane and then, with diabolical cunning and patience through the years, convincing them of his gradually returning sanity, he manages to be declared sane, he would not be allowed to go free. He would be brought back into court to face trial on the original charge.[1]

There is an opposite fear to this one, that sane people are frequently "railroaded" into insane asylums and detained there as prisoners, utterly unable to prove their sanity to unsympathetic authorities. It is a staple of popular fiction, based, perhaps, on every sane man's doubts of his sanity; but the danger is grossly exaggerated. Of course, if the director of some private institution were willing to connive with villainous relatives, it might be done, but it would be an abduction, and the director would run the risk of spending a good many years in the penitentiary.

Certainly consignment to any public institution for the insane is carefully safeguarded. No one can be committed without certification by at least one or two medical examiners appointed by the court or a state board, men whose professional standing is at stake and who are subject to suit for damages. And they cannot proceed surreptitiously. The examination they are required to make would surely arouse the victim's awareness of their purpose, unless he were insane; and if through error or malice a sane person were committed to such an institution, he would be released as soon as his sanity was perceived. All state hospitals are inspected regularly. They are overcrowded, and there is no desire to keep anyone who can safely be let go. If through negligence or incompetence of both the resident authorities and

---

[1] When a person is condemned to death and becomes insane while awaiting execution, he is committed to a mental institution for treatment and cure. When he is restored to reason, he will be executed. This seems, at first glance, to be putting the state to a great deal of unnecessary expense, and the arguments to support it are confused and conflicting. Any other course, however, would be repugnant to humanity.

the inspectors the patient's sanity is not recognized, he can petition the courts for release on a writ of habeas corpus. This won't get him released at once, but it will ensure a hearing. Hospital authorities who prevent an attempt to petition for such a writ—even when they act in good faith—may be personally liable for damages.[1]

The plea of "temporary insanity", which the layman regards —quite rightly—with cynicism, is shown to be specious by the fact that it is rarely entered in cases such as larceny, where psychologists believe it possible, but is reserved almost exclusively for murder cases, where it is highly improbable. The reason is simple. If the plea is admitted, the prisoner may be consigned to a mental institution for life. To a murderer this may be preferable to death, but a shoplifter would rather take the lighter sentence for the crime.

"Temporary insanity" serves, actually, as an "out" for a jury that wants to acquit a defendant in spite of the law, and is used most frequently when the killing results—or is claimed to have resulted—from the sexual misconduct of a spouse. Although journalists have elevated the defence of this particular type of murder to "the unwritten law", it is not always a certain defence. As a matter of fact, except in one state, it is not a defence at all; it is merely an attempt to get the jury so excited that it will disregard the law.

The one state that permits a man to kill his wife's lover is Texas. Elsewhere he runs the risk—slight, to be sure—of an unsympathetic jury. That this statute should exist only in the Lone Star state, where the men are notoriously virile and the women magnificently loyal, is slightly puzzling. It obviously has no significance to Texans, and must, therefore, be intended to encourage newcomers to conform to the local standards. Perhaps it was designed to attract the tourist trade.

The assumption underlying the acquittal of spouses who murder their mates when they come upon them *in flagrante delicto* is that the shock of the discovery temporarily unhinges the

[1] Guttmacher and Weihofen: *Psychiatry and the Law*, pp. 297–8.

moral faculties, though it seems to leave the sighting eye clear and the trigger finger firm.

It may be so. It invests the killer with noble motives while conveniently relieving him of witnesses and, perhaps, an unwanted mate. But Dr Walter Bromberg, formerly director of the Psychiatric Clinic of the New York Court of General Sessions and more recently senior psychiatrist at Bellevue Psychiatric Hospital, has come up with another theory, one not likely to be as appealing to juries quivering with sexual excitement and moral righteousness, but which might in the long run produce more justice and fewer corpses.

Dr Bromberg suggests[1] that "triangle" murders are motivated more by humiliation than indignation, and that the offending spouse is killed as an expiation not of his or her guilt, but of that of the killer, who sees the act as an exposure of his own inner secrets or, perhaps, a publication of his own sexual inadequacy. Dr Bromberg makes a further interesting observation: where the cuckolded man is young, his impulse is to kill the erring woman; where he is older, the man is more likely to be his victim. And Dr Bromberg's explanation of this is that the younger man views the act as an exposure, on his wife's part, of his own sexual incompetence; the older man has the same feelings, plus, it may be, homosexual impulses released by witnessing another man's sexual activities, and these homosexual impulses direct his attack towards the male.

To many laymen such interpretations will most likely seem not only preposterous, but vicious, an attempt to smear brave men who have had the courage to follow the dictates of their consciences and shoot their wives. The adulterer, like the rapist, the exhibitionist, the voyeur, the sadist, the homosexual, the molester of children, and other deviationists, is a "sex offender", and should be removed from the face of the earth immediately upon identification. There is no criminal type regarding which popular opinion is more certain—and about which it is less informed. The sex offender is a fictitious stereotype, and the

[1] Bromberg: *Crime and the Mind,* pp. 160-1.

errors making up the stereotype constitute a serious barrier to proper legislation.

In the first place, there is no class of criminals that specializes in sex offences, as there are counterfeiters, car thieves, or holdup men. A number of sexual offenders are definite psychopaths, dangerous men who should be apprehended and incarcerated; but if a sex offender is one who has violated some criminal law governing sexual conduct, then the majority of American males, as Dr Kinsey has pointed out, are sex offenders. And the number who would gratify illicit impulses if they dared or if occasion offered must be even higher. No one, for example, who attends strip-tease burlesques, night clubs, musical shows with choruses, or even the ballet, can be too indignant with voyeurs. There is as much salacity as high-mindedness in the periodical "exposures" of call girls and vice rings in the daily papers, and the detailed descriptions of sadistic attacks on women do as much to inflame as to abate the evil they ostensibly deplore.[1]

The use of "moron" as a name for sexual offenders is a product of the headline writer's search for words of convenient size. Perhaps, also, there is a reluctance among journalists, as among their readers, to accept the fact that crimes are often perpetrated by "normal" people. It is more comforting to believe that the "insane", "criminals", and "degenerates" do these dreadful things, not ordinary, sane people like the editors who exploit, and the readers who gloat over, the daily fare of sexual crimes.

A moron, in psychological terminology, is simply an adult with a child's mind. A child's mind isn't quite everything that Eugene Field seemed to think it was, but an adult's mind isn't always a thing to thank God for either. There is nothing in a moron, as such, that necessarily makes him commit sexual assaults. The most dreadful sex crimes committed in America in

---

[1] "*Thou rascal beadle, hold thy bloody hand*
Why dost thou lash that whore! Strip thine own back.
Thou hotly lusts to use her in that kind
For which thou whip'st her."
                                        —*King Lear*, IV, vi, 164–6.

the past decade turned out to have been committed by a university student who—except for an inability to spell, which is common to at least eighty per cent of all university students—was possessed of a quite good mind.

There are many illusions about the rapist. He is often thought to be half-crazed with dope or drink, an utterly antisocial fiend, seething with ungovernable lust, and, more often than not, a "foreigner" or a Negro. Dr Blomberg refutes all of these assumptions in a summing up of hundreds of examinations of those accused of sex offences: "The sex offender is more frequently white than Negro, native-born and a professed member of a religious denomination . . . of average intelligence and not a serious user of alcohol."[1] Lynchings are vaguely thought to be the consequence of rape, though less than one-sixth of the almost four thousand persons lynched in the United States between 1889 and 1930 (of whom four-fifths were Negroes) were even accused of rape. The offences that led to mob violence against Negroes were defiance of whites or the assault and killing of whites.[2]

Another error is the assumption that the sex offender progresses from minor offences to major ones—so that an exhibitionist or a Peeping Tom should be sent to jail before he becomes a rapist or a ripper. But "such a graduation is almost unknown".[3] The exhibitionist or the voyeur is acting out some psychic conflict of his own, and would be, if anything, *less* likely than the ordinary man to seek violent gratification.

It is also felt that sex offenders are repeaters, but this, also, is not so. "In the last of the *Uniform Crime Reports* available". Guttmacher and Weihofen inform us, "rape was twenty-third

[1] Bromberg: *Crime and the Mind*, pp. 85–6.

[2] See Arthur F. Raper: *The Tragedy of Lynching* (Chapel Hill, N.C.: University of North Carolina Press; 1933), p. 1; Dollard: *Caste and Class in a Southern Town*, second edition, p. 327. Stronger sexual desires used to be attributed to dark-complected, or "black," men. The *Oxford Book of Proverbs* quotes from Harl. MS 3362 f. 17a (*circa* 1470): "To a red man read thy rede; with a brown man break thy bread; at a pale man draw thy knife; from a black man keep thy wife."

[3] Guttmacher and Weihofen: *Psychiatry and the Law*, p. 111.

and 'other sex offences' twenty-sixth in order of recidivism among the twenty-seven offences listed."

Then it is felt that sex crimes are increasing,[1] and that new and drastic legislation is needed to cope with them. But no authority would endorse either of these assumptions. We simply don't have figures on sex offences of the past, and all comparisons must be conjectural. They may well *seem* to be more frequent because our changing modes permit them to be discussed more freely. Women are more likely to report assaults than they once were, and the newspapers describe them more freely.[2]

The "new and drastic legislation" clamoured for by laymen every time the papers run a fresh series of rape stories is opposed by almost all students of the problem. "There is no need of any new laws to deal with sex offenders", Dr Edward Kelleher told the Illinois State Commission on Sex Offenders in 1951. "What is needed," he said, "is intelligent enforcement of existing laws and more facilities for the treatment of sexually dangerous persons."[3] Dr Karl M. Bowman, after a special three-year investigation of the subject for the University of California's Langley Porter Clinic, found no evidence of a wave of sex crimes, and expressed the opinion that it would do no good to enact harsher punitive laws.[4]

Because most sex offenders are never caught, and because most of those caught are not repeaters, the clamour for sterilization or, more frankly, castration, is particularly nonsensical, and smacks suspiciously of the sort of thing it professes to

[1] Sexual excitation has become such an adjunct of advertising, in ads and store windows, and so large an element of popular diversion in comic strips, movies, magazine illustrations, and on TV—the female bosom, thigh, mouth, and eye are so invitingly and relentlessly thrust upon our attention —that it is a reflection upon either the virility of our men or the chastity of our women that sexual attacks are not more frequent than they are.

[2] One atrocious sexual crime of the past which has almost disappeared with the spread of hygienic knowledge is the assaulting of little girls by men infected with venereal diseases who believed they could rid themselves of the infection if they "gave" it to someone who had never had intercourse. Sexual attacks on children "with intent to give the foul disease" fill a great deal of space in eighteenth-century newspapers.

[3] See the *Chicago Sun-Times*, November 30, 1951, p. 28.

[4] *Time*, March 2, 1953, p. 42.

suppress. Dr Lowell S. Selling, director of the Psychopathic Clinic of the Recorder's Court in Detroit, who examined one hundred and fifty cases with the applicability of this often-urged remedy in mind, is of the opinion that "sterilization or castration of sex offenders would not prevent them from making sex attacks and might actually add to their sex deviations and homicidal mania".[1] Sex offenders are more likely to be undersexed than oversexed.[2] Castration does not eliminate desire, and it would be more likely to add to than to detract from the neurotic conditions from which the criminal offences spring.

A common popular error regarding sexual deviates is that male homosexuals are effeminate, female homosexuals mannish. Some male homosexuals do assume the bearing and appearance of women, but only a small percentage of them. Many overdo the characteristics of their own sex, but most are not recognizable by any outward signs. Frederick the Great was a homosexual, but a great general and administrator. There was nothing effeminate about Oscar Wilde.

Conversely, as Simone de Beauvoir warns us, "nothing could be more erroneous" than to confuse the invert with the "viriloid" woman: "There are many homosexuals among harem inmates, [and] prostitutes . . . and a great many 'masculine' women are heterosexual."[3]

Homosexuality, though still regarded as a crime by many states (up until one hundred and thirty years ago it was a capital offence in England), is now considered by psychologists to be a form of sickness, resulting more from maladjustment than—as is often vulgarly supposed—from physical weakness or glandular deficiency. Some believe that homosexuality is merely an extreme manifestation of a duality latent in everyone. In "normal" persons the one impulse definitely preponderates. In many others,

[1] *Science News Letter*, January 22, 1938, p. 57.
[2] See a summary of the report of New Jersey's Commission on the Habitual Sex Offender, *Time*, February 13, 1950, p. 85. This, if true, refutes one of the oldest fallacies in the world: that prostitution must be condoned as a necessary evil because it provides a safety valve that protects virtuous women against criminal attacks from oversexed males.
[3] De Beauvoir: *The Second Sex*, p. 404.

where the impulses are dangerously even, an attempt to keep that fact below the level of conscious awareness often leads to an excessive demonstration of the one that is socially acceptable. Thus many intentionally "feminine" women are homosexual, and an excess of belligerent virility in a man is suspicious. A man's a man, but a he-man may very well be a homosexual.

The middle class, in its solid respectability, assumes that homosexual males, at least, are to be found chiefly among skid-row degenerates or the idle rich. Kinsey, however, though he found a fair number of both at these levels, discovered the greatest percentage in the middle class by which they are so manfully despised.

Some persons seem to have masculine and feminine feelings, both strong to an unusual degree. Leonardo da Vinci seems to have been one of these, Lord Nelson another, and Shelley a third—all men highly masculine yet at the same time possessing a high degree of feminity without being effeminate. Havelock Ellis felt that this type represented the ideal.[1]

[1] Dr. Caroline Spurgeon in her *Shakespeare's Imagery* (New York: The Macmillan Company; 1936, pp. 114-16), called attention to the extraordinary "femininity" of Shakespeare's unconscious mind, to the remarkable extent to which he drew his imagery from the occupations of women.

CHAPTER SIXTEEN

Poppycock and Mandragora

A NY DISCUSSION of crime and criminals in America today will gravitate quickly to the subject of drugs, for the two are thought to be inseparable; and certainly any reader of the popular press would have to be forgiven for assuming that all criminals were users of narcotics and all users of narcotics criminals.

Actually, four-fifths of the human race uses some sort of drug daily. Some use opium, some hashish, some betel nut, some marihuana, some bromides, some caffeine, and some nicotine. Many combine several. It looks as if life was intolerable to most people without the numbing protection of a depressant or the exciting goad of a stimulant, and perhaps the controlled use of these things is one of mankind's greatest victories over circumstances. Moralists have always inveighed against their use, preferring for their own delectation the headier and infinitely more dangerous drugs of indignation, ambition, and absolutism.

Among the many millions of daily users of stimulants and depressants, some—nobody knows how many—become, as the phrase has it, "slaves" to the drug. It is a necessity for them instead of an aid or a comfort, and some drugs—caffeine, the opium derivatives, and, to some extent, alcohol and nicotine (though not marihuana)—establish themselves through constant use as indispensable to the user's well-being, so that when they are abruptly discontinued there is acute discomfort. And it is the experiencing of this discomfort on withdrawal, according to those who work with narcotics, that marks addiction.

Much thought and study, over many years, has been given to the question of why some users become addicted and others do not. No one can say with certainty, but all who have worked on the problem scientifically agree that the addict is an unstable person to begin with, that his addiction is a manifestation, rather than a cause, of his basic difficulties, and that those prone to addiction are most likely to become addicts under certain social conditions. Drug addicts are drawn from the insecure, the confused, the frightened, and the bored. Most addiction is confined to slum districts and to members of minority groups, young hedonists seeking a thrill to relieve the drab monotony of slum life.[1]

The popular conception of the addict, the "dope fiend", as an emaciated, pallid, wild-eyed, gibbering, desperate creature, in so far as it is not wholly a fabrication of the newspapers, seems to be based on the characteristics of the down-and-outers, the wretched dregs of humanity whom the police have to deal with, and on a failure to differentiate between the symptoms of denarcotization and the actual effects of the drug on the body.

The addict does not need, however, to conform to this stereotype, and most addicts don't. If the police are right in their estimate that we apprehend only a fraction of those who use drugs habitually, then the majority of addicts must be indistinguishable from ordinary people. And so, according to the best-informed accounts, they are. "A normal individual," says Dr Donald Powell Wilson, "can be addicted to large doses of morphine for years without damage to either personality or body. . . . He takes morphine as his neighbour takes his cocktail."[2] He is likely to be unsociable, for he has his own particular pleasure. He may have a poor appetite, and the depressant effect of the drugs will probably make him lazy and unambitious. He is likely, also, to be reserved and secretive, for he must have the drug, and the obtaining of it has been made a crime; but if he can

[1] See M. J. Pescor: "The Problem of Narcotic Drug Addiction," the *Journal of Criminal Law and Criminology*, December 1952, pp. 471–80. The reference here is to p. 479.
[2] Wilson: *My Six Convicts*, p. 340.

afford an adequate supply, he can continue, apparently, to lead a fairly ordinary life.[1]

As has been said, the chances are that the addict takes drugs because he is unstable, neurotic; and the instability that led to the addiction may very well show in erratic behaviour and appearance, but this is a cause, not an effect. All people who use drugs do not become addicts, any more than all who drink become alcoholics—and alcoholism, by the way, will, in the long run, probably show more, in damage to mind and body and social relationships, than drug addiction.

Coleridge is often used as an example: he was an addict to opium, and he made a rather sad mess of parts of his life. He wrote some very great poetry, in fragments and flashes, and his critics often imply that if he had lived a more regular and healthy life he would have written a great deal more. But that is purely a supposition, one opposed to probability, for most people who live regular and healthy lives do not write readable poetry. Coleridge was simply a highly unstable man, and such people often make messes of their lives on nothing worse than yogurt. Both Coleridge and De Quincey, the archetype of the addict, lived to old age, and both men, for all their addiction, produced literary works that few have equalled. De Quincey indulged in and broke the habit three times, and for the last fifteen years of his life seems to have had it completely under control.

It is probably to De Quincey's *Confessions*, which has been accepted as a clinical rather than a poetic report, that English-reading people owe the idea, almost universal among them, that the smoking of opium produces vast and terrible dreams, with overwhelming sensations of fear and guilt. But the *Confessions* reflect De Quincey's specific experiences, and are not a safe guide to the general reaction. He was a dreamer and a great embellisher of dreams, but modern investigations do not support his belief

[1] Pescor: "The Problem of Narcotic Drug Addiction," p. 476. At the time of publishing his article, Dr Pescor was Chief of Medical Programmes in the Regional Office of the U.S. Public Health Service, in Dallas. His article was approved for publication by the United States Public Health Service.

that it was the opium that made him dream. He had waking dreams long before he took opium, and Professor Altick is of the opinion that his dreams were more prompted and shaped by Gothic novels and the weird tales of the German romantics than by laudanum.[1]

It is now popularly assumed that the ingestion of a single grain of unprescribed opium will bind one forever in the grip of addiction. Yet our forefathers, untrammelled by pure-food-and-drug acts and unalarmed by newspaper stories, took opium almost as we take aspirin. Dr Benjamin Rush, in a temperance pamphlet, recommended laudanum mixed with wine as a tapering-off from spirits, and a reporter from East Anglia, where the ague was pandemic, remembered that as a boy he had been told that formerly on market days every woman bought sixpence worth of laudanum for her family and that a fenman would hardly thank you for a glass of beer or a pipe of tobacco unless some opium had been added to it.[2]

So common now, however, is the belief that drug addiction stimulates crime—so stereotyped the conception of the "hopped-up" killer, "crazed" with drugs—that it comes as a shock to read such statements, from responsible authorities, as "There is no relation between morphine or opium addiction and serious crime"[3] or "Drug addiction and crime can be shown to have almost no cause and effect relationship, when compared with the influence of the criminal's personality and antisocial impulses".[4]

Someone must be wrong, for there is nothing on which law-enforcement officers are more emphatic than the relation of crime and narcotics. Lieutenant Kinzie Bluitt, of the Chicago

[1] Richard Altick: *The Scholar Adventurers* (New York: The Macmillan Company; 1950), pp. 260–1. And see Elizabeth Schneider: "The Dream of Kubla Khan", *Publications of the Modern Language Association of America*, vol. 60 (1945), pp. 784–801.

[2] For Rush, see Herbert Asbury: *The Great Illusion* (New York: Doubleday & Company; 1950), p. 27. For the report from East Anglia, see the *Journal of American Folk-Lore*, vol. 40 (1929), p. 115.

[3] Wilson: *My Six Convicts*, p. 342.

[4] Bromberg: *Crime and the Mind*. See also the *American Journal of Psychiatry*, April 1952, pp. 791–2.

Police Force, estimates that "80% of burglaries and 60% of robberies" in that much-looted city are committed by dope addicts.[1] State's Attorney Boyle, not to be outdone by a mere lieutenant, asserted that there were ten thousand addicts roaming Chicago's streets, each stealing from six to forty dollars a day.[2]

That's a lot of larceny. It adds up to three and one half million thefts annually, with an aggregate take of from twenty-two million to one hundred and forty-six million dollars.

The Uniform Crime Statistics for 1948 (the last year for which Mr Boyle at the time of his pronouncement could have had any reliable figures), however, show a certain discrepancy. This report (compiled by the FBI) states that there were nine thousand one hundred and ninety larcenies of fifty dollars and under reported in Chicago for that year. Of course, all larcenies are not reported, but even assuming that twice as many were committed as reported, and further assuming that every theft was for the maximum, it still adds up to only nine hundred thousand dollars stolen. Enough, in all conscience, but something under the State's Attorney's estimate.

There is, unquestionably, some correlation between narcotic addiction and crime. The very purchase of the drugs, except through a legitimate prescription, is in itself a crime. But this is a crime almost solely by legal definition. Fifty years ago it was no crime at all. And it is dangerous simply to say that a crime is a crime and to make no distinction among murder, theft, rape, arson, and perjury, which do harm to others, and which all peoples at all times have regarded as wicked, and the purchase of a substance that harms only the purchaser. Yet this is the principal crime of which addicts are guilty: "Less than one-fourth of all convicts in prison for drug offences have any charge against them other than the possession of narcotics—not even petty theft."[3]

There is, of course, a good deal of petty theft by addicts, and it

[1] The *Chicago Sun-Times*, March 22, 1949, p. 8.
[2] *Chicago Tribune*, October 3, 1949, pt. 1, p. 3.
[3] Wilson: *My Six Convicts*, p. 343.

probably will increase as the increasing scarcity of the drugs and the danger of peddling them drive the illicit prices even higher. The average addict cannot find the needed money honestly very long, and will be more and more driven in his desperation into lawlessness.[1]

But although control of the traffic is a necessity, and though it will seem to many people mere casuistry, it must still be insisted that it is not the drug itself that impels the addict to crime, but the difficulty of getting the drug. Indeed, the actual action of the drug itself would probably *lessen* both the impulse to crime and the ability to commit it. Narcotics *decrease* rather than increase aggressive impulses, particularly sexual impulses. All the addict wants, once he has a supply of the drug, is to be let alone. The addict is escapist, regressive, and passive. "His absence of drive makes it impossible for him to plan a crime skilfully, and he would be inept and maladroit in carrying it out." The legend of the dangerous "dope fiend" may have grown out of "police reporters and even doctors watching the 'show' of denarcotization and its apparent mania".[2]

Actually, alcohol causes "infinitely more murders, rapes, and crimes of violence than do morphine, heroin, cocaine, marihuana, and all other drugs combined". One authority illustrates it this way: "If a man is a murderer in his heart, alcohol may lead him to commit murder; morphine will probably cause him to postpone it." Or, to put it another way: "An alcoholic gets drunk, goes home and beats his wife; an addict to morphine gets 'high', goes home, and his wife beats him."[3] Yet we have seen, in one of the hardest falls on the pavement of Hell ever suffered, the futility of prohibiting alcohol.

[1] Like alcohol and tobacco, opium is incredibly cheap to make. Heroin can be manufactured at a profit for $10 a pound. Yet this same pound may ultimately bring as much as $80,000. As Al Capone once said of a similar situation, this attracts a lot of bright boys.

[2] Wilson: *My Six Convicts*, pp. 342, 343.

[3] J. D. Reichard: "Some Myths about Marihuana", *Federal Probation*, vol. 10, no. 4, Oct.–Dec. 1946, p. 17. Dr Reichard, formerly Medical Director of the United States Public Health Service, was for seven years Medical Officer in Charge of the U.S. Public Health Service Hospital for the treatment of narcotic addicts at Lexington, Kentucky.

The newspapers and magazines a few years ago, in a furor over juvenile delinquency (to which they contributed by their lurid stories), picked on marihuana as a special incentive to crime among the young. It was claimed that the smoking of marihuana is widespread among schoolchildren, that the traffic in it is controlled by an organized and enterprising "ring", that it plays a large part in stimulating juvenile delinquency, causes major crimes and sexual offences, and invariably leads to physical and mental deterioration. The International Narcotic Education Association states that the weed, known (they say) as "the killer drug", leads to physical wreckage, mental decay, and moral degeneracy, and affirms that "many cases of assault, rape, robbery and murder" may be traced to its use. Professor Robert P. Walton, whose *Marihuana: America's New Drug Problem* (1938) is the mine whence much of this colourful stuff is dug, says that it leads directly to "premeditated burglaries" and other crimes, and tells of a youth at Tampa who under the influence of reefers massacred his entire family.

Professor Walton does not stand alone. The latest edition of Osler's *Principles and Practice of Medicine* says that "acute mania may develop" from the use of marihuana, and that "homicides, suicides and assaults, particularly with sex motives, occur". A case is alleged of one who under the influence, apparently to the horror of his better self which was aware but helpless, decapitated a friend. The *Journal of the American Medical Association* takes an editorial stand firmly at Osler's side.

Further corroboration, if any were needed, is furnished by a remarkable experiment conducted by Mr James M. Hepbron, managing director of the Criminal Justice Commission of Baltimore. Governor Harry W. Nice (according to the story as related in the *American Weekly*[1]) had to decide whether to commute the death sentence of a young man who claimed that he had committed his crime under the influence of marihuana. The Governor asked Mr Hepbron to test the effects of the drug for him, and Mr Hepbron, placing a large shopping bag over his

[1] February 16, 1947.

head ("the method most addicts use", he says) smoked several reefers, having taken the precaution to have by him a trusted friend armed with a black jack and instructed to deal with him in the interest of public safety should it be necessary. After five or six of the cigarettes, Mr Hepbron reports, an impulse to divest himself of his clothes and dance nude in the snow (an act "never contemplated when normal") came upon him and might have been put into effect had not the vigilant friend put him under a cold shower. "I was many minutes under that shower," says Mr Hepbron, "before I really came to my senses and won out." He reported to the Governor that "the marihuana-ruled brain is not blank but is robbed of all ordinary restraint". Appalled, the Governor ordered the young man to be executed.

Against such opinions and experiences can be set the experiments of the United States Public Health Service, the report of Mayor La Guardia's Committee on Marihuana, and the convictions of various other scientists and criminologists.

The United States Public Health Service, after a series of experiments, came to the conclusion that "although the drug lessens inhibitions, it does not incite normally law-abiding people to crime". Indeed, the "potentially violent person is quieted [by it] rather than stimulated to action".[1] The marihuana-user giggles and laughs a great deal, seems unco-ordinated and confused, and is subject to alarms and excursions, but he doesn't seem particularly mad at anybody or able to do much about it if he were.[2]

Marihuana does seem to stimulate sexual fantasies (not as much as pin-up-girl pictures and summer dresses but, still, some), but it decreases potency. Indeed, "avoidance of sex is one of the psychological drives to addiction",[3] and the attribution of sex crimes to the influence of marihuana is either the effect of moral

[1] Reichard: "Some Myths about Marihuana," p. 18.
[2] See Walter Bromberg and Terry C. Rodgers: "Marihuana and Aggressive Crime," the *American Journal of Psychiatry*, May 1946, pp. 825–7; Colonel J. M. Phalen: "The Marihuana Bugaboo," the *Military Surgeon*, July 1943; Norman Taylor: *Flight from Reality*, New York: Duell, Sloan & Pearce: 1949), pp. 343–6.
[3] Wilson: *My Six Convicts*, p. 337.

prurience (one of the most powerful stimulants known) or the attempt of some sexual criminal to shift the responsibility for his act. The lurid sexual orgies which the popular periodicals described some years ago as a part of marihuana addiction are highly improbable. One of the features of these saturnalia was the ruin of innocent maidens, but it is peculiar that those maidens bold enough to take part in them would be timid enough to wait until then to make their first experiments in a thrill so easily available as sex. But even if they were, they certainly imposed a handicap upon themselves, for "sustained sexual activity would be [as] difficult to achieve" under the influence of marihuana as in delirium tremens.[1]

The Mayor's Committee, consisting of two internists, three psychiatrists, two pharmacologists, and various public officials in the fields of health and criminology, could find no direct relationship between crimes of violence and marihuana. They did not believe that the drug was habit-forming. They found very little marihuana-smoking among schoolchildren, and were unable to connect the practice with juvenile delinquency. They doubted that there was anything like an organized traffic in the drug. They found that an effective dose definitely impaired intellectual functioning, but did not change the basic personality. They could find no evidence to show that use of the drug led to permanent deterioration.[2]

It is probably a bad thing to smoke reefers. It is unquestionably a bad thing to talk nonsense.

One cannot examine the magic powers popularly ascribed to marihuana without at least mentioning its assumed effect on musicians. Certainly, many musicians think they play better under its influence. Milton Mezzrow writes: "Tea puts a musician in a real masterly sphere. . . . Nothing can mess you up. You hear everything at once and you hear it right." The notes, he says, slide out of the horn "like bubbles in seltzer water", and

---

[1] Wilson: *My Six Convicts*, p. 339.
[2] See *The Marihuana Problem in the City of New York* (Lancaster, Pa.: The Mayor's Committee on Marihuana; 1944).

the music has a richness and a "bigness" it otherwise lacks. Some
players have even gone to jail in their devotion to this conviction,
and even laymen have run risks. A citizen of Queens, New
York, who delights in the song of birds, explained to the police,
when arrested for growing marihuana, that he mixed it with
birdseed to improve the singing of his two hundred and eighty
pet canaries.[1]

But according to experiments conducted in 1944 by the
United States Public Health Service the playing of music, in so
far as it may be determined by ability to distinguish musical
intervals and rhythm, was not improved by the influence
of the drug, even though those taking the tests thought it was.
Critical acumen, however, seemed to be lessened, and that
may have produced some of the sensations that Mezzrow
describes.[2]

In the general furor over drugs, with each magazine and
newspaper seeking new terrors to expose, all sensible distinctions
have been abandoned. Almost any chemical that had a sedative
effect[3] was called a "drug", and the effect of all drugs was
presumed to be the same. Thus the readers of the *American
Weekly* were told that "subjugation" to barbiturates was "as
shattering as the confirmed use of morphine",[4] and many other
publications expressed or implied the same idea. As the use of
barbiturates is almost universal throughout the United States
now, such assertions must have caused a great deal of concern.
But those who were concerned may be consoled by the opinion
of Dr Walter C. Alvarez, one of the country's greatest internists.
Dr Alvarez says that such talk is absurd. He feels that barbiturate
addicts are few and far between, and screwballs to begin with.
The occasional use of a sleeping pill, in his opinion, is almost
unavoidable in our tense, unquiet urban life, and he believes that

[1] *Time*, October 15, 1951, p. 136.
[2] Milton Mezzrow and Bernard Wolfe: *Really the Blues* (New York:
Ramdon House; 1946). See a report by Dr C. Knight Aldrich, *U.S. Public
Health Reports*, March 31, 1944, pp. 431-3.
[3] They have touched very lightly on bromides (which really do have some
dangers), possibly because bromides have advertising dollars to spend.
[4] May 6, 1951, p. 4.

the normal person can continue such occasional use all his life
without any risk of addiction or any serious consequences to
himself.[1]

The professional addictophobes and the sensation-seeking
journalists reply to this by excitedly listing various people who
have died from overdoses of sleeping pills. But these people were
almost certainly neurotics who would have killed themselves
some other way if barbiturates had not been available. People—
many people—kill themselves with razor blades and by jumping
out of windows; yet you cannot therefore prohibit the sale of
razor blades or require all structures to be built without windows.
Society has to be ordered, primarily, for the normal.

So much for the narcotics. They, however, are only a part of
the lore of "drugs". There are aphrodisiacs and anaphrodisiacs,
abortifacients, "pep" pills, "truth" drugs, mysterious inoculations
that render women helpless in the hands of the white slaver, and
certain other gases or potions or emanations, designated merely as
"mysterious", which control men's wills and compel them to do
things

> . . . horrible and awfu',
> Which even to name wad be unlawfu'.

Love, which is more often in need of sedatives than stimulants,
has from the most ancient times been believed to be producible
by various drugs and foods. The list is endless: honey, seafoods,
truffles, onions, garlic, henbane, jimson weed, caper berries,
mandragora, chocolate, satyricon, and prunes are all standard
aphrodisiacs. More exotic are a gander's foot, a jackal's gall,
owl's flesh (which the Hindus believe will excite desire, but at
the same time turn a man to a fool; but, then, the two effects are
always inseparable), the essence of amber, the placenta of a new-
foaled mare, lodestone (the King of Siam, who had seven hundred concubines, had his cooking utensils made of magnetite),
menstrual blood, a mixture of mother's and daughter's milk, and

[1] "Little Danger in Barbiturates," the *Chicago Sun-Times*, May 29, 1953, section 2, p. 2.

salt.[1] There would seem, in fact, to be hardly any substance that could possibly be forced down the human gullet which has not at some time or other been recommended as an aphrodisiac; and in addition there are spells and medicines bought of mountebanks "by which the property of youth and maidhood may be abus'd".

Despite the almost universal belief, however, and despite a flourishing trade based on it, it is doubtful that there are any true aphrodisiacs beyond youth, health, and idleness. Alcohol and opium seem to lessen inhibitions and let nature take her course. Cantharides (Spanish fly) is thought to be infallible, but it is a dangerous, often fatal, vesicant, and the feelings it arouses must bear about the same relation to love as those engendered by stomach ulcers bear to a good appetite.

There are not quite as many anaphrodisiacs as aphrodisiacs, but the list is still curious and impressive. All "cooling" herbs, such as lettuce, cucumbers, gourds, and pumpkins, were, and by some yet are, considered to exercise a tranquillizing effect upon desire. Some herbals listed camphor, and the lapidaries specified topaz. There was formerly a quaintly reasonable belief in Yorkshire that a man could cure himself of thoughts of love by putting on a pair of new shoes and walking in them until he had worn them out.

That certain chemicals were secretly mixed with their food to dull their lust was a conviction held by almost all combatants during the war. The Americans believed that it was saltpetre (potassium nitrate). The English believed it was copper sulphate. The Germans thought their coffee was drugged. The French claimed their wine had been tampered with. Many of the women's auxiliary corps believed that bromides were put in their tea. Marie Bonaparte, in her *Myths of War*, states that feeling ran so high among the French soldiers that morale was endangered and Military Intelligence was compelled to make an

---

[1] A chamberpot filled with salt is, or until recently was, a common wedding present in northeast Scotland. There are a number of aphrodisiac cookbooks: Charles F. Heartman: *Aphrodisiac Culinary Manual* (New Orleans: The Gourmets' Company; 1942), *Cuisine de l'Amour* (New York; 1952); Pilaff Bey (said to be Norman Douglas): *Venus in the Kitchen*, with an introduction by Graham Green (London: William Heinemann; 1952).

investigation. The soldiers had complained that they were unable to obtain the enjoyment from their visiting wives which they had anticipated, and a formal demand was made that those about to go on leave or about to receive visitors should be allowed un-contaminated food. One frugal, angry poilu demanded that the state reimburse him the fifteen francs he had rashly given a prostitute in advance.[1]

There is no evidence, however, that any such substances were administered by any command or that they would have had the effect claimed for them if they had been. Physical exhaustion and fear are strong inhibitors of sex in their own right, and need no chemical support. It is interesting that among aviators, whose lives were especially dangerous, there was a very high degree of impotence, which was attributed to high-altitude flying or the breathing of oxygen.[2] Princess Bonaparte believes that there may have been an unconscious propitiatory gesture as well—such as is made consciously by many primitive warriors,[3] a submissive continence to placate the gods whose powers were so evident.

Aggrieved laymen are convinced that certain drugs will induce abortion and that all doctors know of these drugs, but will not divulge them. But, alas, the secret is that there are none! Thousands of women have died, and hundreds of thousands have been made dangerously ill, by taking ergot and quinine pills or apiol oil, or by administering to themselves or having administered to them potassium-iodide paste, without procuring the abortion for which they ran such awful risks.[4] When an abortion is therapeutically advisable, surgery is invariably employed.

[1] Marie Bonaparte: *Myths of War* (London: Imago Publishing Co.; 1947), pp. 52–8, 61.
[2] See Douglas Bond: *The Love and Fear of Flying* (New York: International Universities Press; 1952), p. 24; William C. Menninger· *Psychiatry in a Troubled World* (New York: The Macmillan Company; 1948), p. 107.
[3] 2 Sam. xi: 8–13. Poor Uriah!
[4] In 1898 the Chrimes Brothers, scoundrels of unusual villainy but also of unusual enterprise, sent out a form letter to between eight and ten thousand English matrons accusing them of committing or attempting to commit "the fearful crime of abortion" and demanding two guineas as the price of not exposing them. Of the 1,785 letters which the police intercepted, 413 contained money. E. S. Turner: *The Shocking History of Advertising!* (London: William Collins Sons & Co.; 1952), pp. 101–2.

A good illustration of the utter confusion of popular pharmacy is afforded by the practice, of which one often hears,[1] of putting benzedrine pills in liquor to give it an added "kick". The absurdity of the practice lies in the fact that the adrenalin-like substances, of which benzedrine is one, are recognized *antidotes* for an overdose of ethyl alcohol. Instead of adding to its effect, they definitely neutralize it. A man who has taken a benzedrine tablet will probably have difficulty getting drunk.

Even more absurd is the widespread custom of putting aspirin in Coca-Cola. Whatever it does, it won't provide a stimulant.

Throughout World War II there were continual rumours of new and mysterious drugs. It was said that German aviators were drugged so that they were indifferent to fatigue and high altitudes. When the great Belgian fortress of Eben Emael, which had been expected to hold out indefinitely, fell within a few days, it was said that the defenders had been sprayed with a "sleeping drug" that had laid them all in quiet slumbers while the Nazis swept in on gliders. The gliders gave it the little convincing touch of authenticity—no noisy engines to disturb the sleepers!

There has been great concern in the newspapers about "truth drugs", which the Russians were thought to be administering to those who confessed at their trials. Mrs Robert Vogeler was quoted as fearing that her husband had been drugged, and similar fears were expressed for William N. Oatis. The Hearst papers obtained a special admission from a Dr Hans Abend, in Berlin, the alleged inventor of these dreaded substances, that Stalin possessed drugs that could make "any living person, religious or not", confess publicly to anything whatever that it was desired to have him admit.[2]

These alarms reached their crescendo in the case of Cardinal Mindszenty, who, according to the English Roman Catholic

[1] See Alson J. Smith: "Is Prohibition Coming Back?" the *American Mercury*, October 1948, p. 462.
[2] This is a game that two can play. Unfriendly English accounts accused the Trenton, New Jersey, police of giving drugged cigarettes to the six Negroes accused of murdering William Horner. See the *Nation*, March 12, 1949, p. 290.

weekly *The Tablet*, had been fed "actedron" before his trial. The *Tablet* was most explicit, and even gave a detailed account of the procedure of the drug's administration. The accused was denied food until he was hungry, and then for two weeks was fed on salt fish only and denied all water. This, naturally, made him so thirsty that when he was finally offered water he did not notice that a small tablet of "potent nerve-destroying actedron" had been dissolved in it. The *Tablet* did not share the folly of the American papers by calling the drug a "truth drug", as that would have granted the factual accuracy of His Eminence's confession; they called it a "will-destroying" drug that left its victim with neither judgment nor memory, "a deadly paralysed vacuum in his head", and "psychologically incapable of saying no to anything".[1]

The force of these allegations was greatly weakened, though, when Vogeler and Oatis, on their release, both insisted that they had been given no drugs at all. And "actedron" was hastily forgotten as soon as it was known that it is merely benzedrine or, colloquially, "pep pills". Hundreds of thousands of American college students have taken these before their final examinations, and while many of them have certainly demonstrated "a deadly paralysed vacuum" in their heads the next day, few have showed any compulsion to be factually accurate or even to repeat what was expected of them.

Medical scientists doubt that any such drugs as "truth drugs" exist. Electroshock treatments sometimes cause a temporary loss of memory, but that would not make the patient deny anything he had said in the past. Scopolamine and morphine might also induce some loss of memory and produce pleasurable dreams, but these would not constitute a confession, and anyone under their influence would show it on the witness stand. Benzedrine addicts are often aggressive and irritable, but they are not unusually suggestible or unable to lie if they want to.[2]

The belief in "truth drugs" may be supported by the generally

---

[1] The *New York Times*, January 22, 1949, p. 4.
[2] *Science News Letter*, March 5, 1949, p. 153.

accepted belief that patients undergoing operations babble their
dearest secrets while under the anaesthetic. Dr Henry K. Beecher,
anaesthetist-in-chief of the Massachusetts General Hospital, in
Boston, says this belief is widespread enough (and, apparently,
hidden crimes are also widespread enough) to cause a great deal
of concern to those contemplating operations.

Dr Beecher says, however, that the concern is needless. It is
rare for people to talk at all when anaesthetized, and there is no
reason why they should say anything then that they would not
say at any other time. "There is no evidence at all," Dr Beecher
insists, "that you can get wilfully suppressed information out of
people with drugs."[1]

One of the most deep-rooted of folk fears in relation to drugs
is that a woman will suddenly be given an injection that will
render her helpless and that she will then be carried away by
sinister people for evil purposes, to be seen by her loved ones no
more. Linda, the heroine of Nancy Mitford's *Pursuit of Love*,
finding herself alone and without funds in the Gare du Nord, is
suddenly alarmed at the thought that some "genial-looking old
woman" might approach her, give her a hypodermic injection,
and bear her off into the white-slave traffic of South America.

Many women share these fantasies of painless ravishment and
there is no lack of anecdotes to support their apprehensions. One
of the commonest is about a girl who goes alone to a movie. An
older woman sits down in the next seat and, when the young
thing is absorbed in the picture, suddenly gives her an injection
of a powerful drug that leaves her helpless but fully conscious.
She then calls an usher and tells him that the girl is her daughter
and is having one of the "fits" to which she is unfortunately
subject. The usher and often a sympathetic manager help the
hellish harridan carry her victim to a taxi and a life worse than
death.

Just before Mrs Oksana Kasenkina's frightful leap from the
window of the Russian consulate in New York revealed the full
measure of her tragic desperation, she had been regarded in some

[1] The *New York Times*, February 24, 1953, 20:7.

sections of the press as a wacky figure of fun. *Time*, in a gay piece entitled "Whites? Reds? Call the Feds!" quoted Mrs Kasenkina as saying that "a man named Leo Costello had lured her to a park bench on Riverside Drive and deftly plunged a hypodermic needle into her arm. Then everything had gone black".[1]

Time was justified in being sceptical of at least that much of Mrs Kasenkina's testimony. No drug is known that acts so quickly except pentathol, and that must be administered intravenously. And any man or woman who could make an intravenous injection on a park bench or across the seat arms in a darkened movie, through clothing and without the subject's consent, is possessed of a manipulative skill so rare that he or she ought to be able to find a more remunerative occupation than shanghai-ing.

The needle is the modern equivalent of the old Mickey Finn, which—while it may not have been wholly the fable that some have suspected it was[2]—was probably administered more in fiction than in fact. The effective ingredient, chloral hydrate, has a harsh and nauseating taste that even the pharmacopœia admits "is not easily disguised". Some say that it can be concealed in pure gin or white mule, and others insist that the Mickey Finn wasn't administered until the prospect was past being able to taste anything. Both may be so, but both militate against the legend. For a man was always "slipped" a Mickey Finn; the whole idea was that, sound of mind and body, and taking, as he assumed, his ease in his inn, he was suddenly struck down by the mysterious potion.

[1] August 16, 1948, p. 20.
[2] Amongst them Howard Riley Raper, in his *Man Against Pain* (New York: Prentice Hall; 1945).

CHAPTER 17

Cursed Hebenon

DESPITE the vast concern with drugs, there is not much popular interest in poisons any more. The gun has shifted the art of the homicide to the getaway. None the less, a few speculations and legends about poisons are worth a passing notice. One still hears, occasionally, that large doses of some poisons are less fatal than small doses. Ground glass is persistently administered to loved ones under the illusion that it is lethal. Sea water is often said to be poisonous, and, as dry ice comes into more general use, there are uneasy rumours about it. The arsenic-eaters live on in the Sunday papers, and there are a few remnants of the old beliefs in vegetable poisons and homicidal trees.

Paul Reichelderfer, in John O'Hara's *A Rage to Live*, utters a common fallacy when he says: "A small dose of some drugs will kill you, but a big dose won't have any more effect than a glass of Benedictine." He is a college man and a Phi Beta Kappa, and his illusion is probably peculiar to the *cognoscenti*—a statement which, since few would be inclined to test it, would pass unchallenged in most company and earn for its utterer the reputation of being a man of vast and unusual knowledge. Pharmacologists, however, would not agree. An excess of poison has sometimes induced vomiting so quickly that most of the poison has been ejected before it could do much harm. But that's another thing.

It is curious how persistent is the belief that powdered glass is poisonous. Rarely does a year pass without there being a murder

trial in which it comes out that someone has been feeding someone else ground glass. Cellini was fed some ground glass. Forty
years ago the Gaekwar of Baroda was suspected of feeding
powdered diamonds to Colonel Phayre, the British Resident. In
1952 Mme Léon Schneider was formally accused of mashing up
light bulbs in her husband's lunch.[1] And so it continues from
year to year.

Efforts to refute the fallacy have been as persistent as the belief
and as unavailing as the substance. Sir Thomas Browne doubted
it, "from the innocency of the ingredients", and fed a dog above
a dram thereof, "subtilely powdered in butter and paste", without
any visible disturbance ensuing. Sir Richard Mead, George II's
physician, an authority on poisons, said that if anyone would give
him two large diamonds, he would be happy to crush one and eat it.

Splinters of glass will, of course, cut the walls of the stomach
and intestines, and various unpleasant consequences, including
death, will probably ensue from these lacerations; but this is a
mechanical injury, not a poison, and it is difficult to introduce
very many splinters of glass surreptitiously into someone else's
stomach. Powdered glass can be introduced, in mushes and puddings, and those who are not finicky about their food or daren't
complain, or who have been prepared by a course of progressively
grittier mushes and puddings, may eat it. But it will have no
serious effect. Indeed, it was recommended, not too long ago, as
a specific for worms, and we all probably ingest a certain amount
of powdered silicon every day. Powdered glass is one of the most
inert of substances, and is more likely to cause acute mental discomfort to those who administer it—as they see their victims
living blithely on—than physical discomfort to those to whom it
is administered.

Dry ice is new enough to have some of the terror of the strange
about it. Its fuming and spluttering suggest something actively
malignant; the freeze-that-feels-like-a-burn that it inflicts is
mysteriously evil. And, needless to say, if one could possibly, somehow, manage to swallow a piece, the effects would probably be

[1] *Time*, May 19, 1952, p. 42.

spectacularly fatal. But, all the same, it is not a poison. We have its substance inside us all the time and go to trouble and expense to get more in. It is simply carbon dioxide—the substance that triggers the mechanism of our breathing and gives carbonated beverages their burpful lure. There are instances in which sufficient carbon dioxide has been released by the melting of dry ice in a confined space—as in closed cars crossing the desert—to limit the amount of oxygen available to less than what is necessary to sustain life; but that is a form of smothering, and makes dry ice, in itself, no more poisonous than a feather mattress or a pillow.

One often hears that sea water, if drunk, will cause one to go mad. Yet sea water was formerly taken (usually early in the morning, fasting) as a purgative, and millions of sportive sea-bathers have swallowed millions of pints of it without demonstrating any madness other than that which took them into the surf to begin with.

Because sea water will not slake thirst, but only intensify it, and will produce severe gastritis to boot, a man suffering from thirst would probably have to be out of his mind to drink it. And that may be the true order of events: shipwrecked men have their minds unsettled through starvation, exhaustion, and exposure, and then drink sea water.

Shipwrecked men have—by the way, and to answer a question often canvassed in poolroom symposia—drunk urine over fairly protracted periods without too severe ill effects. The publications of the Hakluyt Society contain many instances. Among the Chuckchee and Koryaks, tribes inhabiting the area adjoining the Bering Strait, urine-drinking is a part of a social custom. The rich among them take fly agaric for its narcotic effects. The poor have discovered that the muscarine, the essential alkaloid of the drug, is not destroyed in its passage through the kidneys and get their jag by drinking the urine of their more fortunate friends.[1]

While on the subject of unsavoury potations, one has to take cognizance of the assertion that Bedouins and other desert wanderers habitually slaughter their camels for the water in their

[1] Taylor: *Flight from Reality,* pp. 170-1.

stomachs. Thus *Time*'s Frederick Gruin, describing the "mirage-haunted" desert of Sinkiang, noted that "the track through it is marked by carcasses and bleached bones of camels slaughtered by Kazak wanderers for the water in their stomachs.[1]

It may be. Camels do store a surplus of water (though not as much as is commonly supposed), and Prohibition showed us that human beings will drink almost anything. But, even so, killing camels for a drink must be a fairly rare practice, and it is a matter of great satisfaction to be able to record an account of the process by what must be one of the few educated Europeans who has ever had a chance to witness it.

Mr Bodo Oberg writes from Huasco, Hidalgo, Mexico,[2] that from 1906 to 1912 he was an officer in the Colonial Forces of the then German Southwest Africa, where he worked for years with imported North African camels. From time to time it was necessary to kill some of these beasts because of their sicknesses or injuries. Making a virtue of necessity, he seized the opportunity "for examining the improbable tale of the water reservoir".

> In these cases (he writes) we had them watered for the last time a few days before the killing, and had the stomachs treated appropriately by Bushmen: they hanged up the stomach, perforated it in a determined spot and closed the opening again with a kind of strainer made of grass. Then indeed some water dripped out. Bushmen are quite accustomed to this technique of getting water even out of antelopes' (Beisa or Oryx) stomachs, animals that live on the driest steppes on even less water than a camel lives on. . . .
>
> A camel's stomach treated in this way, about five days after the last watering, actually rendered about as much as a gallon and a half of liquid. It had, of course, body temperature. It was slimy, turbid, mixed with particles of fodder, and smelled repugnantly sour. . . .

[1] *Time*, October 20, 1947, in one of those moving "Letters from the Publisher" in which the reader is informed of the difficulties which the staff has gallantly surmounted.
[2] In a personal communication, dated October 19, 1947.

We must admit, therefore, that indeed a camel's stomach contains a certain quantity of conditionally drinkable water and that the old legend has a nucleus of truth. But the practical value of this fact is another question. For even half dead with thirst a traveller will have more hope of saving his life with a live mount than with a dead water reservoir. It is logical to suppose that he would sacrifice his animal only if it became useless to him anyway, say, due to an accident.

Mr Gruin, after surveying the ossueous wastes, adds that he himself drank neither camel's chyle nor antelope's blood (another desert delicacy), but quenched his thirst "more prosaically with Sinkiang's wonderfully succulent melons" obtainable "at oasis towns along the way". But if these *are* obtainable, the Kazaks seem to have been a little hasty.

Returning to poisons—there is an established conviction that potassium cyanide is the perfect poison for suicide, because it acts so quickly that the taker is dead before he can experience any unpleasant sensations. Shelley spoke of it as "the golden key to the chamber of perpetual rest". As most people who have taken it have died very soon after doing so, and as very few people attempt to poison themselves in public, there is not much evidence to go on, but what there is suggests that death from cyanide poisoning is anything but comfortable. H. L. Mencken says that it was the frequent choice of drunk and despondent engravers, who had access to the substance in their work, but that everyone who tried it "passed away in a tumultuous fit and made a great deal of noise". Nor is it now invariably fatal. More than twenty persons are known to have swallowed potassium cyanide and to have recovered.[1]

Mithridates is said to have so saturated himself with poisons, in order to develop immunities and foil those who might try to poison him, that when, after his defeat by Pompey, he had

[1] H. L. Mencken: *Newspaper Days* (New York: Alfred A. Knopf; 1941), p. 173. For the recoveries, see an article by Dr Morris Fishbein, the *Chicago Sun-Times*, July 22, 1949, p. 39.

occasion to try poisoning himself, he was unable to do so and had to order a Gallic mercenary to stab him.

The great modern legend of immunity to poison is that of a group of "arsenic-eaters", generally located in Styria, a province of Austria, or the Tyrol. Lay and learned journals alike testify to the remarkable powers of these remarkable people. It seems that they have discovered that a constant absorption of arsenic (they take it, we are told, in the form of arsenic trioxide) gives their women uncommon beauty and their men, by a happy reciprocity, uncommon vigour and powers of endurance. They have been at it for years and, according to Dr Edward M. Marten, are now born with "an inherited tolerance"—thus going Mithridates one better.[1]

The only drawback to their felicity is that the poison is habit-forming, and while it seems to have no ill effects, failure to continue its use can be fatal—the deprived addict withering away before your very eyes, like the ancient girl in *Lost Horizon*, into the senility and feebleness theretofore evaded. The Austrian government has "of course" tried to put down the practice, but without success. Arsenic is bootlegged into the valleys, where the peasants "spread it on bread and eat it as they would butter".

Incidentally, the excessive beauty of the women or the excessive vigour of the men has led to an extraordinarily high homicide rate among these folk, where murder is safe and sure. You simply invite a fellow arsenic-eater to dinner and maliciously spread the trioxide on his bread a little in excess of his known tolerance. (Apparently there are five-gram men and six-gram men among them, as there used to be five-bottle men and six-bottle men among the Georgian squires.) The autopsy reveals arsenical poisoning, all right, but no jury of addicts will bring in a verdict of murder merely because one of the brethren has over-indulged.

But the credulous are advised to ask one or two questions before they start spreading arsenic on their morning toast. Why,

[1] See Edward M. Marten: *The Doctor Looks at Murder* (New York: Doubleday, Doran & Company; 1937), pp. 160–5.

for instance, is this fortunate adaptability confined to the inhabitants of this one locality? Why do people elsewhere display such dreadful discomfort and grow more ugly and more feeble, vomit, bleed, and lose their hair when they take the least little bit of it? If immunity can be developed, why have there been outbursts of arsenical poisoning in various manufactures where the absorption must have begun with far more minute doses than the Styrians could even measure? How do some people get *chronic* arsenical poisoning? Farmers have been poisoned merely by drinking a few glasses of cistern water after their orchards have been sprayed with an arsenic compound and the wind has blown some of the dust on to their roofs. The miners of Reichenstein, which is pretty close to the Tyrol and not far from Styria, are constantly exposed to a fine powdered arsenic. Unless they are a different species from their neighbours, they should be vigorous and lusty. But they are not. They have cramps, rickets, anæmia, and dropsy. They die young.

If there is anything to this arsenic-eating legend, let's quit wasting our national energies on atomic power and such trifles. Let our manufacturers get to work on the mass production of arsenic trioxide. Most of us have been ugly and feeble long enough.

Except for the impervious-gutted Styrians, arsenic is known to be pretty bad medicine because it is a mineral poison. There is a strong popular belief that minerals are bad, vegetables good. The patent-medicine vendor has always stressed the fact that his nostrums were prepared from herbs—usually from the secret formula of some aged sachem who had spent his life in Nature's bosom. Herb teas and certain mild cathartics derived from herbs have strengthened the general faith in the "wholesomeness" of vegetable derivatives.

Vegetable substances are also thought to be "cleaner" and "purer" than animal substances. Dr Johnson—in an unexpected pronouncement on an unlikely contingency—said that if he ever kept a harem he would dress all the ladies in linen, as more suited to the delicacy and purity he would expect to prevail amongst them. Cottolene, a vegetable shortening, made much in its advertising of the fact that it came from cotton bolls ("one giant mass of roses pure and white, with dewy buds 'mid dark green foliage nursed"), whereas lard, its chief competitor, was derived from the greasy fat of "mud-incrusted swine". The special odour that saints give off, we are told by authorities on these matters, is vegetable, "as of a storehouse of every kind of sweet flowers".[1]

Generalizations are dangerous, however. There are mildly beneficent minerals, such as sodium bicarbonate; while some of the most deadly poisons—strychnine, cocaine, atropine, hyoscine, and aconite—are vegetable.

Where Nature must, for her own inscrutable reasons, grow a poisonous plant, she takes care—in folklore, at least—to have its antidote grow close by, a beneficent provision that makes one wonder why she developed the poisonous plant in the first place. The example most often presented is the dock leaf as a cure for the sting of a nettle. "When stung," a correspondent writes to *Time*, concerning the nettle, "stand still and look: the antidote is always found with it, namely the leaf of the yellow dock. The cure is instant."[2] Others adduce "snakeweed", a mythical plant to which wild animals "unerringly" go for "a sure cure" when they have been bitten by a rattlesnake. Others have pointed out that quinine comes from countries in which there is malaria and that willows grow in damp places where the rheumatic dwell, and that from willows may be obtained a medicine decidedly good for rheumatism. There is no end, though, to this sort of thing. It might as well be pointed out that brambles grow near poison oak so that he who is poisoned by the oak may scratch himself on the bramble. Or one may regard the ague, as Mark Twain suggested, as Providence's means of giving the shiftless dwellers in the river bottoms exercise without exertion.

[1] MacCulloch: *Medieval Faith and Fable*, pp. 89–90. A saint is perceptible, down wind, for about a mile.
[2] *Time*, February 2, 1948, p. 4. The correspondent is supported by a score of proverbs. There is a very dangerous belief that eating the leaves of poison ivy will cure the skin rash a touch induces. It will not.

The sad fact is that some of the most virulent poisons known are of vegetable origin and there is no antidote for them. The most poisonous of all poison plants that have ever proliferated in the imagination of men is the Upas tree. It was slow of growth, and in so far as it had a seed it seems to have grown from the knowledge that the natives of Java and Sumatra tipped their arrows with an especially virulent vegetable poison. Upon the sprout of conjecture that grew from that knowledge was grafted an ancient legend that there was a tree that "shed venom" so that it was fatal to sleep beneath it.[1]

These and other hints were brought together by one Foersch, who professed to have been a surgeon in Sumatra, and published a description of the tree in the *London Magazine* for December 1783. Foersch has never been identified, and there is a suspicion that he was actually George Steevens, a whimsical scholar much given to erudite practical jokes—such as writing obscene notes upon Shakespeare and attributing them to various clergymen. The article—whoever was the author—made a strong impression on Erasmus Darwin, Charles's grandfather, who set down a gruesome account of the mythical tree in the second part of his extraordinary poem *The Botanic Garden*. In this account the tree reached its full stature, and from it all subsequent accounts have been derived. No living thing, Darwin stated, could exist within miles of the Upas tree. It stood in the midst of a blasted heath, decorated with bleaching bones.[2] In the sand were footprints leading to, but none away from, its lethal trunk. The very air above it was poisoned, and birds that attempted to fly over it fell dead into its branches.

The Botanic Garden was a source book for the romantic poets, and the Upas tree passed from it to Blake, Coleridge, Byron, and Pushkin. It was a fine metaphor for romantic despair. Blake saw it as the human mind. Byron saw it as life itself, doomed with its

---

[1] See Dryden's *Aurengzebe* (1685), Act IV.
[2] Erasmus Darwin did not know that decomposition, necessary to strip the bones of their flesh, is the work of living organisms. As there could have been no scavenging animals and no bacteria near the tree, its victims would simply lie there until Gabriel sent some saprophytes.

"ineradicable taint of sin". Coleridge at one time thought of writing about "a whole forest of Upas trees" but abandoned the idea, fortunately, in favour of *The Ancient Mariner*.

From the poets the concept seeped down to the politicians and the editors. It was for two or three generations a favourite metaphor of the learned, but gradually fell into complete disuse as progress and optimism became the more conventional modes of thought. It was last heard from—a sort of dying hiccup, a last spasmodic twitch—in 1947 in a letter to the London *Times* by two Americans, in which President Roosevelt's policies were compared, in their balefulness, to the Upas tree.[1]

In so far as the contemporary imagination has concerned itself with vegetable horrors, it has been in the direction of exaggerating the power of some of the carnivorous plants, of which there are more than four hundred species. Science has not yet discovered one that eats anything larger than insects (though birds, mice, and lizards are claimed to have been among their victims), but the very thought of the much-eaten vegetables turning, in however limited a degree, upon their animal devourers is too delightfully terrifying not to be exploited.

The most impressive fictional use of the idea was in a novel entitled *The Devil-Tree of Eldorado*. Here the tree, a "gigantic vegetable octopus" with sucker-equipped branches hundreds of feet long, writhes in endless quest of prey and hisses most dismally when disappointed. This particular species was a bloodsucker that cast "the fleshy, bloodless husks" of its victims from its fibrous maw when it had drained them. They were not wasted, however, but instantaneously and avidly seized and devoured by "myroglams", a kind of dinosaur that had survived in symbiosis with the tree.

A more scientific account of a man-eating tree was furnished to its readers by the *American Weekly* on September 26, 1920, in a gripping narrative by Dr Carle Liche, who claimed to have seen a young girl eaten by a plant in Madagascar in 1878. The

[1] Mentioned by Mr Geoffrey Grigson in a talk on the Upas tree over the Third Programme of the BBC, June 15, 1947.

victim, who was represented in the illustrations as a lissome, naked blonde with bobbed, marcelled hair, was a member of the cruel tribe of "Mkodos", an outfit that inhabited a forest described, in a phrase that came nearer to truth than anything else in the story, as "practically unknown".

Five years later, in the issue for January 4, 1925, the *American Weekly* was able to present corroboration of its earlier narrative. A Mississippian, Mr W. C. Bryant, had had an encounter with a man-eating tree and had managed to escape with his life and to carry the tale of his adventures to the offices of the *Weekly*. It seems that he had been exploring a "tabooed" mesa on the island of Mindanao in the Philippines when one of these trees had suddenly reached for him with writhing leaves and a great hissing sound, and he had been saved from its deadly grasp only by the presence of mind of a devoted guide, who had knocked him down and dragged him to safety. Bryant himself had been in a sort of stupor, for the tree exuded a subtle soporific.

In the illustrations accompanying this article, the tree was shown with skulls and an entire human skeleton impaled and bleaching on its greedy branches. Some questions were raised by sceptical readers[1] as to the strict accuracy of the account, and the author, in an answering letter, confessed that the drawing had not been meticulously exact. The ground under the tree, as he remembered it, was not as uncomfortably bestrewn with skulls, for example, as the over-zealous illustrator had pictured it; on the contrary, it was smooth and soft, "very inviting to a storm-beset or sun-depressed traveller". And the hissing sound, he believed, proceeded from "a gluey consistence of, or on, the leaves", and not, as certain over-imaginative folk might have thought, from any ferocious inhalations or expirations of the plant.[2]

---

[1] A sceptical reader of the Sunday supplements is the mental equivalent of the one-armed paperhanger.

[2] See Richard Clements: "Truth about Man-Eating Plants," *Discovery* (London), August 1948; Earl Welch: "Man-Eating Trees? Could Be!" *Pageant*, December 1947–January 1948, pp. 58–60; and, especially, Sophia Prior: *Carnivorous Plants and "The Man-Eating Tree"* (Chicago: Botany Leaflet 23, Field Museum of Natural History; 1939).

With these minor corrections the story seems to have reached a stasis. Perhaps it has achieved classic perfection and can go no further. The nude young blonde, anaesthetized and helpless, encircled by the tentacles that embrace, suck, and stab, fulfills all longings of the popular psyche. Lust and pain. Love and death. "Could Be!" *Pageant* defiantly asserted, re-telling the tale in 1948.

CHAPTER EIGHTEEN

The Law is Not Wholly an Ass

THE COMMON man's remedy for all social ills is to pass a law
against them. "There ought to be a law" is the infallible
formula of disapproval; and judges, legislators, and the
Executive labour mightily, in edicts, injunctions, proscriptions,
directives, statutes, ordinances, acts, rules, and regulations, to
meet the popular demand—though sin and crime, often with
assistance from some of the same legislators, seem to flourish as
vigorously as ever.

This is explained, in the vulgar conception, by the existence of
a parcel of rogues known as lawyers, a parasitic tribe that in some
inexplicable way has managed to interpose itself between the
ordering and administering of justice, where it deliberately
obscures plain intent and creates, to its own profit, interminable
delay. The common man has no terms of opprobrium strong
enough to describe the knavish members of this group. They are
greedy rascals who refute good words with gibberish, draw unwarranted deductions from "circumstantial evidence", prefer
precedent to justice, and reverse sensible decisions merely because
a word is misspelled or a comma out of place.

A plurality of accusations, however, like a plurality of excuses,
often conceals the real meaning, and one suspects that the actual
sin of the lawyer and the true basis of the popular aversion to him
is that he is an intellectual. He is interested in classifications and
categories and logic. He has had—however brief and blurred—

a glimpse of the concept of justice. He is a champion of civilization against barbarism in that he seeks to have men live by reason, order, and custom, and, almost alone in our society, understands what is meant by the common weal.

Unlike the other two great intellectual classes to which the common man must turn in his hours of fright and pain, the clergy and the physicians, the lawyer cannot shroud himself in mystery or threaten censure with Hell-fire or disease. The priest and the doctor deal largely with people made docile by fear. The lawyer deals largely with people belligerent and rash with anger, vindictive with disappointment, and aggressive with greed. That some lawyers have profited from the confusions of the law, have split hairs and made the worse appear the better reason, there can be little doubt. But there have never been enough crooked lawyers to meet the demand. No lawyer, says one of them, "has engaged in half the amount of procedural chicanery which clients would like to have exerted in their behalf. When it comes to sheer obstruction, lawyers have actually had to keep clients in check".[1]

The last is particularly interesting, because delay is one of the chief charges that the layman constantly brings against the lawyer. "The law's delay" is listed by Hamlet, in his famous soliloquy,[2] as one of the major burdens of existence.

But it may be questioned whether delay is inherent in the law or even in the predilections of lawyers. The structure of society must bear some of the blame, and the structure of a democratic society must bear a great deal of the blame. The demand that cops and judges "get tough" with criminals, for instance, which one frequently hears from solid citizens (except when the citizens happen to get arrested themselves), is not likely to be gratified so long as we seek to defend the liberties of the individual. The Founding Fathers were all criminals in the eyes of the then-

[1] William Seagle: *Law, the Science of Inefficiency* (New York: The Macmillan Company; 1952), p. 65.
[2] Shakespeare was involved in litigation and no doubt knew whereof he spoke, but, as Dr Johnson observed, this particular complaint was inappropriate in the mouth of the heir apparent to the throne.

established government, and they seem to have deliberately designed a constitution to block and limit the power of the police. It would look as if they thought—rightly or wrongly—that efficient police were a greater menace to liberty than some unpunished criminals. Indeed, some men have gone so far, bolstering their statement with dicta from Supreme Court judges, as to assert that "The inefficiency of the criminal law is the pride of democracy".[1]

It's all, really, in the point of view. The law's delays may be a burden to the plaintiff, but most defendants welcome them, and when any group or class consists of those who will normally be defendants in litigation, that group or class will do what it can to make litigation a protracted and expensive business. The landed gentry were such a class, and the incredibly protracted legislation of the nineteenth century was the result. Corporations are in the same position today. Seagle estimates that "the chances that a corporation will be a defendant rather than a plaintiff in litigation are probably at least 100 to 1", and says that, in consequence, corporation lawyers would probably "render the machinery of justice completely impotent" were it not that their clients also, occasionally, have to appear as plaintiffs.[2]

Legal phraseology is usually infuriating to the common man, who doesn't see why "a plain fact shouldn't be plainly stated"—though the same common man will hear commercials refer to product as "superior" or "better" without demanding to know "superior to *what*?" or "better than *what*?"

Swift, with his usual vigour, expressed the popular view in *Gulliver*:

"It is likewise to be observed," Gulliver tells his Houyhnhnm master, "that this society [of lawyers] hath a peculiar cant and jargon of their own that no other mortal can understand, wherein all their laws are written, which they take special care to multiply; whereby they have wholly confounded the very essence of truth and falsehood, of right and wrong."

[1] Seagle: *Law, the Science of Inefficiency*, pp. 102–3.
[2] Seagle: *Law, the Science of Inefficiency*, p. 68.

The old law French, which was still somewhat in use in Swift's day, would have justified the first part of this charge, but the second is a cherished fallacy. Half the civil suits that come before our courts grow out of the obscurity of "plain" language. The wording of legal documents may be tedious, polysyllabic, repetitious, cacophonic, and humourless, but to anyone not panic-stricken at the sound of "whereas", it usually makes the meaning clearer than it otherwise would be. "The party of the second part" may be cumbrous, and it may be exasperating to have to pay a lawyer to write it, but "him" will eventually fatten a dozen lawyers.

None the less, to the aggrieved litigant legal terminology remains studied pedantry, a part and parcel of the mentality that delights in quibbling and finds a typographical error sufficient reason for reversing a decision.

Actually, cases are never reversed on trifling grounds, though sometimes, more so formerly than today, trifling grounds were used to justify changes that had deeper motivations. Thus, a century or so ago in England, when the bloody book of the law was being read to its cruellest letter, when children were being hanged for stealing rabbits and labourers deported for trying to form labour unions, savage verdicts were sometimes reversed on technicalities. But in most of these cases the error, as Max Radin has said, "was only a pretext".[1] Today appellate courts from time to time reverse verdicts in criminal cases, but never on such trivial grounds as is popularly imagined.

Serious grounds may, of course, seem trivial to the untrained or prejudiced mind, and the papers, in presenting an account of any reversal, "play up" the popular delusion if they can. Thus even the *New York Times* in its report of the dismissal of a

---

[1] In 1841 the House of Lords dismissed charges against the insufferable Lord Cardigan (later to lead the charge of the Light Brigade at Balaclava) for shooting Captain Tuckett in a duel because Captain Tuckett was named in the indictment as Harvey Garnett Phipps Tuckett; whereas no witness could identify the man shot as anything but Harvey Tuckett. But this wasn't the work solely of lawyers; it was the Lords highhandedly defending their privileges. See Cecil Woodham-Smith: *The Reason Why* (London: Constable & Company; 1953), pp. 79–82.

first-degree manslaughter indictment against James Harrison, by Judge Samuel S. Leibowitz, in 1948, shaped the whole story to emphasize the fact that it was the "omission of a question mark in a stenographic report of an alleged statement" made by Harrison, after his arrest for the fatal stabbing of his wife, that led to Judge Leibowitz's action.[1] This is exactly the sort of thing that the indignant layman expects, and the headlines must have caused many a snort and exclamation of disgust. But the full story made it plain that the question mark was by no means a trifle. In the stenographic record Harrison was made to say: "I had intentions of stabbing her———", a clear admission of that premeditation which can make all the difference between life and death for the accused. Whereas, it seems, he had actually exclaimed in horror, rejecting a suggestion of premeditation in a rhetorical question: "I had intentions of stabbing her?" So that the question mark was not a mere flourish of punctuation, but something which made the distinction between a confession and a denial.

The weight that precedent carries with judges is often another source of annoyance to the layman—unless, of course, the precedent happens to be in his favour. And again Swift has given the layman's resentment one of its clearest expressions.

"It is a maxim among lawyers," Gulliver went on, "that whatever hath been done may legally be done again: and therefore they take special care to record all the decisions formerly made against common justice and the general reason of mankind. These, under the name of *precedents*, they produce as authorities, to justify the most iniquitous opinions; and the judges never fail of directing accordingly."

Even when the worst case possible is made out against appeal to precedent, however, it remains the lesser of two evils and, despite its limitations, is one of the cornerstones of justice. Law is what the courts will say it is, and men risk their fortunes every day on the assumption that the courts will be consistent. "Consistency," Max Radin has said in *The Law and Mr Smith*, "is a

[1] The *New York Times*, March 31, 1948.

real and powerful constituent of justice . . . and [an] abstract
consideration of justice that does not take that fact into account
misses the essence of its search." Appeal to precedent may sometimes perpetuate injustice; but a disregard of precedent would
produce chaos and destroy all justice.

The popular mistrust of "circumstantial" evidence is basically
anti-intellectual, a hatred of logic and a dislike of trained experts,
though usually disguised as a desire for "proof" or even "fair
play". Evidence may be direct or circumstantial. Evidence is
direct when sworn to by persons having actual knowledge of the
facts in issue—the witness actually saw the crime committed or
saw the accident. Circumstantial evidence is evidence upon facts
other than those directly in issue in the trial, but from which, by
human experience, the facts in issue may be inferred and thereby
proved. Both can be misleading, but no one who has had much
experience with human testimony would hesitate to accept circumstantial evidence. If an automobile, for example, had been
wrecked in such a way that it would have been impossible to
move it before the police got there, and if the police show photographs that include eighty-foot skidmarks on a level pavement
leading directly to the wrecked car, few opponents of circumstantial evidence would accept the assurance of the driver that he
was going only twenty miles an hour.

There is considerable confusion in the common mind between
moral and legal "oughts", and those who believe in a "higher"
law (of which they themselves are usually the interpreter) often
feel that the "lower" law is no better than chicanery. A strong
article of their faith is that actions should be judged by their
intent rather than by their consequences. They feel that if one
means well, any damage that may occur through misdirected
zeal should be overlooked. But the law cannot always overlook
damage merely because the feasor blundered or was ignorant.
The well-meaning one may find nothing in his own conscience
with which to reproach himself, but he can still have done a great
deal of harm to another, and the other is entitled to redress. Men
and women—to choose a very common instance—who have been

slightly hurt in automobile accidents have often been seriously injured by the zealous ministrations of the misguided helpful, and the law must offer protection against fools as well as against knaves.[1]

One frequently hears in America an assurance that the laws are better in England, and especially that they are "better enforced" there, but any sweeping generalization to that effect may be challenged. It all depends. They certainly hang convicted murderers with dispatch; but whether their briskness in this particular business is admirable or not must surely depend on whether one identifies oneself with the hanged or the hangman. Mr Troy B. Sturgill, who, when running for sheriff of Floyd County, Kentucky, in 1953, urged the mothers of the county to vote for him because he would not abuse their sons when he arrested them, had, at least, a democratic outlook.[2]

In some other respects, British laws might be regarded as inferior to American. Their laws governing real estate are infinitely more complicated than ours. Their divorce laws are antiquated and oppressive, and practically compel collusion and perjury—though the same charge may be made against some of the states in the United States. And British laws governing libel can be used—and have been used—to stifle what in the United States would be regarded as normal freedom of speech. Crime is increasing in England at about the same rate as here, though their "wave" was a little slower getting started. They have fewer per capita murders than we do (George Ade said that was because they overlooked some good opportunities), but theft, robbery, rape, and assault are as flourishing there as with us. Their coming later to these deplorable activities may be owing to fewer automobiles, to fewer guns, to the fact that they escaped Prohibition and had to wait for the coupon system of World War II to destroy their morals, or simply to their conservative natures and sedative climate.[3]

---

[1] Prosser: *Handbook of the Law of Torts*, pp. 220–1.
[2] *Time*, July 27, 1953, pp. 10–11.
[3] Perhaps the most commendable principle of British law is that "The Crown cannot win and the Crown cannot lose." The sole function of the British prosecutor is to find justice not, as so often with us, to procure political advancement for himself by securing convictions.

Among the more noble and pathetic delusions concerning law must be listed "International Law", a term used so frequently that men and women who innocently believe that such a thing exists and allow themselves to become indignant at those who "violate" it are certainly to be excused. But by what consent or conquest was it ever established? How is its existence compatible with national sovereignties? What tribunals are there whose interpretations of it must be accepted, and what officers are there to enforce their decrees? If those who speak of International Law mean thereby only the usages of nations, they are talking in sad circles, for it is to repress many of these usages that men of good will desire international law. People really want in international affairs the same thing that ensures domestic peace—an external authority that compels all men to subordinate themselves to the common good. Without such an authority there is no law, and to get it men must sacrifice more than most seem willing to. Wide is the gate and broad is the way, but few there be that dare even point toward it.

Descending from these philosophic heights, there are many fallacies concerning the practical application of particular laws to everyday affairs—such beliefs as that a man is obliged to save a life if he can, that it is illegal to change one's name without permission of a court, that "the greater the truth, the greater the libel", and that a prefatory "it is alleged" automatically frees a speaker or writer from any liability for the ensuing utterance.

Though all humane and moral feelings cry out against it, a man is not *legally* obligated to save a life just because it may lie in his power to do so. The detached and contemplative citizen is at perfect liberty to watch a fellow citizen drown or get run over or eat a poisoned lollipop without offering so much as a warning. Humanitarians may condemn, but the law is reluctant to countenance nonfeasance as a basis of liability. Indeed, it could scarcely be otherwise; for how could the perception of the danger and the ability to prevent it be established—established so incontrovertibly, that is, as to sustain the serious charge of murder or manslaughter which would have to be made?

There are those, however—such as policemen on duty, parents at all times, and lifeguards during their working hours— who have "a legal duty to act", and can be held responsible for not acting. Furthermore, their liability is automatically assumed by anyone who, by some act of his own, renders it impossible for them to perform their duty. Thus a cautious bather on the beach has no legal obligation to assist an incautious bather in the water. But if the bather on the beach should, in a spasm of zeal, seize the lifeguard's boat and set out to rescue the incautious bather, thus depriving the lifeguard of his power to act, he has assumed responsibility; and if he should lose his nerve and turn back, or allow himself to be diverted by some more attractive bather than the one he set out to assist, he may be held for the consequences. The Good Samaritan and Meddlesome Mattie are not always clearly distinguishable; and the Levite who passed by on the other side, though not the most admirable of men, had certain negative virtues.

Doctors, in particular, are victims of the popular belief that one is required to save a life.[1] Newspaper stories of those who have died "because medical aid has been refused them" are sure-fire indignation-breeders. Most of the cases, when examined, turn out to be not quite what was suggested in the headline: the aid was not sought in time or in the proper way or at the proper place; the doctor was occupied with other patients who had prior claims; or the patient, or his relatives, attached some exasperating or unacceptable condition to the demand for atten-tion. Something of this sort almost always lies at the bottom of these stories; few physicians would refuse to help in a desperate emergency.

But even if one or two did, they have violated no statute. A doctor is under no more legal obligation to exercise his skill than is any other citizen. That many people think he is, and that there is widespread resentment when he refuses, is a tribute to the

---

[1] They are also victims (as well as beneficiaries) of the belief fostered by soap opera and the movies, that they *can* save a life whenever they have a mind to.

high standard that the doctors themselves have voluntarily maintained, but it has nothing to do with the law.

Many insist that doctors are bound by the Hippocratic Oath, a conjuration thought to be imposed on all M.D.s at graduation ("the rock to which the profession of medicine has been moored for some 2,400 years"[1]); but this, too, is a myth. A copy of the *Principles of Medical Ethics*, formulated under the supervision of the American Medical Association, is usually put into the hands of a medical student sometime before his graduation, but the actual oath of Hippocrates would be absurd today. In the first place, Apollo is now regarded as feeble security. Then the parts of the oath enjoining secrecy are in direct opposition to the best modern practice; and the injunction against seduction, though both moral and expedient, would be thought irrelevant. Opponents of euthanasia point sternly to that section of the oath which prohibits the giving of "deadly medicines", but have no objection, presumably, to doctors cutting persons who are "labouring under stone", though that, too, is forbidden.

Those who believe that a man cannot change his name without permission of a court are not wholly wrong, for some states do have statutes that so rule. But most agree with Illinois that a man's name is that by which he is known, and that he may change it at will if he does not do so with intent to defraud.[2] Casanova went under the name of the Chevalier de Seingalt and, secure in his right, saucily told a judge who charged that Seingalt was not his true name that he had found the eight letters idle in the alphabet and put them to use.[3]

[1] Willard Sperry: "The Case against Mercy Killings," the *American Mercury*, May 1950, p. 275.
[2] Prosser: *Handbook of the Law of Torts*, 1057; Elsdon C. Smith: *The Story of Our Names* (New York: Harper & Brothers; 1950), p. 197.
[3] There is widespread superstition that it is bad luck to change one's name. But most of the popes have changed their names on being elevated to the papacy—in fact, it is felt that those who do not will not live out their first year. Many successful writers have submerged their true names in their pseudonyms. Plato would hardly be recognized under his true name, Aristocles; nor Dante under his, Durante. Oliver Cromwell was born Oliver Williams and Stanley, the explorer, was born Rowlands. Sailors think it particularly unlucky for a ship to change her name, yet the luckiest ship that ever sailed, the *Golden Hind*, changed her name, and in mid-voyage, too!

Lord Mansfield's aphorism that "the greater the truth, the greater the libel" is still heard, but it no longer pertains in the United States. In every state except New Hampshire truth, in civil libel, is a complete defence, provided that "it is published with good motives and for justifiable ends".[1] That is, you can't just go around disseminating some shameful thing about a man (such as his having been in the penitentiary), even if it is true, unless you can show that you had some good reason for publishing the fact. Politicians, by the way, are underprivileged in the matter of libel; courts have held that a certain amount of sneering and ridicule must be accepted as the politician's lot.

Perhaps the popular conception of libel is coloured by the fortuitous sound of "lie" in the first syllable.[2] *Libel* does not mean an untruth, but a little book. That was its original meaning. Then it came to mean a paper and then any publication. The essence of libellousness lies in its defamation, which, in turn, may depend on its intent. Wittenberg[3] cites a Louisiana case, however, in which a doctor collected damages for having been *praised* in the *New Orleans Picayune*, alleging that the particular praise (of an operation he had performed) constituted advertising and that advertising damaged his professional standing.

The dangerous belief that responsibility for a defamatory utterance is avoided if the utterance is attributed to someone

---

[1] Prosser: *Handbook of the Law of Torts*, 854.

'The popular feeling about the meaning of many words is unconsciously affected by hearing another word in these words. Thus *fakir* (derived from an Arabic word meaning *poor*) suggests an impostor because it seems to contain *fake* (which is probably derived from a German word *fegen*, to sweep). A man of delicacy would hesitate to mention *shittim* wood in mixed company. People expect *greyhounds* to be grey. The meaning of *belfry* has been shaped by the wholly adventitious *bell* heard in its name. One hears "boo" in *taboo*, "bull" in *bulwark*, "ball" in *ballistics*, "junk" in *junket*, and "sex" in *sextet*. The persistent misspelling of *sacrilegious* is undoubtedly due to the feeling that "religious" is in the word somehow. Dr C. S. Blumel relates that a schizophrenic patient, when charged before a committee of doctors with a fault—by a doctor he particularly disliked—said: "I grant the allegation but defy the alligator." See Allen Walker Read: "English Words with Constituent Elements having Independent Semantic Value," *Philologica* (Baltimore), 1949, pp. 306–12.

[3] Philip Wittenberg: *Dangerous Words* (New York: Columbia University Press; 1947).

else—by being "alleged" or enclosing in quotation marks—is based, apparently, on a misunderstanding of what is meant in the law by "publishing" a libel. It does not mean the invention of, or even an acceptance of responsibility for, but the mere making public of, the defamatory statement. Reading such a statement aloud, or even stating it in a will,[1] has been held to constitute "publishing" a libel. It doesn't require a large audience; "one or more persons capable of understanding" the defamatory remark will do. Even though you don't believe the defamation and make that fact clear in the very act of repeating it, you have not freed yourself from the tort of publishing it.

Similarly, such assurances as "any resemblance to persons living or dead is purely coincidental" offer no protection against libel suits. If a resemblance can be shown, and if it can be shown to be defamatory, it is immaterial that the author or producer did not so intend it. It is immaterial, indeed, that they did not even know of the resemblance. The question "is not so much who was aimed at as who was hit".[2] The assurance of no such intention is irrelevant; you can't get out of a legal responsibility by exempting yourself from it.

In money matters there are a number of deep-rooted fallacies. Perhaps the insistence that men formerly did as they pleased with their own, a natural expression of irritation with tax forms, regulations, and government restrictions, is more a historical error than a financial one, but it is an error all the same. There is a strong feeling that a deposit is a sacred trust, that written contracts are more binding than oral, and that "paid in full" written on a cheque compels the recipient either to refuse the cheque or to regard the entire indebtedness as discharged. Many people believe that firms can be compelled to abide by a price stipulated in their catalogue, even though a typographical error has made the price ludicrous, and that goods sent without permission may be kept and used without payment. "Finders keepers" is more often an

---

[1] This is an exception to the Common Law rule that "liability for personal torts dies with the tortfeasor." The estate can be sued. Prosser: *Handbook of the Law of Torts*, pp. 813–14.

[2] Wittenberg: *Dangerous Words*, pp. 90–1.

I

announcement of intent than a statement of legal principle, but there is a good deal of popular confusion about the ownership of things that are found.

Harassed businessmen, resentful of the government's continual interference with their attempts to turn an honest dollar, often allow themselves to imagine a happier past when this was not so. But it may be doubted if there has ever been a time or place at which any considerable number of people were permitted the untrammelled use of their own property. In Rome there were statutes limiting a man's right to tear down a building, for example, unless it was in ruins or he intended to build a new house on the same site. Feudalism was based on the assumption that the land was held in return for certain services, and every manor was, in a way, a commune, with most elaborate restrictions in its use. In Chaucer's time you could not store French and Spanish wines in the same cellar. The ornaments of your dress, the cut of your clothes, the very material of your shroud were regulated by law. Until the late seventeenth century the minutiæ of everyday business were governed with restrictions that would drive a modern entrepreneur nuts. As a matter of fact—though the assurance will be cold comfort—he probably has more freedom of action today than at almost any other period known.

Those who look back to happier, unregulated days usually have the nineteenth century in mind (when you could be fined for not going to church and when many cities stretched chains across their streets on Sundays), and they can make out a certain case by confining themselves to the frontier or to the world of the small shopkeeper. But when one reflects that this golden age of "free enterprise" and "individual freedom" was the era that introduced conscript armies, colonial empires, the factory system, labour unions, the trusts, protective tariffs, restrictive covenants, zoning laws, the income tax, compulsory education, and the licensing of physicians, engineers, and maritime officers, one is inclined to see it as the cradle not of personal liberty, but of an unavoidable socialism.

One meaning of the word *deposit* is the placing of something in trust or safekeeping, and the common use of this word to describe money placed in a savings account may in part explain the idea, so often and so vociferously expressed, that an insolvent bank has defrauded its depositors. But money deposited in a savings bank is simply a loan. It makes the bank a debtor, not a trustee, and does not, necessarily, give the depositor preference over other creditors.[1]

The common man firmly believes that a written contract is more binding than a spoken contract, and he is right in so far as an oral agreement is more difficult to establish in court if one of the parties chooses to deny that he ever made it. But if there is sufficient credible testimony, a spoken agreement is as binding as a written one. In the Middle Ages, when the majority of men, even of high station, were unable to read or write, there were some quaint procedures designed to secure reliable witnesses. The agreement was often made in the presence of children because they would probably live for many years to testify, and something was done to impress the occasion on the children's minds. Sometimes they were given fruit out of season. At other times, more thriftily, they were thrashed. One lord, making a deed of gift, had his young son, splendidly apparelled, suddenly seized and thrown, with his clothes on, into a pond; and no doubt the youngster, if he was fished out while still living, remembered at least that part of the event.

Even a written agreement, however, is not always binding. The law is no tyrant to compel a man, simply because he has signed on the dotted line, to permit himself to be defrauded. A mere promise, it might be pointed out, even though written and notarized, is not binding at all. It may be repudiated at will. Promises have to be kept only when a "consideration" has been received in exchange or where something has been promised in return. The value of the consideration, though, unless it has been fraudulently misrepresented, is no concern of the court.

[1] Max Radin: *The Law and Mr Smith* (Indianapolis: The Bobbs-Merrill Company; 1938), p. 201.

No man can sign away his legal rights. Thus, one who signs a waiver on entering a hospital can, under certain circumstances, still recover for negligence.[1]

Many a base and cunning rascal has marked "paid in full" on a cheque that is made out for less than the sum owed, on the assumption that the creditor would rather have something than nothing, and that his acceptance of a cheque so marked will constitute a waiver of the remainder of the debt. And many a timid creditor has refused to accept such a cheque for fear that his endorsement might seem an acknowledgment of full payment.

Both hope and fear are unjustified. The notation "paid in full" is unilateral and has no binding force whatever. Even where a creditor has voluntarily given a receipt in full, he may collect more if he finds that there has been an omission in his bill.

There are many exciting stories of a misplaced decimal that bankrupted some great mail-order house, but they are largely fanciful, perhaps the fabrications of an astute publicity department. Few catalogues are now published that are not protected by some warning or reservation, and even if they were not, the firm that issued them could not be compelled to make good on a typographical error because, legally, listing in a catalogue is not an offer to sell; it is an invitation to consider merchandise that is for sale.

Indignation at the antics of advertising sometimes leads sober citizens to demand that manufacturers be compelled to "make good" on the implication of their advertisements. But generally the most that can be hoped for is a cease-and-desist order, and there will have to be something pretty close to fraud to get that much. In an inducement to buy, even the Roman courts recognized a distinction between those promises which were "to be made good" and those which were intended "merely to show off".[2]

[1] Prosser: *Handbook of the Law of Torts*, p. 1082; Radin: *The Law and Mr Smith*, pp. 261–2.
[2] "Sic ut praestentur" and "sic ut iactentur"—Radin: *The Law and Mr Smith*, p. 232.

In time of scarcity during the wars, counters did not always carry what the windows displayed. There was a widespread belief—probably not without foundation—that hard-to-get items were reserved for favoured customers, and many a shopper, denied an article that he had seen in the window, stormed out angrily threatening to invoke the law. But such threats left the merchants unmoved. They knew quite well that there is no law that compels a man to sell his displays, though some authorities argue that if a price is attached to the article on display the display then constitutes an agreement to sell and a sale can be forced by anyone offering the indicated price.

The past ten or twelve years have been so entirely a seller's market that we have almost forgotten the desperate measures to which some manufacturers can be driven by overstocked warehouses; but there are some indications that we may yet again see harassed firms unloading unwanted goods on unwilling customers. And when we do, we shall again hear it said that the recipient is under no obligation to pay for what he never ordered. He is not. But he is not entitled to use what he has not paid for. If he uses the goods sent to him, whether he ordered them or not, he can be compelled to pay for them. If the goods are not used, however, the recipient is under no obligation to pay for them or to return them. The sender must pick up his goods at his own expense.

Many people believe that a cheque for less than a dollar is not only invalid, but illegal. Perhaps they have in mind, or have heard of, Section 293 of Title 18 of the United States Code, which states that "no cheque, memorandum, token, or other obligation for a less sum than one dollar, intended to circulate as money" shall be made or issued. A personal cheque, however, is not intended to circulate as money, and Mr George T. Stimpson, in his *A Book About a Thousand Things* (N.Y., 1946, p. 285), quotes a special statement from the Department of Justice that "the statute does not apply to such a cheque". Even more widespread is the belief that a cheque is invalid if dated on Sunday or a legal holiday, but this, too, is without foundation.

Finders often *are* keepers, but they have no legal right to be. For example, the law of the state of New York provides that a person who finds lost property under circumstances which give him knowledge or means of inquiry as to the true owner and who appropriates the property to his own use without having made reasonable efforts to find the owner is guilty of larceny. The New York City ordinance requires that the finder of lost property must either deposit the property with the legal authorities or at least report the finding to the legal authorities. Nevertheless, the finder of the property acquires a property right in the property against everyone but the true owner, though finding lost property in and of itself cannot result in the transfer of title to the property to the finder. Further scope for legal subtlety is offered by the question whether the object was lost or abandoned.

Treasure is usually claimed by the state, though the finder is allowed a share of it. "Jetsam, flotsam, lagan, or derelict" belonged, in the English law, to the lord of the manor if above the high-water mark and to the Crown if between high- and low-water marks.

There was formerly a grim belief among coastal folk that a body washed ashore was derelict, a conviction that in some instances produced bodies where there might have been survivors. Admiral Sir Clowdisley Shovell, commander in chief of the British fleet, was a victim of this belief. He was murdered in 1707 by an old woman at Porthelick Cove as he struggled ashore after the loss of his ship among the rocks of the Scilly Islands. The hag is said to have observed an emerald ring on the Admiral's finger and to have taken what she felt were the proper steps to ensure the legality of her possession of it.[1]

[1] See the *Dictionary of National Biography*. The *Oxford Book of English Proverbs* (p. 466) quotes, as "a saying of the Cornish": "Master Vier, we cannot pay you your rent, for we had no grace of God this year; no shipwreck upon our coast."

CHAPTER NINETEEN

Our Trespasses

THE DISCOVERY in recent years of the fierce possessiveness that most animals feel about their "territory" gives a natural, if not a legal, sanction to the conviction that many landowners seem to cherish that a trespass constitutes a crime. And not only that, but a crime of so heinous a nature that its commission automatically suspends the Constitution, denies the perpetrator all civil rights, and confers upon the landowner the solemn duties of judge and executioner.[1]

It does not, however, confer a legal sanction. The law still recognizes the trespasser as a citizen with civil rights, even though he may at the moment be committing a misdemeanour. Indeed the trespasser, under certain circumstances, may sue the responsible party for negligence if dangerous objects are left about with which he injures himself while trespassing. The trespasser is not liable in damage for trespassing unless he has inflicted damage, though most courts assume that some nominal damage is inseparable from a trespass.

Some go so far as to believe that even the landlord cannot enter an apartment or house without the tenant's permission. "A man's house is his castle", they assure you; and, swept away by the romantic excitement of the metaphor, seem to feel that the landing is a portcullis, the elevator shaft a moat, and the

[1] The state of Massachusetts takes something of the same stand in its rule that the driver of an unregistered automobile is a trespasser upon the highway with no right of action. (See Prosser: *Handbook of the Law of Torts*, pp. 276–7.)

landlord an invading Saracen to be repelled with fire, sword, and molten lead. Prevalent practice, however, does not support these baronial delusions. Under practically all leases the landlord is entitled to enter to do anything that has to be done to preserve his property or to save himself from liability. The police also may enter for the purpose of making an arrest. Process-servers, it is true, may be denied admission.

In former times many actions for trespass were concerned with fruit trees whose branches overhung another man's property, and there is probably still some litigation based on this situation. Is the owner of the tree entitled to enter upon the other man's property to pick his fruit? If the fruit falls from the tree, does it belong to the owner of the tree or to him upon whose land it has fallen? As the fruit belongs to the owner of the tree, whether on the tree or the ground, he may enter upon the other's property to recover his fruit even without permission, though he may not use force or commit damage in so doing. The owner of the land upon which the fruit falls may protect himself, if he feels strongly enough about it, by compelling the owner of the tree to remove the overhanging branches.

Overhanging fruit trees don't play a very large part in modern urban and suburban life, but the increasing development of building areas facing on golf courses has led to a new problem in trespassing—the entering upon another's property to recover a golf ball. Of course if the golfer (whose ball probably wouldn't be there if he were an expert player) insists on playing the ball out, and in the process removes a generous divot from the house-holder's precious lawn, he has certainly committed wilful damage, and if he is brought before a jury of suburbanite lawn-tenders, things will go hard with him. But if the player walks carefully and merely picks up his ball, it would be hard to prove any damage other than a temporary bending of some blades of grass and the disarrangement of half an ounce of dew. Time was when courts were willing to set a high value on disturbed privacy, but a modern court would probably rule that if the house had been built deliberately on the edge of a course in order to enjoy the advantages of such a location, a few stray balls and an occasional well-mannered trespasser must be accepted as hazards inherent in the situation.

There was a few years ago a strong-willed farmer whose land at one point jutted into the Northbrook Country Club, near Chicago, and who was convinced that it was not only his privilege but his duty to shoot any golfer rash enough to retrieve a ball sliced over the fence. That this was not just a bluff was attested by the fact that in a frantic effort to draw his gun fast enough he managed on one occasion to shoot himself in the leg, and his presence, lurking armed in the bushes, came to be recognized as a definite psychological hazard of the third and fourteenth holes, duly allowed for in estimating par.

Many another man who would hesitate to shoot trespassers still feels that he is within his rights if he keeps and trains a dog to bite them. One sometimes sees "Beware of cross dog" or "Beware of savage dog" or whatever other sort of dog the owner of the property feels will be effectively menacing. But these are either hollow threats or indications of unlawful intent, for a man (says Prosser, in his great work on torts[1]) "may not intentionally keep a savage dog for the purpose of attacking a mere trespasser". A trespasser, it must be repeated, is a wrongdoer, but he is not an outlaw, and intentional battery may not be committed upon him with impunity. The dog is, however, in the quaint language of the law, "privileged" against a felonious intruder.

The warning sign that the owner feels exculpates him[2] may actually incriminate him the more, for it shows that he was aware of the dog's savagery, and the question of his responsibility for any injury that the animal may inflict often rests on whether or not he knew the creature was vicious. There is a popular, half-jesting legal maxim that every dog is entitled to "one bite free", but this does not mean that we must turn the other cheek at least once before we can seek redress. It means, rather, that the dog's

[1] p. 442.
[2] How often do we hear one who has injured another say in insolent and passionate self-defence: "I warned him. I warned him", as though the announcement of a criminal intention purged the deed of all illegality.

owner is not liable to the person bitten unless it can be shown that the owner was aware of his dog's tendency to bite, and that cannot usually be shown unless the dog has previously bitten or attacked someone. Mr Justice Maxey, of the Pennsylvania Supreme Court, in a decision handed down in 1936, attempted to protect the common flank by ruling that "a dog may show ferocious propensities without biting anyone and, if he does so, it is his master's duty to see to it that he is not afforded an opportunity to take 'a first bite' ". And, of course, if the owner himself has posted a public notice of his dog's ferocity, he can hardly plead ignorance of it.[1]

The exasperated gardener who pursues his neighbour's trespassing chickens with murderous rage rarely questions his right to kill them if he can catch them, but unless he can prove self-defence he has no such right. He can bring an action for damages against the owner of the chickens, but he will have to identify the chickens and, unless his rage has got the better of his common sense, he will have to be sure that the damages will cover the cost of the action. Of course if he goes ahead and kills the chickens, then it will be the neighbour who must bring the action, identify the chickens, and be sure it's worth it.

Not the least enraging feature of trespassing is that, if tolerated, it may establish itself as a right. The proving of "squatter's" rights—that is, the establishment of ownership through uncontested, non-permissive occupancy beyond the statute of limitations—is, perhaps, the only place in our law in which bad faith is essential to justifying possession. For, in order to create a title, the possession must have been "open, notorious and adverse". It must be shown, that is, that the squatter did *not* have permission to squat; otherwise, of course, he would simply be a tenant who hadn't paid his rent. It is to establish the granting of

[1] The principle is a very old one. Exodus 21: 28, 29, says that if an ox gore a man or a woman, [so] that they die: then the ox shall be surely stoned, and his flesh shall not be eaten; but the owner of the ox shall be quit [*i.e.*, go free]. "But if the ox were wont to push with his horn in time past, and it hath been testified to his owner, and he hath not kept him in, but that he hath killed a man or a woman; the ox shall be stoned, and his owner also shall be put to death."

permission at all other times that certain private thoroughfares—such as Rockefeller Plaza in New York or the esplanade before the south entrance of the Merchandise Mart in Chicago—are closed one day a year.[1] By showing on this one day (a Sunday is usually chosen) that he has the power to close the street, the owner signalizes that its use as a thoroughfare at all other times is by permission and not by right.

So that it is true, as popular belief has it, that possession, if non-permissive and maintained for the period of time within which action to recover must be brought, will confer ownership. But a squatter's life has its difficulties none the less. The squatter must, for example, definitely establish the date of the commencement of his notorious adverse possession, because if he should be unable to show that it antedated the requisite period, the owner could sue him for back rent.[2] Then he must look carefully into the owner's title. It is injudicious, for instance, to squat upon land owned by an infant, for the statute does not begin to run against an infant until he has attained his majority, and the careless squatter may find himself amerced and rudely ejected in his old age. Or he may find himself involved in unwelcome commitments; in the case of *Nisbet and Pott's Contract* it was held that a squatter is bound by the restrictive covenant of a former owner.

A peculiar belief that once prevailed widely in England and, apparently, still exists there locally, though it never seems to have been accepted in America, is that if a house was built

---

[1] *Reader's Digest*, April 1950, p. 87, quoted a sign which read: "Harmless Trespassing Permitted". The sign was regarded, apparently, as an innocent absurdity; but it may have been on a piece of ground that was used as a thoroughfare and the owner may—by conferring a permission which he could not withhold without difficulty and expense—have been establishing his right to withhold permission and, at the same time, warning that he would prosecute for damage done.

[2] Thus when in 1949 Boys Johnson, of Calgary, filed claim under squatter's rights to the house of Olaf Olsen, Olsen simply reappeared and filed a counter claim for 128 months' rent. See AP dispatch, May 1, 1949 (the *Chicago Sun-Times*, p. 24). After squatting in a vacant house in Memphis for twenty-five years, Fred and Fondo Kountz found that, instead of owning the place, they were in arrears for twenty-five years' rent. *Time*, February 23, 1949, p. 18.

entirely in one night—so that smoke was passing through the chimney before daybreak—the builder would acquire right to the house and to a small plot of land surrounding it. Some of them seem to have been built as late as the turn of the century. In Wales they were called "one-night houses" or "morning surprises". In the Lake District they were called "unthanks" or "without leaves". In *Cry, the Beloved Country*, the Negroes rear their miserable shanty-town in feverish haste through the night so that it will be fully erected by dawn.[1] Perhaps the rationale is that no one can then swear that he saw it a-building— *i.e.*, that it must have been there beyond the present memory of man.

There is a widespread belief that a corpse must proceed to the grave without let or hindrance. Originally it may have expressed —as the *Standard Dictionary of Folklore* states—a fear that some dissatisfied ghost, reluctant to leave this world, would take advantage of the pause to work mischief, but any such thought has been lost, in civilized lands, in the vague feeling that it is "only proper" that a funeral procession should not be stopped or interrupted. Until quite recently it was believed in many places that the passage of a corpse created a public right of way, and funerals were stopped by indignant landowners and their solemnity marred by unseemly scuffles.[2]

An obscure echo of all this may linger in our custom of allowing funeral cortèges to pass through red lights. The Model Traffic Ordinance, drafted by the National Conference on Street and Highway Safety some years ago, forbids the intersecting of a funeral cortège by any but authorized emergency vehicles except "where traffic is controlled by traffic signals or police officers". But some cities have not adopted the ordinance, and others (Chicago among them) have made a specific change in this regard.

---

[1] See the *Journal of American Folk-Lore*, vol. 53 (1942), p. 162; vol. 55 (1944), p. 128. And see Alan Paton: *Cry, the Beloved Country* (New York: Charles Scribner's Sons; 1948), p. 57.

[2] Funerals sometimes went out of their way *in order* to mark a public right of way.

The justification for thus creating a traffic hazard is that it constitutes a mark of respect for the dead. Perhaps there is a touch of sentiment in it—one last traffic violation, as thieves on the way to Tyburn were permitted one last larceny. Maybe the morticians wish to add a dash of sporting interest to an otherwise tedious journey—or hope for new business out of it.

The male householder sallying forth to repel trespassers is probably expressing something fundamental to his masculinity and identifying himself with the maned lion and the valiant wren. But whereas these lowly creatures are probably rewarded for their valour (at least in folk zoology) with the admiring growls or chirps of their mates, the human male often has to face the snickers of his. For within the nest or lair he so often risks a punch on the nose to defend, there is often a regrettable disharmony.

When legal difficulties arise in the bosom of the family many women feel aggrieved because they do not have full equality with men. Their complaints are likely to leave their men more bewildered than sympathetic, for most men, in so far as they have given the question any thought, assume that women have at least equal rights, and probably a host of privileges thrown in. But some inequalities do remain, and some women have made much of them. In many states, for example, women cannot serve on juries. Most states severely restrict the right of a young woman to dispose of her person. Some still assume that if a husband and wife die together in an accident, the wife died first and that, in consequence, her property passes to his heirs rather than his to hers.[1] In many states prostitution is defined as the act of a female. In Kentucky a woman can secure a divorce if her husband is "living in adultery", though the husband can secure a divorce for a single act of unfaithfulness on his wife's part, or even for "lascivious behaviour".[2]

---

[1] In Willa Cather's *My Antonia*, Wick Cutter murdered his wife and then committed suicide. He did not die immediately and in triumphant malignance called on witnesses to testify that she was dead and that he was not, so that his property could not go to her relatives.

[2] Harriet F. Pilpel and Theodora Zavin: *Your Marriage and the Law* (New York: Rinehart & Company; 1952), p. 281.

Aggressive feminists insist that these differences add up to in-equality, and have fought for years to have the Constitution amended so that equality under the law shall not be denied or abridged on account of sex. But as Senators Douglas, Lehman, and Kefauver pointed out in the debate on the proposed amend-ment in 1950, women are also accorded certain privileges and exemptions under the law, and these would be nullified by an equal-rights amendment. Women would lose their dower rights, their right to sue for non-support, their favoured position in many divorce cases, and their exemption from the draft. Whether the gains would compensate for these losses is a question; the feminists seem to think they would.

One sometimes hears it asserted that a married woman is not responsible for any crimes she may commit in her husband's presence, though it is disputed whether this is a privilege or an act of discrimination. Some feminists seem to view it as a con-spiracy to deprive her of her right to go to jail if she wants to. Thus Elizabeth Hawes, in her essay "American Women Don't Get a Break", complains that if an enterprising married woman does commit a crime in the presence of her husband "it is pre-sumed she did it under constraint by him and he is presumably responsible". "In other words," she adds bitterly, "in the whole United States of America it is assumed that no woman in her husband's presence has a really strong mind or will of her own."

Matrons would be ill-advised, however, to indulge their criminal propensities too freely in the security of this belief, for there are serious limitations to it. The statutes of Illinois, which are typical in this respect, state that a wife is fully responsible for her acts unless she can prove that she committed the crime in question "under threats, commands or coercion" of her husband. If she can so prove, then he takes the rap; but in murder and treason even that won't save her.

Custom, if not law, seems to permit any youngish woman to kill her husband with impunity. All that is needed, it would appear, is a reproach and a pistol for the man and a demure countenance for the jury. But now that there are fewer men than women and the need for conserving our natural resources is growing more important, this may change.

Not that men seem to mind very much. They are more concerned with such immediate and practical matters as divorce and annulment, about which clusters a whole galaxy of popular delusions.

From those who oppose divorce (many of whom, being celibate, cannot possibly have any selfish interest in the matter) we often hear that divorce laws should be "tougher". Their assumption seems to be that if divorces were harder to obtain, more couples would stay together and eventually (one assumes) learn to endure each other. It makes a sort of grim sense, though if marriage *is* the basis of social order, as most thinkers agree it is, one wonders why the celibates don't get married themselves.

But Draconian laws have a way of backfiring. Divorce is almost impossible to obtain in Ireland, but, if we may trust Mr Sean O'Faolain, marriage seems to be becoming impossible there too.[1] Some two million spouses in the United States, finding divorce even under our more lenient statutes too difficult, apparently, have separated without its assistance, and the chances are that severer laws would increase this number rather than the number of the tolerantly married.[2] Meanwhile, society would have to shoulder the increased burden of illegitimacy and delinquency.

Less high-minded folk, men especially, are more concerned with the legal aspects of opposite problems. They want to know —to be forearmed—when an affair suddenly becomes a common-law marriage, upon what terms an annulment may be secured, whether "mutual consent" or "incompatibility" are valid grounds for divorce, and whether an advertisement to the effect that they are no longer responsible for their wives' debts frees them from the necessity of paying them. And in almost every case the popular opinion is erroneous.

[1] *Life*, March 16, 1953.
[2] Pilpel and Zavin, *Your Marriage and the Law*, p. 35.

Many men, on reading of the recognition of a common-law marriage, feel that a trick has been played on the man. Since licit unions are often dull, it is natural—if illogical—to assume that illicit unions are uninterruptedly blissful, though the contrary might be nearer the truth. At any rate, many male readers are likely to feel, here was one man living happily in untrammelled sin when the woman trapped him and spoiled the whole thing by making it legal.

The fallacy is that a common-law marriage, while regarded by some as not too respectable these days, is in many states quite legal. The House of Lords, in 1844, ruled in effect that marriage by agreement was not valid by the common law of England, but this was a historical reversal in so far as it affected England, and had no effect in America, where the validity of common-law marriages has been upheld by several important decisions. In our pioneer days, access to ministers or magistrates was not always easy; yet unions and offspring were socially desirable, and the law was quite willing to let young couples dispense with ceremony.[1]

The actualities of early married life often correspond so imperfectly to the expectations of courtship that many a spouse has decided that a fraud has been perpetrated and sought an annulment on the ground that he or she had been deceived by deliberate misrepresentations. But they have usually found the courts cold and unsympathetic. Although one often hears of "the marriage contract", marriage is not a contract in the ordinary sense. The frauds that void other contracts will not necessarily void a marriage, and the union cannot be rescinded or modified by mutual consent.

The misrepresentation has to be vital to the marriage as a biological or a social union before it is likely to be considered grounds for annulment. Concealment of some serious infectious disease might be so regarded; whereas concealment of some ailment that afflicted only one of the two, even though he or she

[1] Joseph W. Madden: *Handbook of the Law of Persons and Domestic Relations* (St. Paul, Minn.: West Publishing Company; 1931), pp. 49–51.

was thereby rendered (in Milton's words) "totally unfit for all the more estimable purposes of matrimony", would not.

The concealment of anything that would have prevented the marriage in the first place will, of course, be grounds for annulment. This would include consanguinity within the statute, insanity (where there are laws forbidding the insane to marry), a living, undivorced spouse, youthfulness below the legal limit, and so on. But except for such matters the law is aloof. Misrepresentations in regard to wealth,[1] character, beauty, social position, or even religion, are not generally regarded as sufficient. Love is more or less a matter of reciprocal misrepresentation anyway, some cynical courts have implied, and the unwary cannot be protected against all predation.

Some innocents have even sought annulment on the grounds that a greater degree of affection was protested before marriage than was demonstrated after, but they have found little comfort. A man is not under oath in a canoe or a porch swing, and cannot be held to scientific accuracy in the description of his feelings at that time. The law, as one court has icily phrased it, "does not recognize the necessity of love in the marriage relationship".[2]

A misrepresentation of person (such as the substitution of one twin for another) would be grounds for annulment, if it could be practised in the first place and detected in the second. Laban

---

[1] An heir or, especially, an heiress in popular conception is one who expects to inherit money; or, as the trustful masses say, "will" inherit money. Legally, however, an heir is one who has succeeded to an estate—not one who will inherit but one who has inherited.

This may seem a quibble, but it has caused many a fortune-hunter many a pang. It might infuse a little caution and avoid regrets if the proper legal terms "heir apparent" and "heir presumptive" were used. An "heir apparent", by the way, is one whose right is indefeasible if he survive the ancestor. An "heir presumptive" is less secure. If the ancestor should obligingly drop dead immediately, the heir presumptive would be heir; but his right to the inheritance may be defeated by the birth of a nearer relative or some other contingency. From among heirs presumptive could probably be culled a list of some of the bitterest human beings who have ever died in penury.

[2] Morris Ploscowe: *Sex and the Law* (New York: Prentice-Hall; 1951), p. 54.

wouldn't find it so easy today to dispose of his sore-eyed daughter.
Concealed pre-nuptial pregnancy has been admitted as grounds
for annulment, though the same does not hold for unchastity.
There have, by the way, been wretches so moral and so base at
the same time as to seek annulment on the grounds of the very
pre-marital unchastity to which they themselves had contributed!
The presence of a shotgun, even though it were entwined with
orange blossoms, would be grounds for annulment; the law
insists that a marriage must be made, at least, in free consent, and
will annul one entered into when either of the parties was
drunk, drugged, or dragooned. The threat of arrest or prose-
cution for rape is not usually considered coercion, though some
aggrieved young men have thought it ought to be.[1]

The phrase of gossip columnists, that the So-and-so's have
"agreed to disagree", must be accepted as journalistic licence.
Mutual consent would seem to be the most civilized of all
grounds for separation, as it is for coming together, but the
laws of most state *deny* a divorce when it can be proved that
the parties agreed to get one. Even in an uncontested action,
the party suing must have legal grounds and corroborating
witnesses. If couples who merely wished to go their separate
ways were allowed to do so, what would become of divorce
lawyers and gossip columnists?

"Incompatibility of temperament", though unquestionably
the underlying cause of many divorces, is recognized as grounds
only in sunny New Mexico. The law is grim on this subject.
The suffering party, Lord Stowell has solemnly affirmed, "must
bear in some degree the consequences of an injudicious connection. . . . Courts of justice do not . . . furnish cures for all the
miseries of life". And his lordship's dictum has found sonorous
echo in the judicial chambers of America. The Supreme Court
of Michigan has asserted that the marriage bond cannot be
severed "merely because parties . . . live unhappily together", and

[1] Pilpel and Zavin: *Your Marriage and the Law*, pp. 260–1, 265, 272, 263,
264; Ploscowe: *Sex and the Law*, pp. 26, 55; Madden: *Handbook of the
Law of Persons and Domestic Relations*, pp. 15–17, 4, 10, 33–5.

it and other tribunals have held that divorce may be granted only when the degree of misery exceeds endurance and threatens the health of one of the partners. Now that mental health has come to be recognized as a necessity, this may open the door to more divorces. A famous example is furnished by the New Hampshire case of *Robinson* v. *Robinson*, in which a druggist was granted a divorce because his wife had become a Christian Science Practitioner. The Supreme Court held that this manifested a degree of incompatibility dangerous to the husband's reason.[1]

Agnes Allen's law, that anything is easier to get into than out of, finds its clearest demonstration in marriage and its responsibilities. The continued appearance of "I am no longer responsible" ads in the paper shows that there still are hopeful males who believe that such a notice frees them from any further obligation to pay their wives' debts. But they are in for an unpleasant surprise. A man is not legally absolved of his duties merely because he announces that he no longer intends to assume them, and one of a married man's duties is to furnish his wife, whether she be in his bed or at his board or not, with such "necessaries as are essential to her health and comfort, according to the rank and fortune of her husband". A woman's idea of what is necessary to her comfort may vary widely from her husband's and in these days of concern for the psyche things may well be adjudged essential which our unenlightened fathers might have classified as luxuries. Some courts have, for instance, considerately included an occasional purchase of jewellery as among some women's "necessaries".

Some men have cut their wives out of their wills and gone chuckling with malicious satisfaction to their graves, but the wives have almost always had the last laugh, for in many jurisdictions the wife may renounce her husband's will and claim a "widow's share", usually a substantial fraction. Many, after securing a divorce and disgorging alimony, have ceased payments on the woman's remarriage, only to find themselves in alimony

---

[1] I. H. Rubenstein: *Contemporary Religious Jurisprudence* (Chicago: Waldain Press; 1948), pp. 78–9.

row. Only California, Connecticut, Montana, New York, and Louisiana make any such merciful provision.[1]

Even the death of the wife will not bring immediate relief, for courts have held that a wife's funeral expenses must be paid by the husband, and some will not even permit him to be reimbursed for them from her estate, holding that this is more his obligation than her just debt. By the time a man has reached the "I am no longer responsible" stage, however, he is usually willing to make an exception in favour of this particular expense.

[1] One man's poison is another man's mate. Aubrey tells us that when Sir Kenelm Digby "married that celebrated beautie and courtezane, Mrs Venetia Stanley, whom Richard earle of Dorset kept as his concubine" the noble Earl delicately ceased payments on the annuity he had settled on the lady. But Sir Kenelm, solicitous of his wife's interests, as a good husband should be, sued his lordship and compelled him to continue his bounty, thereby setting posterity a bold example.

Aux Armes, Citoyens!

The war between Homo sapiens *and* Homo neanderthalensis, *thought to have been won fifty thousand years ago, has broken out with renewed fury and, at the moment, the forces of reason are scattered in dismay while the Jugheads advance in triumph.*

But courage, comrades! The situation is not as bad as it seems. A bull roarer is only a slat on a string, and behind those hideous masks, sedately capering, are merely some Old Stone Age gentlemen who, for all their war whoops, are in a dreadful state of funk. Wisdom must be militant. It was not for nothing that the Greeks, who gave the world Intelligence, conceived of Athena as armed or that Asinius Pollio, when he established the first public library in Rome, placed it in the Temple of Liberty.

We are committed to democracy, that "formidable heresy", and democracy is based on the belief that men can and will be reasonable.

Formez vos bataillons! *We have stood too long in sneers amid the alien scorn.*

Index